Jonathan Swift

A. L. ROWSE

Jonathan Swift

MAJOR PROPHET

with 25 illustrations

THAMES AND HUDSON
LONDON

Contents

To W. S. LEWIS
friend of many years
for his unparalleled contribution
to our knowledge of the eighteenth century

Preface

FOR MANY YEARS I have meant to write a biography of Swift. It was in fact one of my first literary projects, when elected to a Fellowship at All Souls, more than forty years ago. Always ambivalent between the claims of history and literature, devoted to both – though writing poetry long before I confronted the writing of history – eventually I found myself concentrating on the Elizabethan Age.

The fact is that I was too young to write Swift's life: the subject, in particular his relations with Stella and Vanessa, was too difficult for me. All the same, Swift has always haunted me: in looking over early diaries and notebooks for a future volume of autobiography, I came upon a complete synopsis for a play; in the intervening years I have published two full-length essays on 'Swift at Letcombe' (in *Times, Persons, Places*) and 'Swift and Stella at Moor Park' (in *The Spectator*), along with a number of reviews, one of them (in *The Criterion*) an early claim for the proper recognition of Swift's stature as a poet. And Swift's view of human beings has influenced my mind all my life.

After a lifetime I think I understand better Swift's complex and unusual attitude towards Stella and Vanessa, and have been able to contribute a new inflexion – which the reader will find in its proper place – bringing out the difference in social class between the two. These differences were important in the past, and writers without historical sense, or any subtle social sense, have missed the nuances in Swift's attitude towards his womenfolk.

Many years ago I took the trouble to visit the scenes of his and their lives: Dublin, Laracor and Trim, Vanessa's Celbridge, Moor Park in Surrey while it was still a country house in private possession, as in Sir William Temple's day. In recent years I have become very familiar with Moor Park, now a college, through successive invitations to lecture there. I am as grateful to the present Warden and his predecessor for their kindness as we all must be for their devoted care of that delightful place, so much appreciated now by many, while still retaining the charm it had for Swift.

In Ireland people were most hospitable and helpful. I regret that I do not now remember all the obligations that I incurred as a very young man to whom all doors were opened. But I have not forgotten the kindness of the then Dean of St Patrick's, the Very Rev. H. J. Lawlor, who showed me over the Deanery from cellars to attics; several members of the Gwynn family who welcomed me to Trinity College, and again in Cork; generous ladies like Sara Purser and Mrs Fitzgibbon; Joseph Hone, who also wrote about Swift; Lord and Lady Powerscourt, who entertained me at that splendid house, now a burned ruin; Æ (George Russell), Myles Dillon, Mrs Starkie, Frank O'Connor.

They are all dead, but the young man to whom they were kind, now old, has not forgotten them.

All Souls, Lent 1975   A. L. ROWSE

CHAPTER 1

Early Years and Inheritance

JONATHAN SWIFT'S FAMILY had several literary associations, which offer unexpected pointers to his subsequent career. For though his ambitions and his bent were political, his genius was for writing; and it is possible that, if his desires had not been frustrated, he would not have fulfilled himself in his writings – a substitute for power, the pursuit of which was his main motive (as Lord Orrery, who knew him well, perceived) but which always eluded him. This in itself was enough to madden a man conscious of abilities so superior to those of the ordinary run of mortals.

On his father's side he was quite closely connected with Sir William Davenant (who liked to think that he was a by-blow of William Shakespeare): Swift's uncle married Davenant's daughter. Another uncle married a near relation of the poet Dryden, who called Swift cousin. His mother was an Errick, of the decent Leicester clan of Errick or Herrick, from which came the cleric and poet; again, she was related in some way to Sir William Temple's wife, famous for her love-letters to him as Dorothy Osborne. It is no less significant that the Swifts stood in relation to these people rather as poor relations – which is also apt to give a cutting edge to the temper of an insatiably ambitious man.

What men of genius write about themselves is always more interesting than what others write about them, for these are usually persons of very ordinary talents and small perceptions. Swift is no exception, in his *Fragment of Autobiography*, if only for what he does *not* say: he is so reticent, controlled, anxious to draw a veil over what had so hurt his sensibilities, and present a picture he himself *willed*. Never was so wilful, so passionate a man – yet contrarily held in leash by the equal power of his reason. The tension between the two created his genius, his style, which one can read in every line he wrote. But one can also read between the lines, for so powerful a personality forces its way through every crevice. Again, as Orrery says of him, he was open, undisguised and perfectly sincere – we are reminded of what Ben Jonson (whom he much more resembled) said of Shakespeare: 'he was indeed honest [i.e. honourable], and of an open and free nature.'

He was also, like Shakespeare (though, for the rest, he was at the opposite pole), bent on being regarded as a gentleman, rather snobbishly inclined; for men of imagination find interesting people more interesting than uninteresting ones. He tells us that 'the family of the Swifts are ancient in Yorkshire' and cites a member of it who achieved an Irish peerage as Viscount Carlingford. This stands in some contrast to his old enemy, the Duchess of Marlborough's brisk dismissal of any ancient ancestry for the Churchills: 'it is no matter whether it be true or not in my opinion; for I value nobody for another's merit.' (That was all very well for her, for she had become a Duchess; Swift never achieved the meanest of bishoprics – and how he resented it!) His mother, he tells us, was 'descended from the most ancient family of the Erricks', and he takes them back to William the Conqueror. The fact was that they were Leicester *bourgeois*, and Dissenters at that.

The one member of his family Swift was proud of was his grandfather, Thomas Swift, parson of Goodrich in Herefordshire, who achieved some celebrity in his day for his devotion to the Royalist cause, the sacrifices he made for it, the sufferings and persecution he endured. He was very obstinate and courageous, an indomitable man: his grandson took after him. The Swifts were very much a Church family; the grandfather had the income of an independent gentleman from the Church properties he leased, besides his livings. He was thrown out of everything, and had to make way at Goodrich for 'a fanatical saint'. All his life Swift hated fanatics and doctrinaires and illusionists – quite rightly, for the troubles they bring down on sensible people. Grandfather Swift was promised reward for his exceptional services to the King, 'but Mr Swift's merit died with himself'. (Swift was thinking of the grandson, too – and indeed all his life had not much opinion of kings.)

When the grandson, by his own efforts, made himself famous, he celebrated the old Cavalier parson's memory by presenting his church with a chalice, with an inscription. When one goes to Goodrich – that superb rose-red castle, a ruin from the Civil War, looking down upon the Wye – there not far away is the ancestral church, looking as if it had suffered somewhat in the senseless conflict.

Old Thomas Swift had many sons, three of whom sought a career in the opportunities opened up by the Restoration settlement in Ireland – after the uncivil and intestinal wars there, the catastrophes of massacre, Cromwellian conquest and decimation – jobs were going, qualified men were needed. The oldest son, Swift's Uncle Godwin, married a relation of the Ormonds and, an attorney, got a job in running their estates. Altogether he married four times; once he married, 'to the great offence of his family', says the Dean, a daughter of the regicide Admiral Deane. This branch seems to have been pleased by their notorious descent, for they carried on the confusing name of Deane Swift for three generations. Godwin's grandson Deane Swift, the great Dean's first cousin once removed, was a talented youth of literary inclinations. The Dean wrote to introduce him to Pope, in his usual discouraging way, 'although he be related to me; for I am utterly void of what the world calls natural affection, and with good reason, because they are a numerous race degenerating from their ancestors, who were of good esteem for their loyalty and sufferings in the rebellion against King Charles I.'

Young Deane Swift, for all his promise and the interest the great man took in him, never achieved anything much, once he married and settled back in Ireland – merely an essay upon Orrery's *Observations*. He never got down to the edition of Swift's works he scratched away at; Walter Scott, a man of more enterprise and rapidity – apart from anything else – made good use of the materials that Deane had collected. So, perhaps, the great Dean was right in discharging himself of any obligations to a dilettante, and leaving him, rather pointedly, a standish, inkpot and writing materials in his will.

A younger son of the old vicar, Jonathan, married Abigail Errick and died some months before his son was born. The son leaves us in no doubt of his sentiments as to the affair. 'The marriage was on both sides very indiscreet; for his wife brought her husband little or no fortune, and his death happening so suddenly before he could make a sufficient establishment for his family, his son (not then born) hath often been heard to say that he felt the consequences of that marriage not only through the whole course of his education, but during the greatest part of his life.' He himself would never make the mistake of such a marriage; on the other hand, he had not the philosophic justice of mind to reflect that, but for that, his genius would never have come into being – by which these people live for us, and without which they would all be forgotten.

Swift had a sister, Jane, eighteen months older than himself and apparently closer to his mother. But this poor creature made the mistake of marrying a tradesman, a leather-seller, whom Swift had no opinion of. He opposed the marriage, which took place when he was already cutting a figure as chaplain to the Berkeleys at Dublin Castle. Unfortunately he proved right about this marriage, which came to no good; when the husband died, Swift was forced to make his sister the contemptuous allowance of £15 a year – evidently good enough for her, no credit to the Swifts. He later wrote, 'I did not know, nor will ever believe such a breed had either worth or honour.' So much for his family – they were just very ordinary people, such as recur. It was another improvident marriage, one more lesson against entangling oneself with others.

He was born on St Andrew's Day, 30 November 1667, in Hoey's Court, Dublin. His coming into the world, without a father, into an impoverished family, must have been unpromising enough. Then a very strange thing happened to him – everything was strange about this singularly fated man. His nurse, a woman of Whitehaven in Cumbria, doted on him and 'being under an absolute necessity of seeing one of her relations who was then extremely sick . . . she stole him on shipboard unknown to his mother and uncle [Godwin], and carried him with her to Whitehaven, where he continued for almost three years. For, when the matter was discovered [he must have been put out to nurse], his mother sent orders by all means not to hazard a second voyage, till he could be better able to bear it.' There certainly were hazards in those Irish Channel crossings – Deane Swift's only son perished with wife and child on one of them. 'The nurse was so careful of him that, before he returned, he had learnt to spell; and by the time he was three years old he could read any chapter in the Bible.' This was precocious of him; it seems that he was happy with his nurse, for he always thought kindly of White-haven afterwards.

After his return, the boy was sent at the age of six to Kilkenny, which was the best school in Ireland – several clever boys emerged from it in Swift's time, among them his junior, Congreve. The Dean later said, with his usual lack of justice wherever his complexes were touched, that his uncle 'gave him the education of a dog'. This probably meant that he was kept on short commons, for his uncle became straitened in means – the Dean's proud spirit naturally thought nothing should have been too good for him. The reality was that the Swifts were poor, and this had a lifelong effect on the boy whose passion was for independence: he became very saving. Orrery was no bad psychologist, and he says truthfully, 'his pride, his spirit, or his ambition – call it by what name you please – was boundless; but his views were checked in his younger years, and the anxiety of that disappointment had a visible effect upon all his actions.' The fires within must have been early banked up.

He was away at Kilkenny school for some eight years. There he received the usual education of a public school of the time, strictly based on the classics, but particularly Latin. Swift became fairly widely familiar with Latin literature, though not very proficient at verse-making, the *fine fleur* of a classical education. One cannot but suppose that the rough and raw circumstances of a seventeenth-century public school educated him also in 'the facts of life' – to which he exhibited so singular a repulsion all his days. It is a well-known fact of psychology that complete sexual repression is liable to compensate itself with a marked scatological fixation, and this is the direction Swift's mind took.

In 1682, in his fifteenth year, young Jonathan was entered at Trinity College, Dublin, apparently as a pensioner. Again he re-proaches his relations for not doing better for him – it seems that,

ring of himself as English, as he always did ('I am not of this vile
ntry, I am an Englishman'), he would have liked to go to Oxford.
family circumstances made this impossible. Pride made him later
write down his career at Trinity as one of ill-success: 'by the ill-
treatment of his nearest relations, he was so discouraged and sunk in
his spirits that he too much neglected his academic studies, for some
parts of which he had no great relish by nature, and turned himself to
reading history and poetry.' Orrery elaborates for us: 'he held logic
and metaphysics in the utmost contempt; and he scarce considered
mathematics and natural philosophy, unless to turn them into ridicule.
The studies which he followed were history and poetry: in these he
made a great progress.'

In short, perhaps unknown to himself, his genius was feeding on
its natural food and rejecting the rest. But this morose youth made a
lifelong friend of his tutor, St George Ashe, who must have spotted
something exceptional in him. For, again paradoxically, this solitary,
ungregarious spirit had a genius for friendship – on his own terms.

There is no doubt that he was a difficult youth; what was to be
done with him or, rather, what was he to do for himself?

In 1688 the Revolution overthrew James II, and his nephew and
son-in-law, William III, took his place. In 1689 James arrived in
Ireland as a base from which to return to the throne he had so foolishly
thrown away in England for his Catholicism. Ireland was once more
plunged in turmoil – not only the Cromwellian conquest overturned
but the more moderate Restoration settlement undone; William III
had to fight for his throne on Irish soil, after all, in spite of the surprisingly easy submission of the English to their Dutch deliverer.

The background of insecurity, civil war, the domination of a
largely Catholic people by an alien Protestant ascendancy, conditioned
all Swift's life in Ireland. All he says in his *Autobiography* is, 'the
troubles then breaking out, he went to his mother, who lived in
Leicester. And after continuing there some months, he was received
by Sir William Temple, whose father had been a great friend to the
family, and who was now retired to his house called Moor Park,
near Farnham in Surrey: where he continued for about two years.'

His real education was now to begin.

14

CHAPTER 2

Sir William Temple

WHAT WILLIAM SHAKESPEARE OWED to his introduction to South-ampton for the refinement and sophistication of his tastes, that and even more the young Swift owed to his mentor, Sir William Temple, and the charmed circle at Moor Park. For Shakespeare's patron was only a young man, though an earl, and their intimate relations occupied but some four years; while Jonathan's patron was an elderly retired statesman, of wide experience and distinction, and the apprenticeship covered a decade, most of which the uncouth Irishman spent at delicious Moor Park, near Farnham, in its friendly, cultivated household. It is impossible to overestimate what Swift owed to Temple, though he himself eventually disconsidered it, for Temple's failure to provide for him. Swift, too, had reason to gird against Fortune,

> That did not better for my life provide
> Than public means, which public manners breeds.

It is not generally realized how familiar Temple was with Ireland and Irish affairs. For three generations the Temples were involved there. Temple's grandfather had been the most important of the early Provosts of Trinity, who virtually gave the College its organization and character. Temple's father, Sir John, was born in Ireland and had his whole career there, as Master of the Rolls. Even Sir William, whose own career was closely connected with the Netherlands, had lived in Ireland for some years after his marriage. His earliest work was an 'Essay upon the Present State and Settlement of Ireland', and, though he was an exponent of what we should describe as liberal (Whig) principles, he had the sense to see that they did not apply in

Ireland – 'for to think of governing that kingdom by a sweet obliging temper is to think of putting four wild horses into a coach and driving them without whip or reins.'

His father, Sir John, was for many years the active head of the Irish Bar and had been kind and helpful to the Swift brothers, all lawyers and members of it. So young Jonathan came with a recommendation to the great man, Sir John's son, now retired from a lifetime in diplomacy and government, famous as the creator of a Triple Alliance of Great Britain, the Netherlands and Sweden, to resist Louis XIV's dangerous preponderance in Europe. The Alliance did not last; a more enduring work was Temple's negotiation of the marriage between Charles II's nephew, William of Orange, and his niece Mary, which ultimately brought them to the English throne as William III and Mary II. So Temple was *persona gratissima* with Dutch William, though he would never take office again once he had retired.

The truth was that, an upright man and a man of principle, he had not been very effective in the reptilian politics of the Restoration. He had been made use of by the clever men about Charles II and the King himself, more for their purposes than he fully realized; an intellectual rather than a practical politician, with a good deal of an intellectual's self-complacency, he was less influential than he thought he had been. He consoled himself with writing – and he was a very good writer, with a clear, perspicuous style influenced by the best modern French writers. He had lived much abroad, and was well read in French literature.

He was a man of taste, a connoisseur. He had bought Moor Park in the year of the Revolution, 1688, and was making a paradise of the place, in the valley of the Wey with overhanging woods upon the eastern bank, the rim of the estate. A famous gardener, and no less famous for his *Essay* on the subject, he formed a canal and laid out walks and fruit-trees after the Dutch model. The house, not large, was of red brick then and, within, gay with pictures and portraits, books and china. Retired and gouty, somewhat valetudinarian, Sir William still cherished his fame as the exponent of a Protestant alliance against France, and the new King William once and again came down to Moor Park to seek his advice and approbation. Within the house, he was adored by his women-folk; his wife, the famous Dorothy Osborne, rather left the running of it to his sister, the redoubtable Lady Giffard, widow of an Irish knight of County Meath.

To this charmed circle – something of a mutual admiration society – came Swift, now twenty-two, without job or prospects. Temple sent him back to Ireland with a recommendation to the Secretary of State there – nothing doing: there was no opening for him, no Fellowship at Trinity. But this year 1690 saw the turning-point in Irish affairs: the battle of the Boyne was the graveyard of the hopes of Celtic Ireland for a couple of centuries, of which the symbol was the statue of King Billy that stood outside the great gate of Trinity up to our time.

In this biography we cannot go in any detail into Swift's proliferating work, though so much of it is biographical, inextricably entwined with personal events and the events of his time. (The kind of criticism which would deny the importance of the personal and biographical in the work of a writer is never more absurd than in the case of Swift.) His very first writing is a congratulatory ode to King William 'on his Irish Expedition'. Though prentice-work, it already has some surprising touches that foreshadow the mature Swift:

> *What do sceptre, crown and ball,*
> *Rattles for infant royalty to play withal,*
> *But serve t'adorn the baby-dress*
> *Of one poor coronation day*
> *To make the pageant gay:*
> *A three-hours' scene of empty pride,*
> *And then the toys are thrown aside.*

What an odd and radical reflection to appear in a celebration of a king's triumph! And there are other characteristic self-reflecting strokes:

> *We poets oft our bays allow*
> *Transplanted to the hero's brow.*

The earliest efforts of men of genius often have something prophetic of their future in them: there is nothing more important than to observe that there was something *heroic* about Swift's personality, life and work, at the same time as tragic – a tragic hero.

Nothing for Swift in Ireland, Temple invited the young man back on the same unpromising assignment as before: 'he has lived in my house, read to me, writ for me, and kept all accounts as far as my small occasions required.' We note the cool estimation at which the services of the amanuensis are rated; Swift was a careful keeper of accounts, while his handwriting – always a revealing feature – is surprisingly beautiful. It is not notably masculine, a little finicking and self-conscious with a deliberate curling backwards of the stroke in 'd' – the only aesthetic sign one observes in him.

He returned to England in August 1691, and in the next few months we see several signs of what was to come. He spent some time at Leicester with his mother, and there flirted with young women, as was his way. He could afford to, for he had no temptation to go further. 'A thousand household thoughts always drive matrimony out of my mind whenever it chances to come there; besides that I am naturally temperate, and never engaged in the contrary, which usually produces those effects.' This man would be difficult for any woman to catch. But, of course, such a man would be very difficult for ordinary fools, as he proceeded to describe them, to understand. For they had gossiped about him in the town. 'I should not have behaved myself after the manner I did in Leicester, if I had not valued my own entertainment beyond the obloquy of a parcel of very wretched fools, which I very solemnly pronounce the inhabitants of Leicester to be.'

Here is the mature Swift, at twenty-three.

The second foreshadowing of the future is that he experienced the first symptoms of the peculiar disease from which he suffered all his life, which has been diagnosed only in our time: Ménière's disease. He thought that it came from eating a surfeit of summer fruit, so that – abstemious as he was all his life – here was another field of enforced abstinence. In fact it was an incurable disturbance of the inner ear, which came on at intervals, he could never tell when: it gave him attacks of giddiness, vertigo, and nausea – he had to live carefully. When one considers that so much of his life was lived, his work done, under this shadow, one must respect his fortitude. All the same his correspondence is full of this trouble, its symptoms and his disabilities; having mentioned it, we need not go into it all again. At times it made him very deaf, at others querulous; often he could not go out or about his business. In the end, it must have brought about the total deafness and undermining of his faculties in his last years. Considering what he had to put up with, it is amazing what he did. We must understand this conditioning element, always present.

A third pointer is this. On his way to Moor Park he stopped at Oxford. He had friends there: his cousin Thomas was at Balliol College; St George Ashe's son was taking an M.A., *ad eundem*, as a Trinity man. Swift decided to do the same, incorporating cheaply not from a college but from Hart Hall. This was at any rate a qualification for the Church, which always remained a possibility, something to fall back on, though not Swift's first choice.

This was, of course, literature and politics, a combination of the two such as Temple had achieved; but, then, he had been a gentleman of independent means. However, this was the atmosphere of Moor Park, the air Swift breathed there. He arrived back in December 1691, to spend the next two and a half years there; the tradition of the house – not essentially changed, though enlarged in the later eighteenth century – is that he had a small room on the ground floor in the old part that has retained its red brick, along the terrace from the main rooms looking down towards the canal. In these years he gave himself to poetry, apart from his attendance on Sir William, who encouraged his efforts in verse. The fashion of the time was for Pindaric odes in complicated form; Swift worked at them for a couple of hours in the mornings. Sometimes he wrote two stanzas in a day, at other times no more in a week, 'and yet I do not believe myself to be a laborious dry writer, because if the fit comes not immediately I never heed it, but think of something else.' He was very proud of the first heir of his invention to achieve print, the stanzas to the Athenian Society; 'Sir William Temple speaking to me so much in their praise made me zealous for their cause, for really . . . poets cannot write well except they think the subject deserves it.'

ese early odes have been imperceptively depreciated; they not
tell us a great deal about his life at Moor Park, they express its
es – rectitudinous, moralistic, rationalist – but they have strokes
that reveal the mature Swift, impassioned, angered by human folly.
At this time everything he touched turned to verse:

> Whate'er I plant, like corn on barren earth,
>   By an equivocal birth
> Seeds and runs up to poetry.

A young man, he was an idealist, like Sir William; that doctrinaire
Whig, personally incorruptible, had always hoped for the reform of
English government. Hence, too, the long ode on the improbable
subject of Archbishop Sancroft, an upright man who had sacrificed
the see of Canterbury for his convictions (would Swift have done?).
Even on these (early) moral altitudes Swift's contempt for the mob
comes out:

> In vain then would the Muse the multitude advise,
> Whose peevish knowledge thus perversely lies
>   In gathering follies from the wise . . .

The people are described as 'the giddy British populace', there had
been so many overturns, civil wars and revolutions. There is the
universal idiocy of war:

> War! that mad game the world so loves to play,
>   And for it does so dearly pay:
> For though with loss or victory awhile
>   Fortune the gamesters does beguile,
> Yet at the last the box sweeps all away.

There are particular targets too, where the poet scores bull's-eyes:
the pedantry of the Schools, especially the dead scholasticism which
Bacon, Milton and (a nearer spirit) Hobbes had all derided; the
'rudeness, ill-nature, incivility' of academics; the silliness and obtuse-
ness of critics. (As Henry James was to say, two centuries later,
'nobody ever understands *anything*' – he might well have been writing
of the Shakespeare establishment.)

In 1692 something happened to put Swift off writing Pindaric odes: he never wrote another. The young author sought the approbation of his cousin Dryden, at the height of his fame, the acknowledged head of the commonwealth of literature. Understandably, he showed the great man proudly the one work he had in print, the Athenian Ode – to receive no encouragement whatever, but an almighty rebuff: 'Cousin Swift, you will never be a poet.' Dryden was never forgiven for that; the next two poems were written in heroic couplets, then for some years no poetry was written at all. It shows how deeply Swift took this to heart; it was his nature always to take things too hard.

And the next two poems are very revealing. The subject of that to Congreve was an awkward one; for Swift's junior had achieved fame at one stroke with the brilliant success of his first play, Swift himself – the most ambitious soul alive – yet unheard of, Sir William Temple's amanuensis. It was hard to take, and the poem he wrote, hoping that it might make a prologue to Congreve's next play, shows it. It was never used. Swift's envy of his junior's triumph is clear enough:

> *Thus prostitute my Congreve's name is grown*
> *To every lewd pretender of the town.*
> *Troth, I could pity you; but this is it,*
> *You find, to be the fashionable wit.*

Proud as Lucifer, as always, he did not intend to tax the Muse

> *of a mean design*
> *To praise your parts by publishing of mine:*
> *That be my thought when some large bulky writ*
> *Shows in the front the ambition of my wit.*

That day would not be long in coming; within the next few years he would write his first masterpiece, A Tale of a Tub. The inspiration of all his work is foretold in a scarifying couplet of this early poem:

> *My hate, whose lash just heaven has long decreed*
> *Shall on a day make sin and folly bleed.*

In 1693 Temple fell ill; in the poem which his amanuensis wrote to celebrate his recovery we get delightful glimpses of the interior at Moor Park. There is Lady Temple, the charming Dorothy Osborne, less sprightly now, in truth somewhat faded:

> *Mild Dorothea, whom we both have long*
> *Not dared to injure with our lowly song:*
> *Sprung from a better world, and chosen then*
> *The best companion for the best of men.*

The household was run by Dorinda, Temple's sister. Lady Giffard was far from mild, really rather bossy; but she adored Sir William – everybody did – and had been grief-stricken at his illness, for all of them depended on him: everything was centred on the great man.

Here, too, Swift's own peculiar spirit bursts out, in his reproaches to the Muse, i.e. his genius:

> *To thee I owe that fatal bent of mind,*
> *Still to unhappy restless thoughts inclined;*
> *To thee, what oft I vainly strive to hide,*
> *That scorn of fools, by fools mistook for pride.*

It does not appear that Swift strove very hard to hide it; but he could not help himself, he was so obsessed:

> *Madness like this no fancy ever seized,*
> *Still to be cheated, never to be pleased . . .*

and with this, he renounced the Muse and wrote no more verse for several years.

Life with 'the best of men' was not always easy, especially in the subordinate position in which Swift was, and with his nature – madly independent. Someone told him that he was like 'a conjured spirit': if he did not give his overactive mind full employment it would be the worse for him. Temple was complacent and self-satisfied; he was also a rather cool man – and what the young Swift was looking for was a father, and the father's affection he had never known. The great man was moody too. Later on, Swift warned a friend in power, 'never to appear cold to me, for I would not be treated like a school-boy – I had felt too much of that in my life already. I used to be in pain when Sir William Temple would look cold and out of humour for three or four days, and I used to suspect a hundred reasons.' How well one knows the situation! – the genius with one skin too few, engaged in growing a carapace; at bottom, for all his distinction of mind, Sir William was a conventional man: he can never have suspected what fires burned within his subordinate. But Swift loved the place, 'which no time will make me forget and love less'. As an old man he remembered 'the tree on which I carved those words, *factura nepotibus umbram*, one of those elms that stood in the hollow ground just before the house.'

Swift expected too much of an ordinary mortal, even a distinguished one, for he had no father, and was set apart by the fracture of genius. It is likely that Temple never noticed that his secretary was possessed of it – like Rodin with Rilke. On his part, Swift admired him only this side of idolatry, not only his rectitude, his principles – Swift was always a moralist – his justice of mind, his rationalism, but his style and taste. He thought Temple the best master of the English language alive – and indeed he was the finest of models for a young writer: to his clear unadorned prose Swift owed much – and added his own wit and passion channelled into irony. He read widely at Moor Park, not only in the classics but in modern French and English literature, where Temple could show him the way.

The young man could not but be affected by the political interests that still touched the elder statesman. King William came down once and again to consult him and, over his dilemma with regard to the Triennial Bill in 1692, sought Temple's advice. Temple entrusted it to Swift, who took it up to the King in person. (It was not taken.) Swift, as an old man: 'this was the first time that Mr Swift had ever any converse with Courts, and he told his friends it was the first incident that helped to cure him of vanity.' (However, it did not.) Lady Giffard was less sensitive: she knew that the first qualification for Court life was 'to be ready to swallow anything'.

It was a natural expectation for an ambitious young man, with such a patron and such doors open to him, to think that his services would be rewarded with preferment: it was the way men rose, the way his friends – Addison and Steele and (from a much humbler beginning) Matthew Prior – rose. What would the King do for him? What would Sir William? Swift was now thinking of the Church; he was twenty-five, several years had elapsed since taking his degree at Trinity, when normally he should have taken orders – like his cousin Thomas, now provided for. Temple suggested that he waited, until the King provided him with a prebend. 'Though he promises me the certainty of it, yet [he] is less forward than I could wish; because, I suppose, he believes I shall leave him, and upon some accounts he thinks me a little necessary to him.' The fact was that Swift had become indispensable, and Temple did not exert himself to get him an independence by which he might lose him.

Five months more of this indecision and Swift had to come to a resolution. In May 1694 he took the bit between his teeth and declared that he would go back to Ireland and take orders. There must have been a scene, for Sir William 'was extremely angry when I left him – and yet would not oblige himself any further than upon my good behaviour; nor would promise anything firmly to me at all. So that everybody judged I did best to leave him. I design to be ordained September next, and make what endeavour I can for something in the Church.'

Now, to his humiliation Swift found that he could not even take orders without a certificate of 'good life and behaviour' from Sir William. Two or three bishops, 'acquaintances of our family', were willing enough to ordain him, but so long a time had elapsed since taking his degree that he had to have a testimonial. Pocketing his pride, he wrote to Temple in October: 'May it please your honour, that I might not continue by any means the many troubles I have given you, I have all this while avoided one, which I fear proves necessary at last . . . The sense I am in, how low I am fallen in your honour's thoughts, has denied me assurance enough to beg this favour, till I find it impossible to avoid.'

Temple could not in justice refuse this plea, and in January 1695 Swift was ordained in Christ Church Cathedral, Dublin. His Irish connections stood him in good stead enough to provide him with a living in the North, at Kilroot near Belfast. The living – or combination of livings – was a small one, the neighbourhood uncongenial, but at last Swift was independent, if on a small, penurious basis.

With only this at his back, Swift was normal enough sexually to propose marriage. There was in the neighbourhood an eligible female, sister of one of his college friends, an Archdeacon's daughter, Jane Waring. The lady seems to have been a rather feeble creature, with a small dowry, who blew now warm, now cold, in general rather tepid. Swift was nettled – or put on his mettle, and the poor girl received a proposal of marriage that seemed more like the laying down of a gun-barrage, and must have frightened her. The thought of love is apt to go to a writer's head as much as anywhere else, and Swift urged a hundred persuasions. 'Impatience is the most inseparable quality of a lover.' She is wasting her life daily in fancied ill-health, 'though one just and honourable action would furnish health to her and unspeakable happiness to us both'. Then comes the authentic Swift note: 'Why was I so foolish to put my hopes and fears into the power or management of another?' Rejected, he never would again.

His prospects in England were improving. 'I am once more offered the advantage to have the same acquaintance with greatness [i.e. from Temple] that I formerly enjoyed, and with better prospect of interest. I here solemnly offer to forgo it all for your sake.' We shall never hear these accents again from him. She should impose her own conditions. 'I desire nothing of your fortune; you shall live where and with whom you please till my affairs are settled to your desire. In the meantime I will push my advancement with all the eagerness and courage imaginable, and do not doubt to succeed.' Here was a generous and sincere proposition.

It is followed by a protestation never repeated by Swift. 'Surely you have but a very mean opinion of the joys that accompany a true, honourable, unlimited love; yet either nature and our ancestors have hugely deceived us, or else all other sublunary things are dross in comparison. Is it possible you cannot yet be insensible to the prospect of a rapture and delight so innocent and exalted? Trust me, Heaven has given us nothing else worth the loss of a thought. Ambition, high appearance, friends and fortune are all tasteless and insipid when they come in competition . . .' It is an extraordinary declaration, clean contrary to everything we associate with Swift, and everything he came to hold.

'But listen to what I here solemnly protest, by all that can be witness to an oath, that if I leave this kingdom before you are mine, I will endure the utmost indignities of fortune than ever return again.'

The lady rejected him.

He would never again put himself in a posture to be humiliated by a woman. It is curious to think what might have happened if Swift had been normalized and subjugated, roped and tied by the bonds of marriage and family life – he could never have accomplished the astonishing achievement he did, if he had accepted the limitations of ordinary human society. His whole genius depended upon his revolt against those limitations. The extraordinary thing is that he should ever have been willing to submit to them; he had allowed himself to be carried away. But never again; nor did he forgive the woman who had dared to reject him.

A little later, she tried to renew the affair, apparently incited by a rumour that he was marrying someone else in England. She received a wounding, a most humiliating, dressing down, all the sharper for the assurance that he had never thought of marrying anyone but her. Nevertheless, he assured her that 'in England it was in the power of any young fellow of common sense to get a larger fortune than ever you pretended to.' And now, 'are you in a condition to manage domestic affairs with an income of less perhaps than £300 a year? Have you such an inclination to my person and humour as to comply with my desires and way of living, and endeavour to make us both as happy as you can? Will you be ready to engage in those methods I shall direct for the improvement of your mind, so as to make us entertaining company for each other, without being miserable when we are neither visiting nor visited?'

It is the proposition of a master to a servant. Such, and more degrading still, are the questions he would put now; if she could answer them in the affirmative, Swift would receive her, 'without regarding whether your person be beautiful, or your fortune large. Cleanliness in the first, and competency in the other, is all I look for. I desire, indeed, a plentiful revenue, but would rather it should be of my own.'

The whole tone is insulting, intended to humiliate her who had humiliated him. No answer is recorded, as was no doubt intended; Jane Waring never found a husband, though she lived many years to witness the greatness of the man who had once laid himself at her feet.

What a chasm, what a world of difference between these two letters, all the evidence we have as to what passed between them in these few years. This is what this poor creature had done to this proud man. It is as if this proudest of spirits was fated to be rejected, and by people he justly considered inferior to himself. At the same time as his contempt for others invited rejection, the rejection justified his contempt: it was a crux from which he could not escape. Henceforth the pattern was set; it was to recur, in different circumstances, again and again. And it maddened him.

Swift's last period of residence at Moor Park stands in some contrast to the earlier. It is evident that he was happier for being on a better footing; he was now an independent clergyman (with a licence for non-residence at Kilroot), his prospects were more assured. He was to put the failing elder statesman's papers in order, and have the publication of his *Memoirs* – in itself both an introduction to the literary world, giving him a place in it, and a useful literary property. No more poetry – these years were given up to prose, and there emerged from it a major masterpiece, *A Tale of a Tub*.

The circle was now more restricted, with Lady Temple's death, and Lady Giffard sometimes away seeing her grand Court friends – like the Duchess of Somerset, the great Percy heiress, to whom the Temples had been very helpful in her earlier matrimonial disasters. Sir William was ailing, and we see how happy Swift was to take charge.

'Aeolus has made a strange revolution in the rooks' nests; but I say no more, for it is dangerous to meddle with things above us. I now live in great state, and the cook comes in to know what I please to have for dinner: I ask very gravely what is in the house, and accordingly give orders for a dish of pigeons, or, etc.' The fact is – Swift was born to rule. In addition, there was charming company for him now in a girl just growing up, whose education and forming he could supervise, as he had hoped to do Jane Waring's. This far more attractive girl came into his life as Jane went out – and stayed there. This was Stella.

She was Esther Johnson, the daugher of Temple's steward. Her father was dead, and Sir William had taken her into his household, where she filled the place of his own little daughter who had died. The child was the light of his eyes, and provided amusement with her lisping baby-talk, for she could not pronounce consonants easily. This was the origin of the 'little language', filled with endearments, with which Swift relaxed in his famous *Journal to Stella*, written to her and her companion Rebecca Dingley when they were in Dublin and he was busy in London. Miss Dingley was a relation of Temple himself, of good family, but impoverished. They were all in a way poor relations of the great man, hangers-on: everything depended on his life. And now he was gouty and feeble.

He had had a sad disaster, too, in the death of his son. He had possessed influence enough to procure him the splendid position of Secretary at War. All that this young fool could do was to fill his pockets with stones and throw himself into the Thames. What would not Swift have given for such an opportunity – and what a career he would have made of it! For he had an undoubted gift for politics, and a passion for good government.

The charm of the household came to centre upon the girl, whom they called Hetty, but Swift – different from everybody else – Stella. She had been only eight when he first arrived; now she was coming to maturity, dark, intelligent and immensely sympathetic. She had difficulty with her spelling, like most contemporary ladies; but, unlike them, she grew to be well-read, in French too, under his direction. He was training her for the companion he needed; his attitude towards young women was always tutelary, tempering 'love and books together'. He thought it safer, as it was – for him.

After his experience with Jane Waring he was not going to expose himself to humiliation again. Years later, he wrote of Stella, as if from a distance, as was now his settled resolution, that 'he had had some share in her education, by directing what books she should read, and perpetually instructing her in the principles of honour and virtue; from which she never swerved in any one action or moment of her life. She was sickly from her childhood until about the age of fifteen; but then grew into perfect health and was looked upon as one of the most beautiful, graceful and agreeable young women in London, only a little too fat. Her hair was blacker than a raven, and every feature of her face in perfection.'

What they had in common all their lives were the memories of the happy years at Moor Park, her education, and more – but Swift was not going to go further into that now forbidden territory.

The happiness of these years is expressed in the tearing high spirits of the three prose works he wrote there, which go together, though published some years later with a good deal of mystification. A gentleman had to be careful about owning his works – still more a clergyman with such works as they turned out to be.

The Battle of the Books is the most popular and easy of approach. It is Swift's contribution to the controversy that had been started over Temple's *Essay on Ancient and Modern Learning*. We do not need to go into it all here; obviously Swift, though taking up the cudgels in defence of Temple, was not much interested in the issue whether ancient writers were better than modern. The controversy had given an opening for the professors to be rude to each other, as with a similarly pointless controversy in our time about the Rise of the Gentry. Swift laid about him enjoyably: Fellows of All Souls like Creech, the great but overbearing Master of Trinity (Cambridge), Bentley, the aristocratic Boyle of Christ Church, Wotton, the Cambridge don who had answered Temple – whether Oxford or Cambridge, they all get their comeuppance from this outsider.

What a biographer must notice is that, in each of these works, Dryden gets a flout or a jeer. In *The Battle of the Books* Dryden makes a ludicrous appearance in combat with Vergil, whom he had translated. The acknowledged head of English letters has a helmet too large for his head, 'even like the Lady in a Lobster [a reference from Herrick], or like a mouse under a canopy of state, or like a shrivelled beau from within the penthouse of a modern periwig. And the voice was, suited to the visage, sounding weak and remote.' What has not been noticed is that, Swift being Swift, these are likely to be tell-tale features of Dryden's actual appearance, of which we know so little: he probably was by this time shrivelled up, his voice feeble. For in the Apology for *A Tale of a Tub* we are informed: 'Dryden, L'Estrange and some others I shall not name are here levelled at, who – having spent their lives in faction and apostasies and all manner of vice – pretended to be sufferers for loyalty and religion.' So Dryden tells us, in one of his Prefaces, of his merits and sufferings and thanks God that he 'possesses his soul in patience'. Next Swift places Dryden's defence of Catholicism, *The Hind and the Panther*, beside chap-books like *Tom Thumb, Dick Whittington and his Cat* and *The Wise Men of Gotham*. He describes it as 'the masterpiece of a famous writer now living, intended for a complete abstract of sixteen thousand Schoolmen from Scotus to Bellarmine'.

This is what Cousin Dryden got for snubbing the young Swift: he was a dangerous man to offend, with (his own phrase) 'the long sedate resentment of a Spaniard'.

As the contemporary St Paul's rising at the time was the masterpiece of the first half of Wren's creative life and Greenwich Hospital of the second, so *A Tale of a Tub* is the masterpiece of Swift's early career as *Gulliver's Travels* is of the later. For all its rational classicism of spirit, the *Tale* is a Gothick edifice, complicated and rambling, tricked out with digressions and prefaces; though its style is closer to Hobbes, its humour is more like Rabelais. Much reading and reflection went into it – we have a long list of the books Swift read at Moor Park at this time, several of them with a suspiciously sceptical tendency. Such is the tone, as well as really the moral, of the work.

* The kernel of it is the allegory he reflected upon in Ulster, where he was thrown cheek by jowl into the company of Scotch Presbyterians. He hated them, for, to his mind – with the Cavalier background of his grandfather – the Scotch Covenanters had begun the Civil War with their war against bishops and their armies inter-

vening in England. The seventeenth century had been filled with
religious warfare and war itself, and Swift hated the insane enthusiasms
that had given rise to it. Indeed he detested every sort of fanaticism,
political or intellectual as well as religious, for the trouble and suffering
it brought down upon sensible people in the middle of the road.
We in our time, who have seen civilization debased and the world
ruined by the fanaticisms let loose by a Lenin or a Hitler – to name
no others – must sympathize deeply with Swift. He was a major
prophet, as we can see now – as comfortable, cosy Victorian liberals
could not. And he had the raw facts of Irish life constantly at his
door, or in his mind: no wonder he wanted to escape them.

It is not the allegory or the fable of the *Tale* that holds us, any more
than with Samuel Butler's *Hudibras* – very close to Swift's mind, for
the same reasons – but the digressions, that on the Madness of Politics
and Politicians, for example. The later seventeenth century was
dominated by Louis XIV, who had filled Europe with his wars and
alarms, as Versailles with his mistresses. 'The very same principle
that influences a bully to break the windows of a whore who has
jilted him naturally stirs up a Great Prince to raise mighty armies and
dream of nothing but sieges, battles and victories.' In one word, the
instinct of human aggression. There follows the succinct career of 'a
mighty king, who for the space of above thirty years amused himself
to take and lose towns, beat armies and be beaten, drive princes
out of their dominions, fright children from their bread and butter,
burn, lay waste, plunder, dragoon, massacre,' etc. – Heidelberg, the
Netherlands, Huguenots, Camisards, what not. 'The same spirits
which in their superior progress would conquer a kingdom, descending upon the anus conclude in a fistula.' This was what Louis XIV
suffered from.

Not much respect for monarchs or potentates in this radical mind,
with his boundless contempt for human stupidity and folly.

But were the religious any better? 'Who that sees a little paltry
mortal, droning and dreaming and drivelling to a multitude, can
think it agreeable to common good sense that either Heaven or Hell
should be put to the trouble of influence or inspection upon what he
is about?' How much of people's religious hopes (and illusions) is

left after that? We must remember how uneducated and irrational seventeenth-century people were, ready to believe anything, as against the masses of today, with all the advantages of popular education. And it was easy to misunderstand Swift's irony, when he asked: 'Is not religion a cloak, honesty a pair of shoes worn out in the dirt, self love a surtout [overcoat], vanity a shirt, and conscience a pair of breeches which, though a cover for lewdness as well as nastiness, is easily slipped down for the service of both?'

Such passages were dangerous, for enemies were able to point to them as expressions of unbelief. In fact, it hardly needs saying that Swift was in favour of religion to maintain order for ordinary humans, incapable of it without – as we see today, in the breakdown of religious belief all round us. But how much of it did he believe himself? – that was the awkward crux for a clergyman, and a very conspicuous one, hoping to become a bishop. Cardinals had become Popes on less – but they had been careful not to write books about it. The leading Swift scholar, Herbert Davis, once told me that he had seen in the margin of a book, in Swift's hand, against a reference to the Nicene Creed, *Confessio digna barbaris*; and that is, at any rate, what he probably thought.

People are what they dress themselves up in. 'If one of them be trimmed up with a gold chain and a red gown and a white rod and a great horse, it is called a Lord Mayor. If certain ermines and furs be placed in a certain position we stile them a judge; and so, an apt conjunction of lawn and black satin we entitle a bishop.' There is in that the whole of the portentous clothes-philosophy of Carlyle's windy *Sartor Resartus*, with its appalling biblical style, himself the descendant of Scotch Covenanters.

Caught as he was, a clergyman of the established Church of Ireland, a small minority between the embattled Presbyterians of the North, and the Catholic majority in the South, he considered both extremes, Puritans and Papists, as playing each other's game. 'For the frenzy and spleen of both, having the same foundation, we may look upon them as two pair of compasses, equally extended . . . which, though moving contrary ways at first, will be sure to encounter somewhere or other in the circumference.'

Swift was no great favourite with Victorians, and never with liberals, with their childish illusions – but we have contemporary Ireland in ferment once more, like him, to enlighten us.

Fanaticism of any kind was what he hated, for it produced only ✳ revolution and suffering. 'A fanatic strain or tincture of enthusiasm, improved by certain persons or societies of men, and by them practised upon the rest, has been able to produce revolutions of the greatest figure in history' – witness not only Luther and Calvin, of whom Swift could not approve, but Lenin and Hitler. In *The Mechanical Operation of the Spirit*, which may be regarded as a fragment of the *Tale*, he cites the Roundheads, and exposes what inspires these people. We might think of this work as his *Varieties of Religious Experience*, except that he is interested only in the expressions of it and its modes of operation, its distasteful phenomena, as a way of showing up the nonsense it is. 'I laugh aloud to see these reasoners engaged in wise dispute whether they are in the verge of God or the Devil; seriously debating whether such and such influences come into men's minds from above or below, whether certain passions and affections by the Evil Spirit or the Good.' He knew perfectly that the great majority cannot think rationally, so why regard with any respect the results of such discussions?

Since the content of their 'thinking' is of no value, he confines himself to describing the motions. 'It is to be understood that, in the language of the spirit, cant and droning supply the place of sense and reason . . . plentifully fraught with theological polysyllables and mysterious texts from Holy Writ.' When the fanatics got into their form, it was frequent 'for a single vowel to draw sighs from a multitude, and for a whole assembly of saints to sob to the music of one solitary liquid.' To the really elect nothing was to be compared with the gift of 'conveying the sound through the nose, which under the denomination of snuffling hath passed with so great applause in the world . . . In a short time no doctrine passed for sound and orthodox, unless it were delivered through the nose.' Here was the authentic Puritan twang, a nasal whine, which passed over with the elect into New England.

Bad as it is today to live in a society of Leftist liberal cant – about the educability of everybody, and everybody being not only equal but the same, and what not – it must have been appalling to live in the England of the Civil War and Commonwealth, when these hypocrites were on top. And the destruction they wrought! – the sale of the King's pictures, the ruin of his palaces, the destruction of great houses like Raglan and Basing, of monuments, brasses, stained glass in the cathedrals and churches, etc. It must have been agonizing to endure. In our time there has only been the destruction of great cities, the demolition of country houses, the losses of works of art – humans in general being all too easily replaceable.

And how did the canters of his time operate? He had observed them in their conventicles: 'they violently strain their eyeballs inward, half closing the lids [I have myself observed that refinement with old Nonconformists]; then, as they sit, they are in a perpetual motion of see-saw, making long hums at proper periods [I have heard 'Hallelujah' and 'A-a-a-men'], continuing the sound at equal height, choosing their time in those intermissions, while the preacher is at ebb.' As for the preacher, 'I have been informed by certain sanguine brethren that, in the height and orgasmus of their spiritual exercise it has been frequent with them . . . immediately after which they found the spirit to relax and flag of a sudden with the nerves, and they were forced to hasten to a conclusion.'

Throughout Swift's aim is to show up the types he despised in the most absurd postures. There is a digression devoted to the asininity of critics: a critic is one who cannot very well write himself – neither novel nor play, history nor poetry – but will lay down the law to those who can. 'The true critics are known by their talent of swarming about the noblest writers, to which they are carried merely by instinct, as a rat to the best cheese, or a wasp to the fairest fruit. So, when the King is a horse-back, he is sure to be the dirtiest person of the company, and they that make their court best are such as bespatter him worst.' And he had done his best to bespatter Dryden.

Though the mass of mankind cannot think, those whose professional business it is – philosophers and such – often only confuse counsel, they are so hopelessly irrelevant or out of touch with real needs, when not positively subversive.

34

'The philosopher's way in all ages has been by erecting certain edifices in the air . . . I think, with due submission, they seem to labour under two inconveniences. First, that the foundations being laid too high, they have been often out of sight, and ever out of hearing. Secondly, that the materials, being very transitory, have suffered much from inclemencies of air, especially in these North-West regions.' We see that these are like the philosophers of Laputa – having not only no sense, but no senses – and recognize a continuity between the *Tale* and *Gulliver's Travels*.

The book was a bomb, but a time-bomb; it was not wanting in its effect on his career, when people began to suspect him of having written it – though he never acknowledged it. It was published, along with *The Battle of the Books* and *The Mechanical Operation of the Spirit*, in 1704, before he became a public figure. All kinds of people were suspected of the misdemeanour, including the brilliant Whig leader, Lord Somers. When Swift was coming into public notice in 1709, he wrote an Apology by way of explaining away the *Tale*. 'Why should any clergyman of our Church be angry to see the follies of fanaticism and superstition exposed, though in the most ridiculous manner; since that is perhaps the most probable way to cure them, or at least to hinder them from any further spreading?' He had been a young man when he wrote it, 'his invention at the height, and his reading fresh in his head . . . He gave a liberty to his pen which might not suit with maturer years or graver characters, and which he could easily have corrected had he been master of his papers for a year or two before their publication.' There was nothing immoral in the book; he had noticed before that the clergy were 'not always very nice in distinguishing between their enemies and their friends'.

It was all to no avail: the odour of brimstone clung to him all his days. It is said that Archbishop Sharp of York, the Queen's confessor, warned her against the irreligious author of *A Tale of a Tub* – no bishopric for him. The odd thing is that Swift should ever have expected one after publishing such a book. For indeed its attack on all forms of inspiration not only struck at fanaticism but aspersed Christianity as such; and though no doubt Swift thought the Queen and her Archbishop fools, they were not such fools as not to see that.

Such was the irony of life that the fools – 'a crazy prelate and a royal prude' – had the last word. Or, perhaps, not quite: for, when an old man and very famous, turning over the pages, he was heard to mutter, 'Good God! what a genius I had when I wrote that book.'

Swift's sister wrote that Temple had become so fond of (*sc.* dependent on) her brother that he made him give up his living in Ireland 'to stay with him at Moor Park, and promised to get him one in England'. We learn from Swift himself that he was criticized by Irish friends for resigning Kilroot, 'before I was possessed of something else', and for not coming to terms with Miss Waring. By this time he was as anxious to be quit of her as of Kilroot. Temple had a friend in the Whig Lord Sunderland. Swift tells us, 'for my own fortune, as late in my life as it is, I must e'en let it drive on its old course . . . Ten days before my resignation, my Lord Sunderland fell and I with him.' This was in 1698; this year Sir William paid his last visit to the Duchess of Somerset upon her Percy estate at Petworth.

In the New Year, 27 January 1699, Temple died. Swift noted, in his meticulous manner: 'he died at one o'clock in the morning and with him all that was great and good among men.' There followed a most generous and moving tribute to his memory. 'He was a person of the greatest wisdom, justice, liberality, politeness, eloquence, of his age and nation; the finest lover of his country . . . besides his great deserving of the commonwealth of learning, having been universally esteemed the most accomplished writer of his time.' There can be no doubt about Swift's sincerity or his admiration for the man who had done so much to form his mind: 'accomplished' was exactly the right word, not 'profound' or 'original'. We may reserve those epithets for the pupil.

All the same, in the end Sir William failed him. Swift immediately went up to London to urge his claim to a prebend at Canterbury or Westminster which King William had promised Temple for him. How strangely different Swift's life would have been if this had been forthcoming! – less tragic, certainly less heroic, a Prometheus chained to his rock in Ireland. Swift applied to the Earl of Romney, 'who professed much friendship for him'; he relied upon 'this lord's honour, having neglected to use any other instrument of reminding his Majesty of the promise made to Sir William Temple'. He waited and waited in vain; Romney said 'not a word to the King' to bring Swift's petition to his notice. Romney, as a young man – a Sidney – had been notably handsome and been made much of by William: he was a good deal of a favourite. He could certainly have done something for Swift. Years later, the famous Dean characterized him, perhaps too savagely, as 'an old, vicious, illiterate rake, without any sense of truth or honour'. He had not been forgiven.

All these disappointments were reinforcing Swift's complex. Allowing for the element of mischance, there was still something to explain in his failure to achieve security. He had relied too much upon Temple, perhaps thinking of him as a father, too happy at Moor Park. So he had not pushed his career in the professional way others did. As his modern biographer, Ehrenpreis, points out, 'Prior clung, without swerving, to Montagu; Congreve never broke with Dryden or the Court [and, we might add, stuck to Marlborough's daughter, the second Duchess]; Addison and Somers kept up, to the end, a cordial, if sometimes thin, friendship; even the quixotic Richard Steele only left Lord Cutts after a dedication . . . won him a captaincy', and we may add that he never left the Marlboroughs. Years later, Swift put his finger on the explanation himself:

> *Had he but spared his tongue and pen,*
> *He might have rose like other men.*

But this he could not do: the force of his genius, and even the strength of his personality, were too much for him. He had not only a passion but rather a foible for independence; he lacked the obsequiousness and the disingenuousness necessary for rising in the world. That, and too proud: 'little disguises were infinitely beneath persons of pride . . . paltry maxims calculated for the rabble of humanity.'

Nor had Sir William left him independent; merely £100 in his will, along with 'the care, and trust, and advantage' – Swift allows generously – 'of publishing his posthumous writings'. Temple had more reason to be grateful that they were in such competent hands – it is doubtful if he ever realized how much grander a spirit he bred in his house. Like the conventional man he really was, he was much more generous to Stella: he left her a lease of lands in Ireland, and a bag of gold coins some £250 in value. Swift stayed a while at Moor Park, winding up affairs, seeing to the payment of legacies, the purchase of mourning, and Temple's internment in Westminster Abbey.

Some time that year he jotted down memoranda, in his usual manner, 'When I come to be old', which give us an insight into his very soul, and perhaps the ambivalence of his feelings for Temple. He was 'not to keep young company, unless they really desire it; not to be peevish or morose, or suspicious; not to be over-severe with young people, but give allowances for their youthful follies and weaknesses.' And then, a recognizable reminder for anyone who has lived with old men: 'not to tell the same story over and over to the same people.' There are others that tell the same tale: 'not to be too free of advice, nor trouble any but those that desire it, not to boast of my former beauty or strength, or favour with ladies, etc.' We come closer to Swift himself, with his mania for cleanliness in a slatternly age: 'not to neglect decency or cleanliness, for fear of falling into nastiness.' And, lastly, we come very near the bone with – 'not to marry a young woman'; 'not to harken to flatteries, nor conceive I can be beloved by a young woman; not to be fond of children, or let them come near me hardly.'

He still had to provide for himself. In a quarrel with Lady Giffard about the publication of the *Memoirs*, some ten years after Temple's death, he expressed what he felt. 'I pretend not to have had the least share in Sir William Temple's confidence above his relatives or his commonest friends. I have but too great reason to think otherwise.' Fifteen years later still, to Temple's nephew: 'Being born to no fortune, I was at his death as far to seek as ever, and perhaps you will allow that I was of some use to him.'

Being as far to seek as ever, and now without a living, he had to take the first offer that came. Lord Berkeley had been appointed a Lord Justice in Ireland, and offered to take Swift back with him as his chaplain.

His fate was Ireland after all.

CHAPTER 3

Dublin and Stella

SWIFT PROCEEDED TO MAKE the best of what had happened, and for the next few years was happy enough in Ireland. He took the best possible step to make it so, in 1701, by bringing over Stella and Miss Dingley for companionship and thus reconstituting something of the Moor Park background. In England Stella could not have lived comfortably as a lady on her small fortune; Miss Dingley had virtually nothing. Moreover, Stella's property was in Ireland; living there cost only half what it did in England, while the return on money was twice as much. Stella needed no persuasion; her future was inevitably tied up with that of her mentor and protector – and she probably hoped to marry him. She did not (yet) know her man.

With his immense practical capacity Swift presided over the transition, and generously added £50 a year for their support. Publicly, to him they were the 'ladies', and he was careful not to see Stella except in the company of a third person. For in introducing her into Dublin society, mainly clerical and bourgeois, there was a good deal of gossip. Ordinary people never understand anything out of their line – and there was nothing ordinary about Swift. He was always a little conscious of the inferiority of her origins, a steward's daughter, her mother a waiting-woman to Lady Giffard; under his tuition she had blossomed above her station, into the most attractive and cultivated woman of her small circle. In return, the ladies looked after his domestic arrangements, providing for his bachelor household, occupying his quarters when he was away, in the country or in Dublin, for – a free agent, as he had always meant to be, and certainly restless, with all his banked-up energies – he was much on the move, in Ireland as well as in England, and between the two countries. He said later that when he was young he could have leaped over the moon.

He was now provided for, more satisfactorily, near the capital – though again disappointed of better expectations. He received the gift of the vicarage of Laracor, which, combined with two more parishes, gave him the substantial income of some £250 a year. (We must multiply by perhaps twenty for comparable values.) Out of this he paid £50 for a curate to help him with the duty, or when he was absent, as he was frequently. This was twice the amount curates normally received; for Swift could be both generous and mean, as he was both kind and cruel. Absence did not mean that he neglected his small kingdom, with only fifteen Protestant families to attend church, the squire – to Swift's annoyance – a Presbyterian. Far from that, he enjoyed his rural retreat and, with his active spirit, set about improving it: the one-story cabin of his occupation, cleaning out the canal and setting willows along it, planting a garden – which the native Irish never did.

The society of the capital, of the grandees at the Castle, political society, was what his teeming brain needed. And it was not until a year had elapsed that he got a prebend in St Patrick's Cathedral, which gave him a position in Dublin. He soon became the most active member of the Chapter, which was one day to come under his rule and be for ever associated with his name: the great Dean of St Patrick's.

Over the wall, in his rambling draughty palace of St Sepulchre's, ruled Archbishop King, with whom Swift was to have awkward, somewhat ambivalent, relations over many years. Archbishop King was quite a match for Swift: he was an indubitably great man, one of the best men the Church of Ireland ever produced, moreover he had the reins of power. Like Swift a celibate, he had the advantage of being single-minded: all his days he cared for nothing, thought of nothing, but the well-being of Church and people. Twice he had been imprisoned in the troubles the idiotic James II brought upon the country; nothing daunted, he went on his way, spoke his mind and did all the good he could. He was immensely charitable and spent practically all his revenues on good works; he tried all he knew to repair the damage to the churches in the appalling conflicts that had ravaged the country, building churches where there was an opening, raising money, where most of the tithes and property of the Church before the Reformation had now been appropriated to the landlords. One must remember this crippling condition in which the Church of Ireland existed. Strict in the performance of his duties, the Archbishop enforced this upon others, so far as he could; he looked with no friendly eye upon absenteeism or non-resident clergymen.

Swift and the Archbishop were fundamentally at one in their views: a Protestant Church, but under episcopal rule; no truck with Dissenters; the Revolution settlement as the only possible basis for government; an established Church, but given self-respect by conducting its own internal affairs. And, born and bred in Ireland, King thought, like Swift, that the Church should be staffed by home-grown products, not by intrusive Englishmen taking the profits and living out of the country. On the other hand, they differed greatly in temperament. The Archbishop had a well-balanced mind, straightforward, with no difficulties within himself; he was benevolently inclined, nothing ever panicked him – perhaps he had not enough imagination. We might almost say that he was rather euphoric – and, considering the place he occupied, it was just as well.

In the fascinating exchanges between them – a drawn battle – Swift once summed up the difference between them. 'I very much applaud your Grace's sanguine temper, as you call it, and your comparison of religion to paternal affection. But the world is divided into two sects: those that hope the best, and those that fear the worst. Your Grace is of the former, which is the wiser, the nobler, and most pious principle.' No doubt Swift was sincere in saying this, and the Archbishop was a wiser, nobler and more pious man. Swift went on, 'although I endeavour to avoid being of the other, yet upon this article I have strange weaknesses.' He hardly dared say to the Archbishop that he was without Christian hope; but, a man of imagination, he did remind him of the loss to Christianity of half the Mediterranean world, all Africa, the Near East, its original home. 'How far the wickedness of a nation may provoke God Almighty to inflict so great a judgment is terrible to think.'

Which of these two great men saw further? Swift had the difficulties of an underlying pessimism about *la condition humaine* to support, the intuitions, and strains, of genius.

Their relations began awkwardly, and characteristically. In the year 1701, Swift took his D.D.; it was a qualification very proper for a bishop, or a dean. Henceforth – Doctor Swift, as everybody called him; they must have perceived the propriety: the Doctor. The deanery of Derry now fell vacant, which King himself had occupied earlier. It was the best deanery going, and Swift fancied himself for it – he seems to have thought that Lord Berkeley was in favour of his having it. The Archbishop did not even consider him for it; he thought Swift too young. The truth was that he did not really trust the man of genius – too independent, he would always take his own line; to use a favourite cliché with conventional people, Swift was inassimilable.

A few years later, Swift still had hopes of Berkeley, with whose family he was a favourite. The Earl had a chaplain, the learned but dull Dr Milles, at whom Swift laughed. The bishopric of Waterford fell vacant, for which Swift hoped; he had his laugh, but Dr Milles had the bishopric.

Nevertheless, the vicar of Laracor remained an intimate of the Castle when the Berkeleys were there. They were a happy and agreeable family, with yet another young lady for the Doctor to entertain with games and verses, word-games and jokes. Later on, the philosopher Berkeley paid tribute to Swift as 'one of the best-natured and agreeable men in the world'. We must always remember that in society this side to him was uppermost – always provided that he was properly regarded, his complexes not grazed by the stupid or hostile, when he could be merciless. He was a rather short man, whose eyes were his most striking feature: a piercing blue, and rather protuberant, like those of the Hanoverian royal family. (Vanessa – Esther Vanhomrigh – said later how terrifying his eyes could be when he was angry.)

In company he was usually irresistible, endlessly amusing and vivacious, with the infallible appeal (to the intelligent) of intellectual high spirits. He required only a modicum of intelligence and liveliness in others to set him alight. We can see that the real reason for brushing off his sister was that she was dull and unintelligent; for he was nothing but kind to an obscure cousin, Patty Rolt, simply because she was lively and amusing: he constantly gave her presents and not infrequently money.

So – another paradox – the great misanthrope, who had no illusions about humanity, was very sociable and a most welcome guest. He had a large circle of friends – may, indeed, be said to have had an exceptional gift for friendship.

One of the most delightful mementoes of those happy days at the Castle is a *jeu d'esprit*, 'The Humble Petition of Frances Harris, who must starve and die a Maid if it miscarries'. She deposes,

> *That I went to warm myself in Lady Betty's chamber,*
> > *because I was cold,*
> *And I had in a purse, seven pound, four shillings and*
> > *sixpence, besides farthings, in money and gold.*

It really is like nothing else, this colloquial poem: part of the joke is that the lady was a gentlewoman-in-waiting, but the language is that of uneducated people, rattling on, disjointed and disconnected, with no reason in it but plenty of rhyme.

> *So when I went to put up my purse, as God would have it,*
> > *my smock was unripped,*
> *And instead of putting it into my pocket, down it slipped.*
> *Then the bell rung, and I went down to put my lady to bed*
> *And, God knows, I thought my money was as safe as my*
> > *maidenhead . . .*

And so on and on, full of the customary jewels with which the people ornament their speech, without which they can hardly express themselves:

> *Says Cary, says he, I have been a servant this five and twenty*
> > *years, come Spring,*
> *And in all the places I lived, I never heard of such a thing . . .*

In keeping with popular wisdom, they talk of consulting an astrologer to find the purse. The chaplain comes in –

> *Parson, said I, can you cast a nativity, when a body's*
> *plundered?*
> *(Now you must know, he hates to be called Parson like the*
> *Devil).*

The upshot is a petition to their Excellencies to make the chaplain marry the poor lady, in spite of the loss of her dowry:

> *And then your poor petitioner, both night and day,*
> *Or the chaplain (for 'tis his trade) as in duty bound, shall*
> *ever pray.*

It is a very Swiftian twist at the end; he never wrote a poem again quite like it. But at the end of his life he wrote two prose works, which are comparable with the poem. One is the *Complete Collection of Genteel and Ingenious Conversation*, a compilation of the inanities and clichés in which bourgeois people clothe their vacuity of mind. It is an idea like Flaubert's *Dictionnaire des idées reçues*, out of which he fashioned *Bouvard et Pécuchet*, with loving hatred for such types. The other is *Directions to Servants*, inspired by Swift's fascinated observation of below-stairs life and lower-class habits and speech. We see what a world away this was from Sir William Temple's *hauteur* – and, indeed, Swift was always friendly with simple folk, with no pretensions or hypocrisies.

He was, however, most at home with charming and intelligent young women – like Lady Betty Berkeley. One of his best efforts in gallantry is a tribute to the looks of her friend, Biddy Floyd. Swift was a welcome guest, when in England, at Berkeley Castle. One day he left a copy of verses lying about, describing the company engaged in a game of Traffic; when his back was turned, Lady Betty surreptitiously added:

> *With these is Parson Swift,*
> *Not knowing how to spend his time,*
> *Does make a wretched shift,*
> *To deafen 'em with puns and rhyme.*

He remained a life-long friend of Lady Betty, who became a well-known figure in her own right, as Lady Betty Germain: a rich widow, living at splendid Drayton in Northamptonshire, where one sees – or used to see – her room, filled with her possessions, and her collection of rare china and porcelain.

Swift contrived to be in England for the summers of 1701, 1702, 1703 and the early summer of 1704; then for three and a half years, a long stretch for him, he stayed in Ireland. His usual routine was to pay a visit to his mother at Leicester, on his way to or from London, where he was engaged in publishing various volumes of Temple's *Memoirs*, a volume of his miscellaneous writings, and his Letter Book. Of this last Swift translated a number of the letters, originally in French, into his own more terse and vigorous English. In 1704 he published *A Tale of a Tub*, with its dedication to the Whig leader, Lord Somers, and immediately left for Ireland. The book had the *succès de scandale* we have seen, and shortly sold into four editions.

He was beginning to make something of a literary income, though thinking of himself as beyond writing for pay. The money came in handy, for he was not living within his income; in addition to the outgoings with which he taxed himself, £50 a year for 'the ladies', another £50 for his curate, something for his mother, he was prodigal in his charities. It is an extraordinary thing, with this extraordinary man, that, though he was careful and counted every penny, he poured out in charity, regularly, week by week, month by month, year by year, almost as much, in proportion, as Archbishop King.

'The ladies', after a spell in lodgings, were settled in their own house in William Street, a new and fashionable quarter, and Stella's 'person was soon distinguished in society'. While he was away, Swift left the ladies in the care of a promising young clergyman of family, William Tisdall. In 1703 we find Swift writing from London, 'pray let the ladies know I had their letter, and that I obeyed Miss Johnson's commands and waited on her mother.' He follows this up with advice as to Stella's property and investments, and relapses into gaiety by telling Tisdall how to outwit Stella with 'a new-fashioned way of being witty' – a *bite*. In the event, Parson Tisdall, to Swift's embarrassment, almost practised a bite on him.

'I am mightily afraid the ladies are very idle, and do not mind their book. Pray put them on reading; and be always teaching something to Miss Johnson, because she is good at comprehending, remembering, and retaining. I wonder she could be so wicked as to let the first word she could speak, after choking, be a pun.' Anyone of common intelligence could have seen what would happen; apparently Swift, with his uncommon intelligence, did not. Young Mr Tisdall fell for Stella, who was his age, not Swift's, and contemplated proposing marriage.

Mr Tisdall, seven or eight years younger, thought of Swift as *in loco parentis*, applied for advice, and received a dusty answer, questioning whether marriage would not be a clog upon his rising in the world, and whether his income was sufficient to make both of them happy and easy. The young man, who must have been pretty obtuse – or, perhaps, merely normal – was much put out by this: he described Swift's reaction as 'unfriendly, unkind, and unaccountable'. It was, however, all too easily accountable. Tisdall was able to assure Swift that his income was sufficient to marry on, and that his prospects were even better.

Now it was Swift that was nettled, as we perceive from the answer he wrote, in which he put forward his position with all the power at his command: 'I will, upon my conscience and honour, tell you the naked truth.' But, of course, the naked truth could not be stated, namely that he wanted to keep Stella to himself. So the young man was treated to a virtuoso performance, which was also true, but hardly the main point. 'If my fortunes and humour served me to think of that state, I should certainly, among all persons on earth, make your choice. Because I never saw that person whose conversation I entirely valued, but her's: this was the utmost I ever gave way to.' And then, somewhat disingenuously, however 'sincerely' Swift felt in writing it: 'this regard of mine never once entered into my head to be an impediment to you.' Even the clearest of heads are apt to be clouded as to their own motives, or – as in Swift's case – could not admit them, perhaps even to himself.

'The objection of your fortune being removed, I declare I have no other. Nor shall any consideration of my own misfortune of losing so good a friend and companion as her, prevail on me, against her interest and settlement in the world, since it is held so necessary and convenient a thing for ladies to marry.' There is a sting in that phrase – the implication is that he did not see the necessity. He concluded with the splendid and moving phrase, 'time takes off from the lustre of virgins in all other eyes but mine.'

The decision was now Stella's – Swift had shifted the moral onus onto the woman. One can hardly feel, after this declaration, that Stella was a free agent; for it meant that he wanted her for himself, but on his own terms. She accepted them, and refused the Revd Mr Tisdall. She may have hoped to marry Swift. But why assume – as people do – that everybody should marry? What about Miss Dingley, with whom Stella was on terms of 'particular intimacy'? Marriage may not have appealed to her any more than to Swift. What a fate to bear the Revd Mr Tisdall's children! Anyone who knows the eighteenth century knows what a lottery it was – the infant mortality, the deaths in childbed. Stella may well be thought to have chosen the better portion – and assured herself of a place in history and the world's regard, alongside the man who had chosen her.

Nor did Swift forget to remind her that Tisdall's feet stank.

Though Swift's career in the Church was at a stand, and he remained a mere Irish vicar while the second-rate and third-rate sailed past him, so far as his grand Whig acquaintance were concerned – Somers, Halifax, Sunderland, Wharton, the Whig Junto, were at any rate out of power – Swift had the consolation that his powers as a writer were coming to be known. At first, only among the elect, among other writers; for there was something mysterious about the Irish clergyman, and he added to it by the deliberate mystification with which he published his own work anonymously. Here was another crux: partly for reasons of prudence, partly for propriety, since he was a clergyman, partly out of an innate love of secrecy and private jokes, he would not acknowledge his works; while at the same time he craved recognition and the fame they deserved.

At this time he was little known, though approaching forty; for him everything was maddeningly belated. It was this mystery that added to the scandal of *A Tale of a Tub*; it certainly was successful, selling four editions in a year, but he could not claim his masterpiece for his own, and never did. He was known to the world at large simply as the editor of Sir William Temple's papers. Few can have known the author of the squibs and verses with which he amused himself and let off his high spirits – when he hadn't the vertigo – like crackers. A fundamental fact about him has not been noticed: literary fame was even dearer to him than office in Church or state. He set a higher value upon the children of his genius, for he would not forgo them for any prospect of preferment. We shall notice that in some notable instances, one of them unpardonable. What this means is that, to himself, he was first and last a writer.

It took other men of genius to penetrate the mask. Among the first was a nasty, but perceptive, attack by the disingenuous Dissenter, Defoe. 'A late happy author, among his mechanical operations of the spirit', had diagnosed enthusiasm as but wind; but his own vapour 'flew upward in vivid strakes of a livid flame called Blasphemy, which burnt up all the wit and fancy of the author, and left a strange stench behind it that has this unhappy quality in it, that everybody that reads the book smells the author though he be never so far off – nay, though he took shipping to Dublin to secure his friends from the least danger of a conjecture.' This was very near the bone: Defoe, who earned his living as an intelligence-man – in other words, a spy – evidently knew.

So did Addison, a very different kind of man, as charming as he was successful in all he undertook, cosseted by fortune and fame – he never had any trouble about recognition, all too generously admired, though his talents were genuine. He and Swift met, apparently, at the St James's Coffee-house and took to each other at once. This was much to the credit of both of them; for Addison already had all the success Swift longed for, five years his junior, and already at the top of literary life in London. On the other hand, he was shy and reserved in company, where Swift blazed and scintillated. Pope tells us, 'Addison was perfect good company with intimates; and had something more charming in his conversation than I ever knew in any man. But, with any mixture with strangers, and sometimes only with one, he seemed to preserve his dignity much, with a stiffer sort of silence.'

He was a well-balanced man, as well he might be, since life had been to him in every way good. He had started with advantages, where Swift had had handicaps. The son of an Anglican dean, he enjoyed a Fellowship at Magdalen for years – where Addison's Walk still recalls him – and he was never wanting patrons. At this moment, he was an under-Secretary of State with over £700 a year. He was to go much further; he ended by becoming Secretary of State himself and marrying a countess. He was always popular. We remember him as the creator of the *Spectator*.

Addison had the generosity to recognize in the Irish vicar a superior spirit – 'the most agreeable companion, the truest friend, and the greatest genius of the age'. What a contrast with the snivelling Defoe! Addison welcomed Swift into literary life, introducing him notably to Steele, a fellow-Irishman who originated the new literary journalism with the *Tatler*, to be followed by the more famous *Spectator*. Soon Swift was on friendly terms with Matthew Prior, poet and diplomatist, and Ambrose Phillips, popular for his pastorals. The doors to literary life were thrown open to the remarkable outsider; he became an insider, an intimate with this group, all Whigs, really much more at home with them than with the great whose approbation he sought. Swift reported to Phillips: 'the triumvirate of Mr Addison, Steele and me, come together as seldom as the sun, moon and earth: I often see each of them, and each of them me and each other; and when I am of the number justice is done you as you would desire.'

Addison was the favourite; as often as he and Swift 'spent their evenings together, they neither of them ever wished for a third person to support or enliven their conversation'. Swift showed an unexpected deference to Addison's judgment over the charming fable he wrote, 'Baucis and Philemon', about the visit of two saints disguised as beggars to a village. They are rejected by all but a couple of poor people, who take them in, feed them – and are suitably rewarded.

Their cottage turns into a church, the cottager receives the preferment
he asks for:

> 'I'm good for little at my days –
> Make me the parson if you please'.
> He spoke, and presently he feels
> His grazier's coat reach down his heels,
> The sleeves new bordered with a list
> Widened and gathered at his wrist.
> A shambling, awkward gait he took,
> With a demure dejected look,
> Talked of his offerings, tithes and dues,
> Could smoke and drink and read the news,
> Or sell a goose at the next town
> Decently hid beneath his gown.
> Contrived to preach his sermon next
> Changed in the preface and the text,
> Carried it to his equals higher,
> But most obsequious to the squire.

This is very much Swift. But there is a further literary interest.
He said that, in this poem of not two hundred lines, Mr Addison
made him 'blot out fourscore, add fourscore, and alter fourscore'. All
Addison's 'improvements' were in the generalizing taste that was to
prevail with eighteenth-century verse, refined and insipid. 'A small
kilderkin of beer', the fried bacon 'tossed up in a pan with batter'
were disapproved; 'full up' became 'replenished'. We can now compare the original version with that published, and Swift's is far better,
concrete and vivid – and, as for literary decorum, more in keeping
with low life.

Addison cut out passages like those that exactly expressed the character of the beggars:

> They called at every door, 'Good people,
> My comrade's blind, and I'm a creeple.
> Here we be starving in the street,'
> 'Twould grieve a body's heart to see 't.

The instinct of the man of greater genius was better; he was not only
in keeping with the more powerful tradition of popular poetry going
right back to Chaucer – as against Addison's gentlemanliness – but

reaching forward to the demotic realism of today. Swift's verse has life in it, like Kipling's – who remembers Addison's? There is a further point, well observed by Ehrenpreis: the poem is an example of humour which is 'neither sentimental nor mocking, but deeply sympathetic. Whenever Swift writes about decent, humble people, this tone tends to appear, though never more benignly than in "Baucis and Philemon".'

Swift achieved far more *réclame* under the pseudonym 'Bickerstaff', under which he perpetrated a hoax against the popular almanac-maker and astrologer Partridge. Hundreds, if not thousands, of fools attended upon this charlatan's prognostications, brazenly fore-telling all kinds of events. Swift spitted him with a prognostication foretelling Partridge's death on a certain date. When the time came crowds besieged Partridge's door, and he was driven to declare in print that he was not dead. All to no avail: Bickerstaff pursued him with more ridicule, and kept the game up with replies to himself.

This kind of thing is hardly to our taste, but Steele tells us that Swift's squibs and pamphlets created a fashion: anything in that line sold. What we should notice is that underneath the joke is the serious Swift: he hated people who battened on the irrationality of the mob, astrologers and almanac-makers as much as Dissenters. His elegy on Partridge has an element of cruelty as well as of the comic:

> *Here five foot deep lies on his back*
> *A cobbler, starmonger, and quack . . .*
> *Who to the stars in pure good-will*
> *Does to his best look upward still.*
> *Weep all you customers that use*
> *His pills, his almanacs or shoes.*

The poor man had only been gaining a livelihood out of people's foolery – but this was precisely what the Doctor could not stand. Merciless, he went on with the persecution; for a time the charlatan was overwhelmed. He wrote to the postmaster of Ireland protesting against the rumours set going 'by a parcel of rogues about my being dead'. But he who puts his money on human foolery has the last word: Partridge, stunned for a moment, recovered his following and, when he died, left a tidy fortune.

What with one thing and another the Doctor was a constant fountain of japes and jokes, full of original ideas whether in prose or verse. Steele paid tribute to it: 'a certain uncommon way of thinking, and a turn in conversation peculiar to that agreeable gentleman, rendered his company very advantageous to one whose imagination was to be continually employed upon obvious and common subjects.' Steele proceeded to make use of this new friend's uncommon way of thinking, working up suggestions from Swift for the *Tatler*, to which himself made some contributions.

He was less successful with his serious pieces at this time, though his *Argument against Abolishing Christianity* is a masterly piece of irony. A straightforward defence of his position was more difficult, as always for a moderate against extremes. Intellectually Swift was a Whig, wholly committed to the Revolution settlement, a rationalist who had no use for Tory Divine-Right-of-Kings nonsense, beginning to pop up its head again, with a Stuart who was a devout Anglican on the throne, in Queen Anne. The intellectual tone and temper of the time were changing from the free-and-easy libertinism of the Restoration – even Congreve was put out of countenance and shut up by Jeremy Collier's attack on the licentiousness of the stage. Similarly with free thought: thought was not so free, in the reign of Queen Anne, as it had been. Intellectually, Swift belonged to the previous age, the rationalist world of thought of Sir William Temple.

A Whig in politics, Swift described himself later as a High-Churchman in religion. No philosopher, he always went straight for people's motives – a most effective short cut in argument. Moreover, it has the advantage of obviating the necessity of taking seriously the arguments in which they dress up their pretences. So we may return the compliment upon Swift by saying that he took up a High Church position simply because he was a churchman: he had taken service, and this was the regiment to which he happened to belong. If it had been another, he would have taken a different stance.

In his *Sentiments of a Church of England Man*, he has little that is convincing except that there are faults on both sides, Tory and Whig. This was true enough, even to a truism: the Whigs were alienating the Church by making up to the Dissenters, the right-wing Tories playing ball to their game by attacking Dissenters for Occasional Conformity, i.e. taking the sacramental test on occasion to qualify for office. Later, Swift said that he had warned the Lords of the Whig Junto that they would end by alienating the Church. This was far-sighted of him: it was exactly what happened and gave the Tories their majority during 1710–14. But no political leaders welcome such threatening advice from an independent-minded follower – as we saw in our time with the protagonists of Appeasement: they turned against the people who warned them what the consequences would be.

So Swift's militant defence of the Church was largely an extra-polation of his own interests as an officer in it. No wonder he was unable to meet the argument of a rationalist Fellow of All Souls, Tindal, that a state church had no separate authority from the state that maintained it, and gave up the attempt to answer Tindal's *Rights of the Christian Church Asserted.* Tindal was an All Souls lawyer who had been a Catholic under James II, and then – seeing through the silliness of both sides – became a deist. He was not popular in college, because he cheated: being a teetotaller, he had no difficulty in answering the other Fellows' arguments after dinner. However, Tindal could be attacked as immoral – and was.

The pious Queen, who had received much acclaim on ascending the throne by a reference to her 'entirely English heart' – a back-hander at her brother-in-law, Dutch William – added to her popularity with the Church by remitting the First Fruits, i.e. the first year's revenues on bishoprics, deaneries and larger benefices. These were to be paid into a fund to augment smaller livings, known as Queen Anne's Bounty. A suggestion came up from the Irish Church that this act of royal beneficence should be extended to Ireland; Swift put himself forward in the matter, and was eventually chosen to represent the Irish Church and push it home in London. It was hoped that his well-known connexions with the Whig peers would help. On Swift's side it provided a grand opportunity to present himself to the political leaders in London to urge his mission. This drew closer the ties between Archbishop King, no mean politician himself, and the Church's accredited agent; it also provided Swift with his licence (renewable) for non-residence.

In Ireland Swift made good friends with the new Lord-Lieutenant, the Earl of Pembroke, and formed a close intimacy with a scholarly connoisseur, Sir Andrew Fountaine, who accompanied him. The number of Swift's acquaintance was very large – it is difficult to understand how he kept pace with them all, political, literary, clerical, personal. Addison paid the best tribute to Swift's company, when he himself was in Dublin as secretary to the Whig Lord Wharton, and Swift went straight to Laracor to make up his duty: 'I think it is very hard I should be in the same kingdom with Doctor Swift and not have the happiness of his company once in three days.'

Again, he longed to 'eat a dish of bacon and beans in the best company in the world'. When Addison was over again with Wharton in 1710, Swift was at Laracor, his ladies close by at Trim. The secretary besought Swift to come up to town: 'I long to see you. I love your company and value your conversation more than any man's.' Soon they were affably drinking tea – the new, fashionable, expensive beverage – in Dublin.

We are indebted to Swift's fascinating correspondence with Archbishop King – careful and guarded as it is on both sides, but between equals in ability, if not in station – for a brilliant analysis of the political crisis of 1708. The triumvirate that had conducted the war against Louis XIV with such success consisted of Godolphin, head of the Government as Lord Treasurer, his closest friend Marlborough, its executive arm overseas, and – on a lower level – Harley, indispensable as manager of the House of Commons. The country was tiring of the war; so was the Queen, whose duty it was to represent the mind of the country. On this she was advised by Harley surreptitiously, and through her waiting-woman, Mrs Masham, whom Sarah, Duchess of Marlborough, had unwisely planted on her. The Whigs, inspired by the commercial interests and high finance of the City, committed themselves to the war aim of extruding Louis XIV's grandson from the throne of Spain and the Spanish Empire, where they wished to force open the door to British trade.

For the prosecution of the war Godolphin was thus impelled to lean more and more on the Whigs, who were keen to support it. Harley, in touch with opinion in the Commons, which spoke for the country at large, closed with the Queen to get rid of Godolphin and take his place. It was a very audacious scheme, and it was premature. The front of Godolphin and Marlborough was as yet too strong; they had the immense prestige of their successful conduct of the war, and the peers in Council would not follow Harley. It was he who went – maintaining his secret line to the Queen, who, for her part, never forgave Godolphin. She bided her time, as she could afford to; for, though the Government was secure in Parliament for the next two years, it was increasingly out of touch with the country, as would be made clear at the next election.

This was the situation when Dr Swift, after much manoeuvring, at last got an interview with the Lord Treasurer. Godolphin was fonder of horses than of writers; a man of the old generation, he had little idea of using writers for the purposes of propaganda; nor had he any liking for the *tracasseries* of party politics, at which Harley was such an adept. (Sir Winston Churchill saw Harley, not without justice, as another Baldwin – an artful manager, disingenuous, with a Dissenting background.) Godolphin was old and tired and irritable, but he was a politician of immense experience, reaching back to Charles II, and Swift's account of his reception is entrancing.

The great man treated the Irish parson very much *de haut en bas*. He was passive in this business, and supposed that the Lord-Lieutenant would deal with it. After a good deal of sparring, he expressed the opinion that, since the Queen's grant, 'not one clergyman in England was a shilling the better'; while in Ireland, the sum at stake was so inconsiderable that it was almost nothing for the Queen to grant. But, if it were granted, it should be 'received with due acknowledgments; in which case he would give his consent; otherwise, to deal freely with me, he never would.' Swift replied, in the equally oblique language of politics, that 'he had the misfortune to be altogether unknown to his lordship, else I should presume to ask him whether he understood any particular acknowledgments.'

After more beating about the bush, Swift got the Lord Treasurer so far as to say that he meant 'better acknowledgments than those of the clergy of England'. More polite palaver and 'I then begged his lordship to give me his advice, what sort of acknowledgments he thought fittest for the clergy to make'. To this he got the answer, 'I can only say again such acknowledgments as they ought.'

Both the Lord Treasurer and Swift knew perfectly what was meant: that the Church should drop its opposition to the repeal of the Test imposed upon Dissenters. This was the condition the Whigs made for their support; Godolphin was under pressure to accept. He therefore insisted upon a *quid pro quo* for the grant of First Fruits to the Church of Ireland. The old denizen of the race-course at Newmarket, his one and only passion, knew how to make and frame a bargain.

For Swift, this meant a double crisis, public and private. Hitherto he had been sanguine about the success of his mission, in spite of having to spend time in dancing attendance on ministers, some of them holding out hopes, or even assuring him that the job was as good as done. Now, at the highest level, he experienced his moment of truth. What he regarded as just treatment for the Church could never be expected from the Whigs; the grant of the First Fruits, upon which his standing in the Church in Ireland depended, from the Whigs would be at the expense of the Church's position and prestige. This forced him to re-think his whole position in relation to the Whigs, and the contacts (and fond hopes) of a lifetime going back to his apprenticeship with Sir William Temple.

How severe the blow was may be seen from the retrograde step Swift contemplated in his dismay. There was a plan for sending Lord Berkeley as Envoy Extraordinary to the Emperor at Vienna; Swift was willing to go along with him as secretary of embassy – a diplomatic appointment, an entirely new venture. Berkeley was unwilling to go, though Swift was. The report reached Archbishop King, who warned him that he was too old to leave an ecclesiastical career for one in diplomacy. Swift replied with what was not so much a hint as a reproach, and a justified one. 'I agree with your Grace that such a design was a little too late at my years. But, considering myself wholly useless in Ireland, and in a parish with half a score . . . I was a little tempted to pass some time abroad, until my friends would make me a little easier in my fortunes at home.'

Archbishop King had promised Swift the first good prebend in St Patrick's that should fall and, Swift commented bitterly, 'great men's promises never fail.' When 'the golden prebend' fell vacant through the death of a relative, the Archbishop awarded it to another. Two days after this, he recommended Swift to put in for the deanery of Down; the Whig Lord-Lieutenant, Wharton, installed his chaplain in it. Swift, to an Irish squire, Charles Ford, now becoming an intimate: 'I believe you are by this time satisfied that I am not grown great, nor like to do so very soon; for I am thought to want the art of being thorough-paced in my party, as all discreet persons ought to be.' That was it.

Swift's last acts before returning to Ireland in June 1709 read like a deliberate rounding up of the past. He paid a call on Lord Halifax, whom he had long known, exponent of pure milk-of-the-word Whiggism. Picking up a French book on a table – Swift was an inveterate collector of books, beyond his means – he begged it as a gift; and then asked this member of the Junto to remember that this was 'the only favour he ever received from him or his party'. Astonishing as it is to be confronted with this statement, after ten years of waiting, it was the simple truth. In a parting letter, Swift wrote jestingly, 'pray, my lord, desire Dr South to die about the fall of the leaf; for he has a prebend of Westminster which will make me your neighbour.' Halifax replied with appropriate, and accustomed, insincerity. A quarter of a century later, Swift had not forgotten this eminent figurehead: 'I never heard him say one good thing or seem to taste what was said by another.'

Appropriately, too, there was a breach with Moor Park. The last volume of Temple's *Memoirs* posed a problem: there were reflections Temple had made upon some persons still alive, or who had relations alive to resent them. What was Swift to do? He had already postponed publication as long as he could. It had been left entirely to his discretion; he was Temple's literary executor, and the text he was publishing had been gone over with Temple and contained his last corrections. It was the undoubted text from which to print. But Lady Giffard possessed an earlier draft, which, she claimed, was the original. Swift could not risk having this unauthoritative manuscript published, or, since it was being handed round, pirated. He published, and was damned by her.

At once there was an outburst from Lady Giffard's friend, the Duchess of Somerset: her aunt, Lady Essex, was still alive, upon whose husband Temple had made strictures. The Duchess was sure that Swift had done this deliberately; this made it 'unpardonable and will confirm me in the opinion I had before of him – that he is a man of no principle either of honour or religion'. So this woman was an enemy, and entrenched close to the Queen – one sees what these people at the top thought about him. Lady Giffard was a woman of action: she published an advertisement in the public prints, declaring that Swift's volume was printed from an unfaithful copy and was not authoritative. The exact opposite was the case; but there was no arguing with Lady Giffard, though Swift tried it.

He reacted, as he always did when treated unjustly, with angry determination to get his own back (his was not a Christian spirit of meekness, offering the other cheek). He broke off relations with Lady Giffard, vowing that he would not see her again until she begged his pardon – and that was very unlikely. The Duchess he reserved, along with Lord Treasurer Godolphin, for another occasion, like a spider hoarding up flies.

Swift came back to Ireland in July 1709, to nurse his health, and spent the next fourteen months there. Most of 1709 he was ill off and on, with his recurring fits of giddiness. Nevertheless, he was as active – or restless – as ever; in Dublin enjoying the entertainments of Castle society, particularly now that Addison was there. Of the new Lord-Lieutenant, Wharton, Swift disapproved as a dissolute debauchee – we must remember how strait-laced Swift was in matters of sex: he hated lechers, taking out his own repressions in coprophily.

Ireland was full of friends with whom he could stay, only too pleased to have him. In those days when travel was difficult and people had to provide their own entertainments, the world was more hospitable: people stayed with each other for weeks on end. Swift had a new friend in Charles Ford, a delightful companion, a scholarly bachelor, with an eligible small estate at Wood Park, halfway between

Dublin and Laracor. Once the 'ladies', Stella and Dingley, stayed there for six months. Swift was grateful to various friends who looked after them and entertained them while he was in England. In Ireland they had the first claim on his time and attention. No wonder his cousin Thomas wrote one day to a friend 'to know whether Jonathan be married or whether he has been able to resist the charms of both those gentlewomen that marched quite from Moor Park to Dublin, as they would have marched to the North or anywhere else, with full resolution to engage him.' Facetious or no, ordinary people could not understand the situation.

Everybody played card games, and Swift was a dab at ombre, picquet and 'whisk'. He enjoyed good food, and especially good wine, the best tea and coffee which he liked to roast himself. (One of his presents to Patty Rolt was a coffee-roaster.) With all the charges on his income and his charities he was for ever giving presents; he lived beyond his income when in England, so he economized on himself, though his tastes were simple but apt to be expensive. In Ireland he could save, especially living with friends or at Laracor, where he could fancy himself the improving squire he should have been. He planted a quickset hedge all round his glebe, to keep out (or in) the cattle; he pruned and cut his willows; he planted fruit-trees. He was set on regular exercise for his health, walking a great deal as well as travelling about on horseback; rather exceptionally for those days, he liked swimming.

When in London he thought fondly of his country retreat, writing one day to Stella, 'Oh, that we were at Laracor this fine day! The willows begin to peep and the quicks to bud. And now they begin to catch the pikes and shortly the trouts. And I would fain know whether the floods were ever so high as to get over the holly bank or the river walk: if so, then all my pikes are gone; but I hope not.' Or at another time we have a pretty inset from his crowded life in London: 'I should be plaguy busy if I were at Laracor now, cutting down willows, planting others, scouring my canal, and every kind of thing. If Raymond goes over this summer you must make them a visit, that we may have another eel and trout fishing; and that Stella may ride by and see Presto [his name for himself with her] in his morning gown in the garden, and so go up with Joe to the hill of Bree and round by Scurlock's Town. O Lord! how I remember names, Faith, it gives me short sighs: therefore, no more of that if you love me.' As, we may be sure, she did.

It was at Laracor that he heard the news of his mother's death, in April 1710. He had been a good son, regularly stopping with her at Leicester on his way to and from London; no doubt he helped to maintain her. Writing everything down as he did, he took pen and wrote – after his own year of sickness: 'I have now lost my barrier between me and death. God grant that I may live to be as well prepared for it [God did not], as I confidently believe her to have been. If the way to Heaven be through piety, faith, justice and charity, she is there.'

This is what he thought of his mother; for himself, we may underline the word *If* . . .

The irony of this was that, unknown to himself, he was on the threshold of the most brilliant period of his life, the most powerful and most feared, most in the public eye – as he would never again cease to be. Fame and greatness together at last: this was what he had always intended from early days. Years later he told Pope that his ambition had always been to have himself respected and received as an equal by the great, on the strength of his own abilities and worth. He was, of course, far superior to them, but this was the key: 'all my endeavours from a boy to distinguish myself were only for want of a great title and fortune: that I might be used like a Lord by those who have an opinion of my parts – whether right or wrong it is no great matter. And so the reputation of wit or great learning does the office of a blue ribbon, or of a coach and six horses.'

CHAPTER 4

The World, the Power and the Glory

SWIFT DID NOT ANTICIPATE the good luck that would be his with the complete turn-round in English politics in the summer of 1710. There was no reason why he should: all his important contacts were with the Whigs, and they were being turned out. Harley at last brought about the *coup* he intended in 1708, and not a moment too soon. The overwhelming need was for peace; the Whigs had missed the best possible chance of making it in 1709, when Louis XIV – aggression at last beaten out of him – offered the humblest terms that could be expected from him. Their rejection enabled him to appeal to the patriotism of his people for renewed effort. Marlborough's victory at Malplaquet was won at a terrible price in loss of life – Queen Anne could not but grieve, 'Will this bloodshed never cease?' She and Harley were at one in their determination to bring about peace; they were completely right in interpreting the will of the country at large, but the political obstacles and difficulties, both at home and abroad, were enormous.

Harley appreciated this, and would much have preferred a coalition of moderate Whigs and moderate Tories to carry through peace by agreement. But he found the Whigs united on the slogan, 'No peace without Spain', which appealed to the commercial classes and financial interests. They had behind them the majority in the Lords, the vast European prestige of Marlborough, and behind him the Netherlands, the Empire and Hanover. The Elector George would be the next King of England, after the ailing Queen – Marlborough and the Whigs had the future with them. So time was short: Harley would need every ounce of support, every voice and pen he could command, if he were to carry his audacious campaign to a conclusion.

Nothing of all this was evident to Swift when the first signs of the impending change of government reached Dublin. When the Lord-Lieutenant asked him when he intended for England, 'I said I had no business there now, since in a little time I should have no friend there that had any credit. And his Excellency was of my opinion.' Everyone was perplexed at the new turn, and – as is so often the way in politics – the tide swept much further up the beaches than was good for the country. Godolphin had made a great mistake: tired of being sniped at by the clergy, he put the High Church Dr Sacheverell on trial for a fire-eating sermon he should have disregarded, and this gave the Tories the chance to raise the silly cry, 'The Church in danger'. It swept the country. This ruined the prospects of moderation: henceforth Harley was, in a sense, the prisoner of his majority. His sensible sister had foreseen the trouble the Sacheverell prosecution would cause – the Harleys were moderates, with a Whig background: 'what is mankind that a nonsensical harangue from a pragmatical insignificant man should make such terrible work.' And, after it had done its work, 'this business will in all probability break the Whigs. My foolish fears are it will raise the Tories to their old madness. The extravagance of every party is to be dreaded.'

Swift had had no success with his mission on behalf of the Irish Church, constantly fobbed off by his grand Whig acquaintance. Apparently the bishops were reluctant to renew his commission, but Archbishop King saw that the new turn might present a fresh opportunity. Swift grasped his chance, and at the last moment caught the Lord-Lieutenant's yacht leaving in August. For the next three years his life is illuminated as never before, by the famous *Journal to Stella*. It gives a precious insight into the inner workings of the mind of a man of genius, and of his feelings for Stella, which can only be described as a kind of love – *his* kind of love, of him who thought like no one else.

On arriving in London he wrote in September, 'I am perfectly resolved to return as soon as I have done my commission, whether it succeeds or no. I ne'er went to England with so little desire in my life.' Later that month, 'we shall have a strange winter here between the struggles of a cunning, provoked, discarded party and the triumphs of one in power. Of both of which I shall be an indifferent spectator, and return very peaceably to Ireland, when I have done my part in the affair I am entrusted with.' His mind is much more with his two girls in Ireland – MD he calls them, short for 'my dears'; sometimes they are PPT, or poppets; he is their Presto (i.e. Swift), their 'good boy' always thinking of them and their well-being. This is the famous 'little language' with which the overtaxed brain relaxed and played games – which has given so many headaches to commentators, particularly psychologists. There is no need for it: baby-talk is the language in which people talk to their pets.

Now he is buying china for Stella, the fashionable taste for which Queen Mary had brought over from Holland, and been taken up by great ladies like Lady Betty Germain. 'I loved it mightily today. What shall I bring?' Lady Betty has invited him to Drayton, the Berkeleys to Berkeley Castle: he will go to neither. 'The Whigs were ravished to see me, and would lay hold on me as a twig while they are drowning, and the great men making me their clumsy apologies, etc.' ' 'Tis good to see what a lamentable confession the Whigs all make me of my ill usage; but I mind them not. I am already represented to Harley as a discontented person, that was used ill for not being Whig enough; and I hope for good usage from him. The Tories drily tell me I may make my fortune, if I please; but I do not understand them, or rather, I do understand them.'

'I laugh to see myself so disengaged in these revolutions.' Never mind. 'I wish MD a merry Michaelmas. I dined with Mr Addison and Jervas the painter at Addison's country place.' Jervas was painting the portrait we have of Swift. 'Faith, I hope in God Presto and MD will be together this time twelvemonth: what then? Last year I suppose I was at Laracor; but, next, I hope to eat my Michaelmas goose at my two little gooses' lodgings.' Meanwhile they were keeping his lodgings warm for him in Dublin.

And he was writing a lampoon. On arriving, he called on Lord Godolphin, and was received more coldly and morosely than ever. The Earl was in a bitter mood; after a lifetime of service to Queen Anne – much of it in the intimacy of private friendship, where he was Mr Montgomery to her Mrs Morley and the Marlboroughs'

Mr and Mrs Freeman – he had been summarily dismissed and commanded by letter to break his white staff of office, without even a farewell interview. He received no sympathy from Swift, who had received none from him in his days of power. So the White Staff was lampooned in verses that went all over the town: 'Sid Hamet, the Magician's Rod', (Godolphin's first name was Sidney).

> As ready was the wand of Sid
> To bend where golden mines were hid,
> In Scottish hills found precious ore,
> Where none e'er looked for it before.

This was a reference to the Act of Union with Scotland in 1707, the enduring memorial to Godolphin's statesmanship at a moment of danger. But it was a shocking imputation that Godolphin had made any money out of it.

> Sid's Rod was slender, white and tall,
> Which oft he used to fish withal;
> A Place was fastened to the hook,
> And many score of gudgeons took.

(Swift, however, had not been one of them.) So the poem went on:

> Sid's sceptre, full of juice, did shoot
> In golden boughs and golden fruit.

One thing that is quite certain about Godolphin is that, for all his years in office, he made no money out of the state. When he died, two years later, everybody was surprised to find that he was no richer on leaving government than he had entered it. But Swift's insinuations were effective propaganda and reached their target. Henceforth he was a partisan. This was what it was to offend this dangerous man, with a pen ever at the ready.

When he met Harley next month, he had a very different reception, 'the greatest respect and kindness imaginable'. For two hours he sat alone with the minister now at the centre of power, 'where he heard me tell my business, entered into it with all kindness, asked for my powers and read them, and read likewise a memorial

I had drawn up and put it in his pocket to show the Queen – told me the measures he would take, and in short said everything I could wish. Told me he must bring Mr St John [Secretary of State] and me acquainted, and spoke so many things of personal kindness and esteem for me that I am inclined to believe . . . that he would do everything to bring me over. He has desired to dine with me (what a comical mistake was that!) I mean that he has desired me to dine with him, set me down at St James's Coffee-house in a hackney-coach. All this is odd and comical, if you consider him and me. He knew my Christian name very well.'

To us, acquainted with the ways of modern politicians, this strikes a rather pathetic note. In genius there is often an element of naiveté, hence the freshness and spontaneity of its reactions. Harley was a forerunner of the modern politician: he was above all a man for public relations. He knew the value of the press and propaganda, or at least the uses to which they could be put. Godolphin, a man of an older generation, above all a courtier, was above such things; so he lost out to a junior and a subordinate, upon whom he was inclined to look down.

Within a month the First Fruits business, which had hung fire for so long, was set going. The Queen was alerted, her grant assured; but still it took months being cleared through various offices, drawing up the documents, settling the form it should take. Now that the principle of the thing had been won, by Swift's access to Harley, the Irish bishops wanted to take the credit from him – and indeed he never did receive proper acknowledgment that it was he who brought it off. This was part of the regular patttern: it seemed that, precisely *because* he was so keen to have it, it was always denied him. Others, far inferior to him, had no such difficulty.

His relationship to Harley became close, quite unlike that he had not enjoyed with the Whig grandees. They became personal friends, on a basis of mutual tastes and liking. The charm of Harley was as a private person, where he had none of the insufferable airs of the grandees; his manner was the same in public as in private. He, too, like Swift had a Whig background and was a man of the centre, not a party extremist; an educated man, he shared Swift's bookish tastes; they could exchange quips about the classics over their wine together – both of them connoisseurs, though Harley drank too much. At an early meeting the minister could quote back verses of 'Sid Hamet' to the charmed author, who did not read his own poetry well. This was not mere flattery, though Swift was naif: Harley genuinely loved literature, which meant nothing to Godolphin, in spite of the poet for whom he was named and his close association with John Evelyn.

On the political side Swift never fully had Harley's confidence: no one had. Swift did not know the difficulties Harley had with the Queen, or what he suffered from the unscrupulous rivalry of his Secretary of State, St John, jealous of his leadership. This was politics, and Swift was not a professional. It says much for his qualities as a friend that he remained on good terms with both these politicians, all through their quarrels, which ultimately ruined their party.

At the beginning Harley made a mistake. He knew the expensiveness of the political and social life Swift was leading, and how hard he was working for the Government in taking over the *Examiner*, writing a weekly article for it. The political line these articles took often followed Harley or St John's suggestions, Swift provided the arguments, the original turns of thought, the style. In this cultivated small society literature and politics went hand in hand; politicians could appreciate good writing, if they could not write themselves – and some could, St John notably, for example.

Harley sent Swift a bank-bill for £50 towards his expenses. It was returned: it was made clear that Swift could not be rewarded on the same level as a Defoe. Like Shakespeare in relation to his patron, Swift was an independent gentleman. Not at all well off, he was at the same time rather grand about money. He did not write for money; he worked hard to raise subscriptions for Prior and Pope's works, but would accept nothing for himself. Later, he refused an offer of £500 for his collected *Examiners*. There was a lofty principle at the back of it all: 'If those who possess great endowments of the mind would set a just value upon themselves, they would think no man's acquaintance whatsoever a condescension, nor accept it from the greatest on unworthy or ignominious terms.'

He would never have been able to manage all that he did – living like a gentleman, with a man-servant, the expensive vails (tips) customary at every turn when attending or dining or stopping with the great, helping to support 'the ladies' and his sister, innumerable charities and presents and outgoings – if he had not had an exceptional head for management. (He would have done quite as well as Godolphin or Harley at the Treasury.) He kept an account of every penny; he picked the coals off the fire when he went to bed at night.

More precious to us than dead politics is the intimate revelation of his life in London in the *Journal*. The book is astonishingly modern in the gritty completeness of its detail – more like a contemporary work by Samuel Beckett or Pinter or Sillitoe, but that Swift's book has more genius. (It exerted a recognizable influence upon Joyce.) One might think of it as a Dutch interior, except that it has no stillness: it is jumping with life, more like a Teniers, or perhaps a Hogarth. He changed his lodgings this year, but kept close to the neighbourhood of St James's – the Palace for attendance at Court, the Park for exercise.

This year he moved to lodgings in Bury Street, off Pall Mall, about where Waterloo Place now is – up two pairs of stairs, where he had a sitting room and a bedroom, with a cubby-hole for Patrick, who kept a tame linnet and got drunk three times a week. Swift wanted to dismiss him, he was so negligent and unreliable, but 'the ladies' pleaded for him. They were indeed constantly in Swift's mind, so much so that it is as if they were in the room with him. He usually wrote to them at night, when the day's business was over, or in the mornings before he went out, often writing in bed.

21 January 1711: 'It has snowed terribly all night, and is vengeance cold. I am not yet up, but cannot write long: my hands will freeze. Is there a good fire, Patrick? Yes, sir. Then I'll rise, come take away the candle. You must know I write on the dark side of my bedchamber, and am forced to have a candle till I rise, for the bed stands between me and the window, and I keep the curtains shut this cold weather. So pray let me rise, and Patrick – here, take away the candle.'

Or the day is over, with all its politicking – 'that you shall know one day, when the ducks have eaten up all the dirt. So sit still a while just by me while I am studying, and don't say a word, I charge you. And when I am going to bed, I'll take you along, and talk with you a little while. So there, sit there. – Come then, let us see what we have to say to these saucy brats, that will not let us go sleep at past eleven. Why, then, I am a little impatient to know how you do.' His mind is full of their concerns, how they are getting on without him – are they taking enough exercise? How about pretty little Stella's eyes? And her spelling? 'Oh then, you kept Presto's little birthday; would to God I had been with you. I forgot it, as I told you before. Rediculous, madam; I suppose you mean ridiculous: let me have no more of that. 'Tis the author of the *Atlantis*'s spelling [i.e. Mrs Manley's, a lower-class writer to whom he was being charitable and kind]. And can Stella read this writing without hurting her dear eyes? O, faith, I'm afraid not. Have a care of those eyes, pray, pray, pretty Stella.'

From a famous man it was enough to turn any young woman's head. 'I got MD's fourth today at the Coffee-house. God Almighty bless poor dear Stella, and her eyes and head: what shall we do to cure them, poor dear life? Your disorders are a pull-back for your good qualities. Would to heaven I were this minute shaving your poor dear head, either here or there. Pray do not write, nor read this letter, nor anything else, and I will write plainer for Dingley to read from henceforward, though my pen is apt to ramble when I think who I am writing to.' This shows which of them he is thinking of; sometimes he dreams of her, and then awakes all confused. But at night, 'God Almighty protect poor dear, dear, dear, dearest MD'. And then, 'Paaaast twelvvve o'clock' – it is the watchman outside calling midnight.

This touch reminds us that there is *one* other work in the world like the *Journal*: Pepys's *Diary* – but, then, it was unpublished and a dead secret. Swift was prior.

He bared his soul to 'the ladies' – they were his family – boyishly proud of his success in London after a lifetime of frustration, naively boastful of his work, sharing everything he could with them, even confessing that he liked talking politics with Stella, though there were things he could not yet divulge. His 'Description of a City Shower' was something new in coarse realism; contributed to Steele's *Tatler*, it was much admired.

> Now from all parts the swelling kennels flow
> And bear their trophies with them as they go:
> Filth of all hues and odours seem to tell
> What street they sailed from, by their sight and smell.
> They, as each torrent drives with rapid force
> From Smithfield or St Pulchre's shape their course,
> And in huge confluent join at Snowhill Ridge,
> Fall from the Conduit prone to Holborn Bridge,
> Sweepings from butchers' stalls, dung, guts and blood,
> Drowned puppies, stinking sprats, all drenched in mud,
> Dead cats and turnip-tops come tumbling down the flood.

This piece of virtuosity should appeal to the modern kitchen-sink school of writing – in fact the smell from the sink in his lodgings contributed to the poem as well as forcing Swift to quit. On its appearance, 'they say 'tis the best thing I ever writ, and I think so too. Pray tell me how you like it.' They teased him by expressing no enthusiasm. In London, when he dined with Rowe (the first editor and biographer of Shakespeare), there was Prior; 'and they both fell commending my "Shower" beyond anything that has been written of the kind: there never was such a Shower since Danae's, etc.'

Politics were drawing Swift away from Addison; going to sit with him one evening he 'found *Party* had so possessed him that he talked as if he suspected me and would not fall in with anything I said. So we parted very drily, and I shall say nothing to Steele; but if things stand as they are, he will certainly lose it [his government job], unless I save him.' Swift thought that he had contrived to save Steele's job for him; he did not know that Harley had made an attempt on his political virtue too. Nothing would seduce Addison: he was a convinced Whig, a regular party man. 'Mr Addison and I hardly meet once a fortnight: his Parliament and my different friendships keep us asunder.' In spite of the Tory landslide, which Harley privately regretted, Addison easily retained his seat; Swift generously said that, if he had a mind to be King, he would be chosen. By the end of 1710, 'Mr Addison and I are as different as black and white, and I believe our friendship will go off, by this damned business of party.' Such are the amenities of politics.

All kinds of prospects were opening out before the disregarded vicar of Laracor. Swift was at Court for a Thanksgiving day (for Marlborough's victories), when the Queen passed by in state with all Tories around her, not one Whig, so thorough was the change of ministry. To the ladies that night he reported, 'the Queen made me a curtsy and said, in a sort of familiar way to Presto, "How does MD?" I considered she was a queen, and so excused her.' What fun he provided the ladies with, as well as executing their commissions for china or for a petticoat, constantly advising Stella how best to invest her capital – he was good at investing his own savings – going to bed in the furred nightcap Dingley had made for him.

Now the rumour was that he was to preach before the Queen. 'Mr Harley and St John are resolved I must preach before the Queen, and the Secretary of State has told me he will give me three weeks' warning. But I desired to be excused, which he will not. However, I hope they will forget. For, if it should happen, all the puppies hereabouts will throng to hear me and expect something wonderful, and be plaguily balked; for I shall preach plain honest stuff.' Everybody knew that preaching before the Queen was the preliminary to a bishopric. Those of his sermons that are preserved are, indeed, plain honest stuff, no rhetoric, no cant, a minimum of doctrine rationally argued. On a rumour that he was to preach at St James's one Sunday, 'an abundance went, among the rest Lord Radnor, who never is abroad till three in the afternoon'. How delicious to be a personage at last! 'I am thinking what a veneration we used to have for Sir William Temple, because he might have been Secretary of State at fifty' – and here was St John at barely thirty; while 'Harley complained he could keep nothing from me . . . It is hard to see these great men use me like one who was their betters, and the puppies [i.e. bishops] in Ireland hardly regarding me.'

All through the year 1711 there was an atmosphere of crisis and suspense: no one knew whether the new ministry, though backed by the Queen, would be able to carry through a peace. It was being negotiated secretly by St John, with Swift's friend Prior as undercover emissary. The coalition of forces against it seemed insuperable; the moneyed interests were with the Whigs, and they held up credit, damaging the Government's prospects. Harley kept coolly on his way. Then in March 1711 there was a sensational attempt on his life, when he was stabbed at a committee by a French *émigré*, Guiscard. There was a scene of confusion, Guiscard was run through by St John – everyone, except the clergy, wearing swords in those days of insecurity (now returning on us). For some days Harley's life was in danger – this produced a revulsion in his favour: for the first time he became a national figure, people realizing that he was the pivot upon whom peace depended.

We can see how Swift felt from the *Journal*: 'O dear MD, my heart is almost broken.' From this time all his references to Harley are of the utmost affection – henceforth, whatever the strains and disagreements of politics, the cord was never broken. St John, jealous of the sympathy everybody felt for Harley, gave Swift an inaccurate account of the affair for the *Examiner*, making out that the attack had been meant for him. While Harley was out of action, but recovering, St John sought to make hay while the sun shone. To curry favour with Mrs Masham – Sarah Marlborough's poor relation had taken her place in the affections of the Queen – he gave the command of an ill-considered expedition to Quebec to her brother, who made a mess of it. This played into the hands of the Whigs – Marlborough would have made no such mistake.

Duchess Sarah had been dismissed from her offices by the Queen, driven to distraction by her teasing and tormenting, in January 1711. But the Government had to proceed cautiously with Marlborough, still in a key position. His services to the country had been transcendent; but they had been transcendently rewarded. The palace of Blenheim was rising, at the nation's expense, to commemorate the greatest victory of this never-defeated man. He and Sarah had made themselves millionaires out of their various *traitements* – altogether he made over £60,000 a year (multiply by perhaps twenty!) out of his command alone, apart from what Sarah had made out of hers, and what both made out of their careful investments. It was too much. Though Marlborough was not to blame for the failure of the peace negotiations in 1709 – the Dutch were much more so – he did not strive officiously to bring them to heel, and his own appointments, at £60,000 a year, to an end.

It was necessary to diminish this over-mighty subject; so he had to be attacked, though not too strongly for, while he remained at the head of the Allied armies, the Allies had to be taken into account, and he remained the strongest card the Government had to play in the secret negotiations with France. It was a tricky business – but one that 'Robin the Trickster', as his enemies called Harley, was well qualified to pursue. On his recovery he kept Marlborough in play and in the command, and saw to it that he did not resign. Harley received his reward, the regular recognition of his headship of the Government, was made Lord Treasurer and Earl of Oxford. The jealous St John, twenty years his junior, was bent on an earldom too; some months later he was made a viscount, to his mortification. This did not improve his feelings towards his superior.

Swift was in complete agreement with the government line, above all on the paramount necessity of peace. The ministry was right, too, on the hardly less important consideration that, if the chance of peace were not grasped now, the terms would alter against us. Further, since the Allies – Empire and Netherlands – had obstructed peace in 1709, it was for Britain to press on now and look after her own interests. This was much to the mind of the country gentlemen, who formed the majority of the politically conscious nation.

Swift worked manfully for the cause, writing articles weekly for the *Examiner* from November 1710 to June 1711, putting forward the arguments and adding others of his own, urging the case for peace now. His mission for the Irish Church achieved, he had something vastly more important to do, and the Government found him indispensable. No one wrote with such brilliance, irony and wit – or, for that matter, conviction. There can be no doubt that he was convinced that the ministry was pursuing the true interest of the public. This was the answer to those party-minded people who called him an apostate – he was rather less of a partisan than they were.

He had arrived at more far-reaching conclusions of his own. The long-continued war with France – it had been going on ever since the Revolution, from 1689, with a short intermission, i.e. for a whole generation – was bringing about a change in the balance of social forces within the country. The creation of the National Debt and the Bank of England – Whig achievements – went along with a marked expansion of the moneyed interests against the stabler elements of society, the landed interest, gentry and farmers, i.e. the people at large. In this sense Swift's position was one with the majority. When one considers that the Whigs and the commercial classes were closely allied with the Dissenters, the Tories and the country people with the Church, one sees the fundamental consistency in the position Swift had at last arrived at – his grandfather in him prevailing over Sir William Temple.

Still, he was no extremist. Like Marlborough's descendant, Sir Winston Churchill – born, like Swift, on St Andrew's Day – he bestrode party boundaries, too big a man to be a good party man. Swift could not but admire Marlborough's greatness – the greatest Englishman alive, but bestriding the world like a Colossus and obstructing the peace. It was necessary to attack him, and in the right quarter: he was inconceivably ambitious, and beyond measure avaricious. And now Marlborough made his opponents right by demanding to be made Captain-General for life. This fortified Swift's arguments that such unprecedented elevation was a danger to the constitution. There was a further consideration that could hardly be raised openly in so many words – the Queen was a bad life, actuarially speaking: what would happen at her death? The Hanover family were to succeed by Act of Parliament; but they were Germans, the Queen hated the thought of them and kept them out of England. Nobody knew them – except Marlborough: what line would he take when the time came?

To the very end of 1711 the suspense held. Negotiations were going on surreptitiously at Versailles; there was an awkward moment when Matt Prior was arrested at Dover by an official as a suspicious agent, and the news came out. Swift had to put people off the scent by a brilliant piece of entertainment, turning it to ridicule. After finishing with the *Examiner*, his time was more fully occupied than ever writing his major political tract, *The Conduct of the Allies*. This was one of the most effective broadsides ever delivered: it sold prodigiously and exercised immense influence on the mind of the nation, i.e. those people capable of taking it in. It was a trenchant statement of the Government's case; for it Swift needed to be briefed, particularly by St John, in whose hands the negotiations were. This brought him more closely than ever into constant contact with both St John and Harley, though the two men were increasingly at loggerheads.

The tract was all the more effective politically for being more partisan than anything Swift had yet written – he had to work in St John's arguments on points at issue in the current negotiations, as well as the insinuations that make the small change of politics. To achieve their purpose there was at last a full onslaught on Marlborough, that can hardly have represented Swift's, or even St John's, real opinion. This was politics. Let us disregard what is ephemeral – on the major issue Swift was overwhelmingly right: there must be a peace. Expressed in an unforgettable phrase, this becomes: 'Ten glorious campaigns are passed, and now at last, like the sick man, we are just expiring with all sorts of good symptoms.' Was the war never to end, until the Habsburg Emperor had been placed on the throne of Spain? The Spanish people had made it clear that they would never accept him. Would not the addition of Spain to the Habsburg Empire give it the overbalanced ascendancy in Europe which we were combating in Louis XIV?

Then why go on, simply to subserve the selfish obstinacy of the Allies? English interests were being sacrificed, the country drained of resources, for the benefit of the Marlborough family – and the gramophone record was turned on against the Churchills again. These tactics paid; it was sound strategy to turn the flank of the opposition to peace by blaming the continuance of the war upon the intransigence of the Allies. For all the specious party arguments contributed by St John, the pamphlet was most effective in identifying peace with patriotism and thus rallying most of the Tories behind it. The exception was the extreme wing of Diehard Tories, led by the Earl of Nottingham, who thoroughly earned his nickname of

'Dismal', both for his face and his politics. He made a disgraceful bargain with the Whigs: they would not oppose his Occasional Conformity Bill (aimed against the Dissenters), if he would join them in opposing the nation's most urgent need, peace. What a lot these party politicians were!

Swift lampooned this Diehard Tory in 'An Excellent New Song . . . of a famous Orator against Peace'. 'Dismal' made a rewarding target:

> *An Orator dismal of Nottinghamshire,*
> *Who has forty years let out his conscience to hire,*
> *Out of zeal for his country and want of a place,*
> *Is come up, 'vi et armis', to break the Queen's peace.*

There follows his Speech:

> *Whereas, Notwithstanding, I am in great pain*
> *To hear we are making a peace without Spain . . .*

So to the ludicrous conclusion:

> *I'll Speech against Peace while Dismal's my name,*
> *And be a true Whig while I am Not-in-game.*

And that was about the long and the short of it.

However, when the issue came before the House of Lords in a crucial debate, the unprincipled combination between Whigs and Diehard Tories carried the day: a majority of eight carried the motion that 'No Peace could be safe or honourable to Great Britain or Europe if Spain and the West Indies were allotted to any branch of the House of Bourbon.'

The Whigs were jubilant and expected the collapse of the Government; indeed Halifax had offered Harley an accommodation if he would only drop the Peace. St John lost his nerve – as he was to do, more disastrously, on the Queen's death in 1714. Harley now showed real leadership: he persuaded the Queen to create twelve peers to carry the Peace through. This constituted an important precedent: the threat to create a sufficient number of peers made the House of Lords give way over the Reform Bill in 1832, and again over the Budget of 1909. Middleton Murry, who wrote a good biography of Swift, comments justly, 'if in 1950 a President Truman could call a General MacArthur to order and subordination, it was partly because in 1711 Oxford had told Marlborough that he must obey or be dismissed.' The will of the nation, as represented by Queen and Commons in 1711, and by President and Congress in 1950, must prevail over any commander-in-chief. At the end of the month Marlborough was dismissed from all his offices.

During that critical year we find Swift spending whole mornings with the Secretary of State, consulting, putting their heads together, then dining together; and spending his evenings increasingly with Harley. These leaders at the head of affairs greatly appreciated Swift's company; for all their elevation they were personal friends. Only a man of integrity could have kept friends with both for long. A small men's club was formed, only a dozen or so, of which Swift was the tutelary genius and allowed almost to be a dictator of its proceedings. It was partly a game, but it also answered to something deep in his nature, starved all his life of recognition. Now he laid down the law; he pretended to exclude the Lord Treasurer. The club had its quota of Dukes – Ormond, a good friend, and Beaufort, who wanted his brother-in-law, an earl, elected: Swift excluded him. To Stella, boasting like a schoolboy: 'I was at Court and church today. I generally am acquainted with about thirty in the Drawing-room, and I am so proud I make all the lords come up to me.' He made it a rule that great ladies had to seek his acquaintance first; most submitted. 'The Secretary showed me his bill of fare to encourage me to dine with him. "Pooh", said I, "show me a bill of company, for I value not your dinner".'

In verse, a year or two later, he describes his situation:

> And now, the public interest to support,
> By Harley Swift invited comes to Court,
> In favour grows with ministers of state,
> Admitted private, when superiors wait.
> And Harley, not ashamed his choice to own,
> Takes him to Windsor in his coach, alone.
> At Windsor Swift no sooner can appear
> But St John comes and whispers in his ear:
> The Waiters stand in ranks; the Yeomen cry,
> 'Make room', as if a duke were passing by.

We see how this kind of thing went to his head, how intoxicating it was. But there was always a sting in it:

> *My Lord would carry on the jest,*
> *And down to Windsor takes his guest.*
> *Swift much admires the place and air,*
> *And longs to be a canon there,*
> *In summer round the Park to ride,*
> *In winter – never to reside.*
> *'A canon!, That's a place too mean:*
> *No, Doctor, you shall be a dean;*
> *Two dozen canons round your stall,*
> *And you the tyrant o'er them all:*
> *You need but cross the Irish seas*
> *To live in plenty, power and ease.*

Not even from that side had there come any offer; for all that he had procured for the Irish Church, he was still vicar of Laracor (it might just as well have been Llareggub).

At Windsor that summer, where Swift lodged in a canon's house for quiet – he was writing hard for the ministry: 'the Queen was abroad today in order to hunt, but finding it disposed to rain, she kept in her coach. She hunts in a chaise with one horse, which she drives herself, and drives furiously, like Jehu, and is a mighty hunter, like Nimrod.' Another day, 'the Queen was hunting the stag till four this afternoon, and she drove in her chaise above forty miles, and it was five before we went to dinner. Here are fine walks about this town. I sometimes walk up the Avenue [planted by the Queen's uncle, Charles II].'

Next day, 'there was a Drawing-room; but so few company, that the Queen sent for us into her bed-chamber, where we made our bows, and stood about twenty of us round the room; while she looked at us round with her fan in her mouth, and once a minute said about three words to some that were nearest her. And then she was told dinner was ready, and went out.' There is a note of disappointment, almost of caricature in this; she was a silent woman – Sarah Marlborough had become so bored of being closeted with her, with no conversation. Only twenty people in the room – she must have caught a glimpse of Swift.

On a Sunday, 'we had a dunce to preach before the Queen today, which often happens.' Nothing whatever had come of Harley and St John's earlier suggestion that he should preach before her – there must be someone blocking the way. 'Lord Treasurer and the Secretary thought to mortify me, for they told me that they had been talking a good deal of me today to the Queen, and she said she had never heard of me. I told them that was their fault, not hers, etc. And so we laughed.' And then, 'but what care I? I believe I shall die with ministries in my debt.'

But, of course, it was her fault: this dull creature must have refused to have the most famous writer in her kingdom presented to her.

It was certainly not Harley's fault: he never spoke of the difficulties he had with this obstinate woman – her father's daughter all right – and there must be someone backing her up. Swift had no doubt who this was. The Duchess of Somerset had succeeded Sarah Marlborough in office – Anne was much attached to her, a friend and almost an equal; Mrs Masham, a good friend to Swift, had the Queen's affection, but she was on a lower level. The Duchess of Somerset knew Swift only too well, and she was an enemy.

A great heiress, sole child of the last Percy Earl of Northumberland, she had had a most unhappy matrimonial career. When only a girl she had been married off, by her guardians, to a Cavendish, who died the next year. She was then married to Thomas Thynne of Longleat, whom she could not bear, and fled, without consummating the marriage, to the protection of the Temples in Holland. The adventurous Count Königsmarck was Thynne's rival and, intending a duel over her, held up Thynne's coach in Pall Mall. One of his retainers shot Thynne with a blunderbuss – one sees the scene sculpted in relief on his tomb in Westminster Abbey. Within four months of the murder of her husband she was married to the Duke of Somerset, with whom she was miserable: he was insufferably stuck up, and made rows with her servants. The Queen was sorry for her; she was only too glad to have Anne's protection to keep away from her husband.

That December Swift wrote a wicked poem about her, clever and

diabolical, even when one makes allowance for the brutality of the
age. The Duchess was red-headed, so –

> *Beware of* Carrots *from Northumberland:*
> *Carrots sown* Thynne *a deep root may get,*
> *If so be they are in* Somer *set:*
> *Their* Connings Mark *thou, for I have been told,*
> *They assassin when young and poison when old.*
> *Root out these* Carrots, *O thou whose name*
> *Is backwards and forwards always the same;* [Masham]
> *And keep close to thee always that name*
> *Which backwards and forwards is almost the same* [Anne],
> *And England, wouldst thou be happy still,*
> *Bury those Carrots under a* Hill.

Hill was Lady Masham's maiden name. This was what Swift was
capable of when mortally offended; he believed that the Duchess
had poisoned the Queen's mind against him.

Spurred on by his complexes, he did not perceive how unforgivable
it was – there was a vein of stark insensitivity in him wherever they
were touched: they blinded him – and compensated him with merciless
merriment. He was very pleased with his verses; they were printed
in black letter, tricked out as an old prophecy found in a cloister
grave at Windsor: 'The Windsor Prophecy'. To Stella: 'My "Prophecy" is printed and will be published after Christmas day; I like
it mightily. I don't know how it will pass. I believe everybody will
guess it to be mine.' Lady Masham, like a good friend, warned him
against publishing it – it would anger the Queen. But it was too late,
dozens of copies had got about: ''tis an admirable good one, and
people are mad for it.' He wondered if Stella had seen a copy in
Ireland, and what she would make of it.

It is inconceivable that, after this, he could hope for preferment in
England: the damage was irreparable. It may be that he didn't care,
had practically given up hope. 'When I expected we were all undone,
I designed to retire for six months, and then steal over to Laracor.'
Unwontedly, he quoted Shakespeare:

> *A weak old man, battered with storms of state,*
> *Is come to lay his weary bones among you.*

A few months later: 'How affectedly [i.e. much affected] poppet talks of my being here all summer; which I do not intend, nor to stay one minute longer in England than becomes the circumstances I am in.'

He was unrepentant, and in all the dangers of the crucial year 1714 wrote implacably:

> By an old red-haired, murdering hag pursued,
> A crazy prelate and a royal prude;
> By dull divines who look with envious eyes
> On every genius that attempts to rise,
> And, pausing o'er a pipe, with doubtful nod,
> Give hints that poets ne'er believe in God . . .
>
> Now Madam Coningsmark her vengeance vows
> On Swift's reproaches for her murdered spouse,
> From her red locks her mouth with venom fills,
> And thence into the royal ear instils.
> The Queen incensed, his services forgot,
> Leaves him a victim to the vengeful Scot.
> Now, through the realm a proclamation spread
> To fix a price on his devoted head . . .

This refers to the proclamation put out against him by the Scottish peers who felt insulted in *The Public Spirit of the Whigs* – party bitterness was rising to new heights with the increasing ill-health of the Queen and the fears as to what would come after her.

Swift had no reason to be grateful to her. His sending abroad 'The Windsor Prophecy' shows that he set store by his writings above everything and would never sacrifice any heir of his invention for any consideration; it could not have come from a politician seeking reward for service, nor from a clergyman in pursuit of preferment, least of all from a Christian.

Though he could do nothing for himself, he was constantly doing good turns for other people, and had set himself to do so from the first. He had helped Congreve to keep his government appointment, when he was now practically blind with cataracts. Swift was continually being pestered by people for jobs, and was always willing to help in the case of people he knew and could answer for. Now it was getting Patty Rolt's husband out of Port Mahón, or Mrs Manley's hopeless spouse. 'Well, I will do Mr Manley all the service I can, but he will ruin himself . . . If I hear any thoughts of turning out Mr Manley, I will endeavour to prevent it.' He got a suitable post for his Irish friend Ford as official Gazetteer, £200 a year besides the perquisites. 'It is the prettiest employment in England of its bigness, yet the puppy does not seem satisfied with it . . . 'Tis impossible to make any man easy.'

He made it a matter of principle to help the wits, though they were rivals. He several times tried to help the poet Parnell. His endeavour to help Steele led to a sad misunderstanding, owing to Harley's secrecy and disingenuousness. Steele claimed that the ministers were laughing at Swift, in allowing him to think that *he* had protected Steele in his job. This at once grazed Swift's raw nerve; he replied that he had never reflected on Steele and, going further, denied that he had written any of the *Examiners*. This was the regular posture he affected to protect his anonymity, but it was not true. Steele resented Swift's charge that 'Addison had bridled me in point of party', and retorted that he wrote not 'out of terror of your wit, or my Lord Treasurer's power, but out of pure kindness to the agreeable qualities I once so passionately delighted in, in you'. Swift was angered by the allusion 'to a clergyman, of some little distinction, as an infidel: a clergyman who was your friend, who always loved you, who had endeavoured at least to serve you, and who, whenever he did write anything, made it sacred to himself never to fling out the least hint against you'.

The ulcerated party struggle was pulling old friends apart.

Arrogant towards the great, out of pride – and, I suppose, inner insecurity – he was kind and considerate to humble acquaintance and those in need. The result was that his lodgings were besieged by scroungers of a morning, like the levee of a minister. Patrick was supposed to keep them out, but – here was 'one of the Queen's Music, a German, whom I had never seen, got access to me in my chamber by Patrick's folly'. He wanted a job in the Customs for a friend; not content with that he had a project for raising £10,000 upon operas, 'and one word of mine', etc. Here was a penalty of fame; sometimes he was driven to go out early in the morning to avoid these solicitations.

Then there was the awkwardness of being caught *in flagrante delicto* with ministers. He was walking in Hyde Park one morning with Secretary St John, when 'the Duke of Marlborough's coach overtook us, with his Grace and Lord Godolphin in it; but they did not see us, to our great satisfaction, for neither of us desired that either of those two lords should see us together.' In September that year, 1712, 'the Whigs have lost a great support in the Earl of Godolphin. 'Tis a good jest to hear the Ministers talk of him now with humanity and pity, because he is dead and can do them no more hurt.' Swift had been no better about him: Godolphin had been an upright and honest servant of the state. The release of party bitterness over the Peace was so great – with the Whigs threatening to send Oxford to the Tower, and the Tories responding with a campaign of calumnies against Marlborough, quite unrestrained – that the Duke decided to go into exile and wait for a better day. He did not return until the day of the Queen's death.

Swift now made a new friend in old Lady Orkney, 'the late King's mistress, who lives at a fine place five miles from hence [Windsor] called Cliveden. She is the wisest woman I ever saw; Lord Treasurer made great use of her advice in the late change of affairs.' She was a Villiers, of that family which exerted such a fascination upon three generations of Stuarts. Now she was as much charmed with Swift as he was with her. She was making a writing-table for him with her own hands – an appropriate present from one who had known so many secrets of state to another. Archbishop King was glad now to have as his correspondent someone at the centre of affairs, who could inform him as to the real inwardness of events. The Archbishop and the vicar of Laracor dealt gingerly with each other; each had a first-class political brain, and the pros and cons of the Treaty of Utrecht in the making – what a lengthy and tortuous business it was – are set forth nowhere more clearly than in their correspondence. When ultimately hammered out, it proved a satisfactory conclusion for Britain of the long struggle with France, and formed a firm foundation for the settlement of Europe over the next generation.

Swift's pen was the sharpest weapon fighting for it in Britain. After his *Remarks on the Barrier Treaty*, with its strictures on the Dutch for their usual fault of 'giving too little, and asking too much', there followed his bitter attack on *The Public Spirit of the Whigs*. Over this, he ran into danger; the printer was prosecuted for libel; Swift was protected by the ministry, but was becoming as much a target of attack in pamphlets, broadsides, verses, insults, as he had been active against others. More important to him was his *History of the Four Last Years of the Reign of Queen Anne*, which he was writing; from early days, inspired by Temple, he was ambitious to become an historian. Moreover, he wanted to be made Historiographer Royal: this was to be his qualifying piece. Actually, his was not an historian's make-up: he was too much of a moralist, and – something better – a poet and creative artist.

The strain of overwork and anxiety was telling on him: in addition to his frequent attacks of giddiness, in April he was laid out by shingles, the details of which he goes into with unsparing detail, as eighteenth-century people did or Americans do today. In those days everybody seems to have been ill off and on – in this respect the *Journal* reminds one of the *Case-Books* of Simon Forman, the Elizabethan astrologer and medico.[1] Little wonder, when one considers the insanitariness, the filth and ordure, the infections, the bugs and bacteria, the fact that no one took a bath, the food they ate and how much they drank, the gout everybody had – which covered a multitude of ailments. Only the tough survived. Queen Anne lost every one of her sixteen or so infants (or pregnancies), and died at forty-nine. Swift was careful about his health and took regular exercise, but he was always dosing himself with pills and was often sick for days together.

His head was always active, with one scheme after another, if not political tracts then verses or prose essays. Always an exact writer, a stickler for style, he was at this time keen on the project of an academy to keep the well of English pure and undefiled. To

[1] cf. my *Simon Forman: Sex and Society in Shakespeare's Age*.

this he recruited the interest of the ministers – men of educated tastes, particularly Bolingbroke, who devoted his better talents in a subsequent life of exile to writing, and won more enduring fame in that occupation.

The Deist controversy continued and, after the Oxford Tindal, a Cambridge rationalist weighed in – Anthony Collins, a Fellow of King's, with a trenchant *Discourse of Free-Thinking*. The implication was that free and open discussion would be the end of orthodoxy. He had previously tilted against Archbishop King's old-fashioned views on Predestination. Now Swift took on Collins, no doubt welcoming the opportunity to appear on the side of orthodoxy, himself so much impugned by the orthodox. Swift's effort took the form of a brilliant piece of irony, since he could hardly traverse the main position. What his serious argument came to was that the reasoning of ordinary uneducated persons in matters of faith and conscience was quite unreliable as a guide for them; these things were better in the hands of experts trained to that end. 'The bulk of mankind is as well qualified for *flying* as *thinking*.' This was true enough – and, though they have since learned to fly, they still have to learn to think, if ever. 'By *free-thinking*, men will *think* themselves into *atheism*.'

This was just what clever Mr Collins hoped. Swift was not an atheist, and was perfectly sincere in thinking that atheism, for ordinary people, would only make them much worse. His very title, indeed, though ironical, expressed his estimate of ordinary folk's faculties, *Mr Collins' Discourse of Free-Thinking, Put into Plain English for the Use of the Poor*. Swift did not hold the view that people were without the capacity for reason; a rationalist himself, he went so far as to allow that plain reason and common sense were not without influence if allowed to penetrate. But will people take the trouble to think, even those who have the capacity? He was a believer in *making* them think: he was essentially didactic and tutorial, a moralist. In these circumstances it was better for people to have a church to go to, the Established Church, approved by historical tradition and by society at large. This was about all it came to; it is hardly surprising if the orthodox, who believed in their various, and conflicting, brands of nonsense, agreed in their attitude towards him – *non tali auxilio*.

The full-length book which occupied most of his time in 1712–13 was his *History*, for which he had begun collecting materials before his illness. Earlier he had the intention of writing a complete history of England, but he got no further than the reign of Henry II before laying it aside. For inside information as to the events of the last few years he was indebted to Bolingbroke, of whom he was seeing more now – Oxford was drinking heavily, his will-power being sapped by it. Swift hoped that the work would qualify him to become Historiographer Royal and proposed it – anything for recognition from that inaccessible, sullen, obstinate quarter. It was not forthcoming.

He was becoming desperate. Deaneries were falling vacant all round him. There was the deanery of Christ Church. He was friendly with Christ Church folk, was made welcome there, and liked to think of himself – the perpetual outsider – as a Christ Church man. The deanery went to his friend Atterbury, a high-flying Tory, a Jacobite at heart, in favour of the Pretender – Queen Anne's half-brother – as her successor. (Such were the factions opening up among the Tories, to ruin them.) Upon Atterbury's promotion to the deanery of Westminster, Smallridge – another of Swift's acquaintance – succeeded him. Now the deanery of Wells fell vacant. In January 1713 Swift was driven, humiliatingly, to write to the Lord Treasurer: 'I most humbly take leave to inform your lordship that the Dean of Wells died this morning at one o'clock. I entirely submit my poor fortunes to your lordship.' The deanery was vacant for a year before it was filled, by another. But the rumour went about that Swift was to have it; he had the mortification of having to receive congratulations upon it, while the rumour reached Ireland and Stella. He wrote angrily: 'talk not to me of deaneries: I know less of that than ever by much.'

By April 1713 there were three deaneries vacant: Wells, Ely and Lichfield. Swift determined to take things into his own hand and force matters to a conclusion. He sent a message to the Lord Treasurer that he did not take it ill of him if the Queen was determined to do nothing for him; but 'I had nothing to do but go to Ireland immediately, for I could not with any reputation stay longer here, unless I had something honourable immediately given to me.' He certainly meant to go; he was packing up his things, 'for I will leave this end of the town as soon as ever the warrants for the deaneries are out.' He accepted the fact that he would not be appointed to one of them. To Stella: 'do you think anything will be done – I don't care whether it is or no. In the meantime I prepare for my journey, and see no great people. Nor will see Lord Treasurer any more, if I go.'

At the last moment a way opened up. An Irish bishopric fell vacant, the Dean of St Patrick's could be appointed to it, and Swift could be put in his place – for it was not in the Queen's gift, but the Lord-Lieutenant's, and the Duke of Ormond was his friend. The move was concocted between Oxford and Ormond, and could be presented to the Queen without a breach of her precious conscience or a departure from her mulish obstinacy. Swift had practically to appoint himself Dean of St Patrick's.

He can hardly have been expected to be grateful, though there were compensations. 'The Archbishop of York, my mortal enemy, has sent by a third hand that he would be glad to see me: shall I see him or not?' A couple of lines were devoted to him later:

> *Poor York! the harmless tool of others' hate:*
> *He sues for pardon and repents too late.*

The Duchess of Somerset had more coming to her – all this had banked up undying resentment, in the most unforgiving of men: they would only go on in history, like flies in amber, through him. 'I was at Court yesterday, and a thousand people gave me joy – so I ran out. I dined with Lord Treasurer and his Saturday people as usual, and was bedeaned.' It was a very hierarchical world.

His elevation gave him little pleasure – just like his fate, it had come too late and in a manner that gave him no satisfaction. Thirteen years of waiting, years of what services to literature and politics, filled to the brim and overflowing with the sickness of hope deferred. So far from deriving any pleasure from such belated recognition, robbing it of all value in his eyes, he merely counted the cost. Psychologically characteristic, it was completely understandable. The dean's house he would have to buy, for £800; what with that, and First Fruits and patents, it would cost him £1,000 to enter upon his deanery.

When he went over to be installed, he was in no good temper and also sick with his old giddiness. He wrote of his deanery as of the place he had been 'thrown into'. Archbishop King was not glad to welcome so powerful a neighbour just over his wall – and took the opportunity to give away Swift's small prebend before he could confer it upon his deserving curate at Laracor. The Archbishop reported that, while in Dublin, Swift 'behaved himself with an appearance of contempt to everybody here'. He was in truth not pleased; he was besieged with official callers, 'all to the Dean, and none to the Doctor'. After a month, 'at my first coming I thought I should have died with discontent, and was horribly melancholy while they were installing me; but it begins to wear off, and change to dulness.'

He was happier at Laracor than in the great gloomy house 'they say is mine'. The ladies moved to Trim to be near him and keep him company. All the same, 'I am condemned to live again in Ireland, and all that the Court and Ministry did for me was to let me choose my station in the country where I am banished.'

CHAPTER 5

Cadenus and Vanessa

DURING HIS THREE YEARS in London Swift came to have a home from home with the Vanhomrighs. They were a family with property in Ireland and Irish associations; it is likely that Swift had known them in Dublin. He would certainly have known of them, for the father was a successful merchant there, of Dutch extraction, who made a fortune as Commissary-General to William III's army, and became Lord Mayor. He died in 1703, and his widow brought her young family over to London; she set up house in Bury Street, where Swift had lodgings. Mrs Vanhomrigh was well-connected, extremely hospitable, and saw a great deal of society. Swift became an *habitué*, along with a couple of other bachelors, friends of his, Sir Andrew Fountaine, the connoisseur, and Charles Ford. They were all either Anglo-Irish or had Irish interests; Stella too would have known of them, though not known them.

Though these things matter little to us, it is important to realize, as few have done, that differences of class and social distinctions loomed large to eighteenth-century people. Miss Johnson, daughter of a steward, whose mother was a waiting-woman of Lady Giffard, was not on a level with the Vanhomrighs. Stella was not a figure in Castle society in Dublin: her place was with Swift's clerical acquaintance – he had educated her above her station. Ungallant as it is to say so, there was something housekeeperish about Stella; she and Miss Dingley performed that function for the restless bachelor always on the move. There was nothing of that in the Vanhomrighs' eldest daughter, another Hester or Esther, who has become famous in Swift's story as Vanessa. Stella was not Vanessa's social equal.

As early as November 1710 Swift writes to Stella, 'What do you mean "That boards near me, that I dine with now and then"? I know no such person: I don't dine with boarders. What the pox! You know whom I have dined with every day since I left you, better than I do.' This sounds like a slightly uneasy conscience; though his letters show that he was constantly dining or spending his evenings with the family, he makes his references as casual as possible and does not dwell on it: he is playing his attachment down. Even so, Stella's feminine jealousy was alerted. Three months later he has to reply to her: 'You say they are of no consequence. Why, they keep as good female company as I do male; I see all the drabs of quality at this end of the town with them. I saw the two Lady Bettys there this afternoon' – one of them being the Berkeleys' daughter, the other the Ormonds'. There is a defensive note in this; 'female company' – he does not mention the male company that found the Vanhomrigh household so attractive. And the most telling circumstance of all: there are only two or three references in the whole of the *Journal* to the eldest daughter, whom he called Vanessa, and more endearing names – its chief attraction.

Vanessa was born in 1688 – two years older and more mature than she was admitted to be: thus seven years younger than Stella, with whom her personality stands out in sharp contrast. Stella's was strong enough certainly, but disciplined, under control – under Swift's tuition, repressed and accepting the conditions laid down by him. Vanessa was in some ways more masculine: what Swift admired about her was that she was open, frank and direct; she had no feminine deceit or disingenuousness. She was also unrepressed – I think, clearly spoiled, apt to give way to her moods, which Swift charmingly named 'Governor Huff', or 'Governor'. Of course, he spoiled her too, quite turned her head. She was not afraid to tease him or play tantrums or other games with him – she was his equal, though so much younger. Stella had been made a lady of; Vanessa *was* a lady.

We know what she looked like: a well-poised head upon slender swan-like neck, strong features, straight aquiline nose and fine eyes – though not black, unlike Stella's; a noble forehead, wearing her own hair well drawn back. Distinctly a personality, there was something commanding and aristocratic about her.

Swift never forgot when he first met her – in the inn at Dunstable, where they all happened to be travellers, and where she spilled coffee in the chimney – he several times recalled the scene, it became a kind of *Leitmotiv* of their relationship. The confirmed bachelor enjoyed feminine society, but what he sought was something more intimate. In all the pressure and strain of his political and social life, he was recapturing something of his youth by undertaking the education of this girl, as he had done years before with Stella at Moor Park. Both girls were much above average intelligence and needed a tutor and mentor. There was a difference: with the society in which the Vanhomrighs moved, rather extravagantly, he could talk politics with Vanessa. They knew many of the same people, and naturally came to have more in common, more to talk about.

It is natural enough that there should be some falling off of intimacy – or at any rate, immediacy – in the later letter-journal to Stella, for she was not in touch with events in England, which absorbed him. He was less in touch with Irish concerns, frustrating and unsatisfying as they had always been. Stella and Dingley were now living a wholly Irish life: this was what they represented more and more to him. Vanessa was intimately bound up with his English life – and intended to become more so.

When Swift moved to Chelsea, Mrs Vanhomrigh gave him a little study in her house, where he could read and write; he kept his best Doctor's gown and periwig there; when it rained he was sometimes there all day, though never for the night. His terms with Vanessa were, to begin with, tutorial: he could never resist the temptation of affectionately bullying his women-folk into reading more, improving their minds. Vanessa did not read enough, or take exercise enough. Now, 'little Missessy . . . Adieu, till we meet over a pot of coffee, or an orange and sugar, in the Sluttery, which I have so often found to be the most agreeable chamber in the world' – I take it, her bedroom, where she received her friends of a morning.

Soon he began to find her rather pressing, and indicated an indirect warning to be more discreet. 'There is not a better girl on earth. I have a mighty friendship for her. She has good principles, and I have corrected all her faults; but I cannot persuade her to read, though she has an understanding, memory and taste that would bear great improvement. But she is incorrigibly idle and lazy – she thinks the world was made for nothing but perpetual pleasure. Her greatest favourites at present are Lady Ashburnham, her dog, and myself. She makes me of so little consequence that it almost distracts me. She will bid her sister go downstairs before my face, for she has "some private business with the Doctor".'

One would have thought that this was warning enough not to make occasions to be left alone with him – a contrast with his rule in regard to Stella. But the lady would not take telling. Swift's weakness was that he had, underneath his aggressive exterior, a tender and compassionate heart; all people who knew him well recognized that – and Vanessa took advantage of it, always appealing to it to get her way. One summer when he was at Windsor – public figure as he was, exposed to criticism and malicious gossip – she proposed to come and visit him, with the insufficient escort of a young brother. He sent a half-hearted warning that as soon as she arrived he would leave. However, he promised 'I will come as early on Monday as I can find opportunity, and take a little Grub Street lodging, and dine with you thrice a week, and tell you a thousand secrets, provided you will have no quarrels to me.'

The weakness of this strong man stands exposed: he stood a little in awe of her, her moods and tantrums. She seems to have come down to Windsor after all, and proposed to visit Oxford, where Swift was also well known. He writes in alarm, 'I would not see you for a thousand pounds if I could . . . Why, then, you should not have come [i.e. to Windsor], and I knew that as well as you . . . I doubt you do wrong to go to Oxford . . . and if I do not inquire for acquaintance, but let somebody in the inn go about with you among the colleges, perhaps you will not be known.' It looks as if she had proposed to make use of his acquaintance there – indiscreet enough, to be sure, in linking their names together.

Since they saw so much of each other in London, and even made trips together, they did not need to write; and how they spent their time together is mostly unknown. What is left of their correspondence is very fragmentary, much of it undated; impossible as it is to make out the full story, we must avoid conjecture. There is some uncertainty at the centre of it, though the outlines are clear enough.

On leaving in June 1713 to be installed as Dean of St Patrick's, he wrote, 'it is impossible for anybody to have more acknowledgments at heart for all your kindness and generosity to me.' One senses a difference from his patronizing attitude towards Stella; this is written to an equal. But there is also a certain distance in it, or the desire to keep a certain distance. 'I will write a common letter to you all, but directed to you.' Vanessa seized the opportunity: 'Now you are good beyond expression in sending me that dear voluntary from St Albans. It gives me more happiness than you can imagine or I describe to find that your head is so much better already.' She ended: 'it is impossible to tell you how often I have wished you a cup of coffee and an orange at your inn.'

From Chester he wrote to the mother: 'I reckon Hess and Moll are widows as well as you, or at least half-widows.' He tries to keep the sister in the picture, as he had done with Dingley and Stella, not to be associated alone. But the flirtatious tone he always adopted with women exposed him the next minute: 'I desire you will let me know what fellows Hessy has got to come to her bedside in a morning.'

Before he wrote to her from Dublin she took up her pen again and again. 'Here is now three long, long weeks passed since you wrote to me. Oh! happy Dublin that can employ all your thoughts . . . Confess: have you once thought of me since you wrote to my mother at Chester? . . . Besides, you promised the letter should be directed to me.' Such feminine recriminations are always a bore to any man of intelligence. She wrote again: ' 'Tis inexpressible the concern I am in ever since I heard from Mr Lewis that your head is so much out of order. Who is your physician? For God's sake don't be persuaded to take many slops.' And so on. Anyone who has been pursued by such solicitations should know that they are usually exaggerated and never disinterested.

This betrays itself in her next letter: he had not replied. 'If you are very happy it is ill-natured of you not to tell me so – except 'tis what is inconsistent with mine.' This is pretty clearly a reference to Stella, of whose existence she was well aware, though she never refers to her. She goes on, 'I have often heard you say that you would willingly suffer a little uneasiness, provided it gave another a vast deal of pleasure. Please remember this maxim, because it makes for me.' Here, paradoxically, was Swift's Achilles' heel – his kindness of heart; what is no less noticeable is her commanding tone. How different from Stella!

When Miss Vanhomrigh did get a reply, she cannot have found it very satisfactory. 'I had your last spleenetic letter. I told you when I left England I would endeavour to forget everything there, and would write as seldom as I could.' He was at Laracor, where he preferred his 'field-bed and an earthen floor', before the Deanery they thought fit to throw him into. He was hedging and fencing, 'a work much more proper for a country vicar than driving out factions and fencing against them. And I must go and take my bitter draught to cure my head, which is spoilt by the bitter draughts the public hath given me . . . Nay, if you do not like this sort of news, I have no better. So go to your Dukes and Duchesses, and leave me to Goodman Bumford and Patrick Dolan of Clanduggan. Adieu.'

While he was away the rift between Oxford and Bolingbroke became irreparable; it is to just this time that the former dated his real loss of power, though he clung on to office. His devoted man of affairs and Swift's friend, Lewis, wrote to him, 'we are all running headlong into the greatest confusion imaginable.' Archbishop King wrote to him from Bath, where he had hoped 'to find a recess from faction and business, but now I find that it is a happiness reserved for heaven'. He added, 'an odd thought came into my mind on reading that you were among willows – imagining that your mistress had forsaken you, and that was the cause of your malady. If that be the case, cheer up: the loss may be repaired, and I hope the remedy easy.' This is an odd thought indeed, coming from the celibate Archbishop, who had never mentioned the subject of marriage to Swift before and never did so again. But he was one of those who knew Stella.

Shortly after, Swift was writing to Archdeacon Walls, who made himself useful to the bachelor Dean in domestic matters, but whose own wife was for ever breeding: 'the old fellow you are pleased to be so free with is a very honest gentleman, though he has not your faculty of increasing the Queen's subjects.' We need not read too much into this, but it is another indication that Swift was not strongly sexed – years before, when young, he had described himself as temperate. He seems to have had no difficulty in remaining continent – perhaps repression had done its work; certainly sex was not allowed to raise its ugly head.

Discontented in Ireland, and much needed by the ministers in England, he left Dublin at the end of August. He resumed his *Journal*: 'the ladies tell me they are going to live at Trim, I hope they will pass their Christmas at Dublin.' Irish business pursued him. Though he had no ear for music, he was determined to have as good a choir as possible – it served both cathedrals, St Patrick's and Christ Church. 'If we want a singer, and I can get a better, that better one shall be preferred, although my father were competitor.' (An odd thought – he never referred to his father: had he been a singer?)

There was some question of his being made Prolocutor (or Speaker) of Convocation, when it met. He did not expect it; 'although I have done more service to Ireland, and particularly to the Church, than any man of my level, I have never been able to get a good word.' Later, when it became obvious that they would not choose him: 'I would see you all whipped before I would venture myself in any manner to come over on a fool's errand; and for what? For a place I would rather be without; neither would I take it upon any other score but being chosen freely by a vast majority, which would let the world see they thought me a man fit to serve the Church. Since they have not chosen me they show they do not think me such a man, and consequently they and I do not deserve each other.' Fair enough: he had had more than enough of being rejected – and by inferiors – when willing to serve.

But he was an ill man to offend. The party struggle was waxing ever fiercer. The Tory majority in the House of Commons, driven on by the October Club, instigated by Bolingbroke (who had no belief), was taking an aggressive Church line, hoping to proscribe Dissenters with their Schism Act. Swift was becoming more fiercely partisan, with the movement of the time; it was ironical that his Toryism came from his position in the Church, with which he had taken service – like a soldier, now an officer, in an army. Only this excuses him for his next move. The Archbishop of Armagh was the Primate in the Irish Church; earlier, Swift had recognized that Archbishop King, the real leader of the Church in Ireland, was the only man for the post. On the death of the Primate this year, whom King naturally expected to succeed, Swift recommended to the ministry a safe, second-rate High Church Tory, Bishop Lindsay. Archbishop King was a moderate Whig – and too good a man to make any reproach. Swift may have thought to excuse himself when he wrote to a third party, 'I should be thought a very vile man, if I presumed to recommend . . . my own brother, if he were the least disinclined to the present measures of her Majesty and ministry here.'

From now on Swift was subjected to the further strain of a rift within himself between Oxford and Bolingbroke. His private affections were with the former, but he was drifting and drinking, could be got to take no resolution as to the policy to pursue. As Swift summed up, 'in your public capacity you have often angered me to the heart, but, as a private man, never once.' Bolingbroke had a line, and the energy to pursue it, though Swift no more wholly trusted him than others did. His line, rather than policy, was based on the high-flying Church majority in the Commons, bent on the exclusion of the Dissenters from civic rights. This was in sympathy with the Queen's views; Swift agreed with it and argued for it.

Oxford could not; he was always a moderate, and at this moment, his power crumbling, he turned to the idea of a combination with the Whigs. They would not respond. Even more serious, he had lost the confidence of the Queen. He supported the idea of bringing over the Electoral Prince, the future George II, to acquaint himself with the country he was one day to rule. This finished Oxford with Anne. He then began to make secret soundings with Anne's half-brother, James Edward, the Pretender. So also, more seriously, did Bolingbroke. Swift, who was perfectly loyal to the Protestant Hanoverian line, established by the Act of Succession, had no knowledge of these treasonable doings that soon were to ruin the Tory party and exclude them from power for half a century.

Beyond the conflict of personalities, the political situation, which expressed itself in and through personalities, was intractable. The Tory majority in the Commons made a sensible accommodation with the Whigs to tide over the succession impossible; the Queen made an accommodation with Hanover impossible. What was to be done? Swift saw that the rift between the two leaders was ruinous, and did all he could to bring about a reconciliation. 'I would never let people run mad without telling them and warning them sufficiently.' He made a supreme attempt to bring the two leaders to an understanding at a meeting he contrived at the Mashams'. 'I expostulated with them both, but could not find any good consequences. I was to go to Windsor next day with my Lord Treasurer; I pretended business that prevented me . . . and sent them to Windsor in the same coach, expecting they would come to some *éclaircissement*. I followed them to Windsor, where my Lord Bolingbroke told me that my scheme had come to nothing.'

Swift realized that all depended on the Queen's life. He wrote to the Earl of Peterborough abroad, 'the Queen is pretty well at present, but the least disorder she has puts all in alarm; and when it is over we act as if she were immortal . . . Our situation is so bad that our enemies could not have placed us so ill, if we had left it entirely to their management.' Since he could do no good he decided to withdraw into the country. His printer reported to him there, 'everybody is in the greatest consternation at your retirement, and wonders at the cause.' It was indeed a danger signal: he at least realized that the situation was beyond repair.

He found a retreat with an old acquaintance, John Geree, at his rectory a few miles from Wantage high up under the lee of the Berkshire Downs. Letcombe Basset is a breezy and delightful spot, with its clear chalk stream, growing watercress, running down to Letcombe Regis, the larger village in the plain below. The garden, with its outlook over miles and miles of open down, still has an ancient mulberry tree; when I was there many years ago the gardener said, 'They do say that a gentleman wrote a book under that tree.'

Was this a folk reminiscence of Swift writing *Some Free Thoughts on the Present State of Affairs* just at that time? He was also occupying himself with his *History*, to qualify himself for the post of Historiographer Royal, which Bolingbroke had promised him. This was to prove only another disappointment: at the end of July, 'as to the Historiographer's place, I now hear it has been disposed of these three weeks to one Madox. So there is an end of that, and of twenty reflections one might make upon it. If the Queen is indifferent in those matters, I may well be so too.'

Within a week of his arrival Swift reported to Vanessa: 'I read all day, or walk, and do not speak as many words as I have now writ, in three days. This is the first syllable I have writ to anybody since you saw me . . . I care not threepence for news, nor have heard one syllable since I came here. The Pretender, or Duke of Cambridge [the future George I], may both be landed, and I never the wiser. But if this place were ten times worse, nothing shall make me return to town while things are in the situation I left them.'

While the ministerial crisis in London was prolonged by Oxford's refusal to give up office, Swift affected to be absorbed only in country talk. 'Farmer Tyler says the white mead at Chawdrey has not been so bad in the memory of man, and the summer barley is quite dried up; but we hope to have a pretty good crop of wheat.' Bolingbroke chaffed him, 'I confess I laughed, and very heartily too, when I heard that you affected to find, within the village of Letcombe, all your heart desired.' He bade him come back and help in the changes that were imminent. Swift had no confidence in them. Lady Masham had gone over to Bolingbroke; Swift begged Arbuthnot, his dear friend, to advise her, 'who in my opinion is going upon a very dangerous adventure without one creature to direct her'. At the end of July the Queen dismissed the Lord Treasurer, as she had Godolphin.

But the prolonged struggle wore her out; on 1 August she died. That day the vicar of Wantage forwarded the news to Swift in his remote eyrie. Two days later Bolingbroke wrote his famous letter: 'the Earl of Oxford was removed on Tuesday; the Queen died on Sunday. What a world is this, and how does Fortune banter us . . . I have lost all by the death of the Queen, but my spirit.' Bolingbroke was still a young man; the gambler would spend the rest of his life out of power, much of it in exile. The most touching account of the Queen's last days came from her doctor – no wonder everybody loved Arbuthnot: 'my dear mistress's days were numbered even in my imagination . . . but of that small number a great deal was cut off by the last troublesome scene of this contention among her servants. I believe sleep was never more welcome to a weary traveller than death was to her.'

In the midst of these alarms Vanessa broke the rules and arrived on Swift at Letcombe, and via Wantage, a posting-town where people knew of the public figure residing near by; moreover it was a Whig town. 'You should not have come by Wantage for a thousand pounds. You used to brag you were very discreet: where is it gone?' Looking back over their relationship, 'I think, since I have known you, I have drawn an old house upon my head.' He now had to go to Ireland, to take the oaths upon the new King's accession. When he wrote to her from there, it would be always under a cover; when she wrote, it should be addressed by someone else, and she to write nothing personal, for letters were likely to be opened. If she came to Ireland, 'I shall see you very seldom', for everything gets known in a week. He was now in an exposed position, and 'these public misfortunes have altered all my measures and broke my spirits'. He ended by assuring her of his 'perfect esteem and friendship' – the terms upon which he wished to keep their relations. As for hers, 'I would not answer your questions for a million, nor can I think of them with any ease of mind.'

Evidently, alone with him at Letcombe, she had confronted him with the question what precisely she meant to him and what his intentions were. The progress and character of their relations up to this date are described in 'Cadenus and Vanessa', in which Cadenus stands for Decanus, the Dean. Though given a mythological framework in the eighteenth-century manner, it is one of the most remarkable poems of the age, or of any age, for its psychological realism, subtle and equivocal.

The situation it describes is equivocal, and follows what we have so far seen of it from the outside; here is the inside story.

Vanessa came to call the Dean later on, fondly, 'Cad' – so she cannot but have approved the poem. He is described as he saw himself:

> Cadenus is a subject fit,
> Grown old in politics and wit,
> Caressed by ministers of state,
> Of half mankind the dread and hate . . .
> Cadenus many things had writ –
> Vanessa much esteemed his wit.

He is anxious, for obvious reasons, to make himself appear older than he is, Vanessa younger, for he wants to keep their relations on a tutorial basis:

> Vanessa, not in years a score,

(in 1713 she was twenty-five)

> Dreams of a gown of forty-four:
> Imaginary charms can find
> In eyes with reading almost blind;
> Cadenus now no more appears
> Declined in health, advanced in years:
> She fancies music in his tongue,
> Nor further looks but thinks him young.

This remarkable young woman is not taken with the usual feminine interests, dress, gossip, putting on airs, attracting beaux; she sets store

> In judgement, knowledge, wit and taste;

and the Doctor undertook to improve her mind.

> Cadenus, common forms apart,
> In every scene had kept his heart,
> Had sighed and languished, vowed and writ
> For pastime, or to show his wit.
> But time and books and state affairs
> Had spoiled his fashionable airs;
> He now could praise, esteem, approve,
> But understood not what was love.

What exposed him in this relationship was the principle that guided him in these matters:

> *That virtue, pleased by being shown,*
> *Knows nothing which it dare not own,*
> *Can make us without fear disclose*
> *Our inmost secrets to our foes –*
> *That common forms were not designed*
> *Directors to a noble mind.*

This principle, despising ordinary people's common forms, really governed his inner conduct with Stella, though he was careful not to offend outward conventions. Stella had accepted; but Vanessa, whose frankness and directness he admired, did not play the game. She fell for her tutor and, worse, declared her love. Swift was taken aback at first:

> *Cadenus felt within him rise*
> *Shame, disappointment, guilt, surprise.*
> *He knew not how to reconcile*
> *Such language with her usual style . . .*
> *His thoughts had wholly been confined*
> *To form and cultivate her mind.*

His first reaction was to blame himself; and, then, what would people say, since the young lady was very eligible, and there were plenty of young men she could choose before himself, elderly and an unsuitable choice? Appearances were against him, people would think he had taken an improper advantage of his position, would laugh at him and say

> *That scholars were like other folks:*
> *That when platonic flights were over*
> *The tutor turned a mortal lover.*
> *So tender of the young and fair? –*
> *It showed a true paternal care:*
> *Five thousand guineas in her purse?*
> *The Doctor might have fancied worse.*

Hardly anyone, but Swift, in this situation would have resisted. However, the next movement of his mind betrayed him: sheer male vanity. Again, hardly anyone but Swift would have admitted it, or even have recognized it; for men do not ordinarily know that vanity is a dominant masculine characteristic – they think it a feminine feature – and do not realize that women get them by flattering their vanity. Swift did:

> His pride began to interpose,
> Preferred before a crowd of beaux,
> So bright a nymph to come unsought,
> Such wonder by his merit wrought –
> 'Tis merit must with her prevail,
> He never knew her judgement fail . . .
> 'Tis an old maxim in the Schools
> That vanity's the food of fools –
> Yet now and then your men of wit
> Will condescend to take a bit.

He is laughing at himself – and, indeed, irony was his strongest line of defence against the battery of the emotions. All the same, in spite of being well aware of it – and this is so true to life – pride opens him to her attack. (As with Bernard Shaw, it is the woman who pursues.)

> So when Cadenus could not hide,
> He chose to justify his pride,
> Construing the passion she had shown
> Much to her praise, more to his own.

Self-deprecating as this is in effect, it is sad to have to say that Stella's lifelong devotion did not appeal to his pride: he took her for granted. With Vanessa,

> Nature in him had merit placed,
> In her, a most judicious taste.
> Love, hitherto a transient guest,
> Ne'er held possession of his breast –
> So long attending at the gate,
> Disdained to enter in so late.

Dignity and age forbade love: he preferred friendship, which offered

> A constant, rational delight,
> On virtue's basis fixed to last,
> When love's allurements long are past.

This was his regular signature tune with women, but Vanessa would not stand for it, and he began to weaken:

> *Cadenus, who could ne'er suspect*
> *His lessons would have such effect,*
> *Or be so artfully applied,*
> *Insensibly came on her side.*
> *It was an unforeseen event,*
> *Things took a turn he never meant.*

It was in vain to plead that he did not know how to make love – *she* would teach him.

> *The nymph will have her turn to be*
> *The tutor, and the pupil, he –*
> *Though she already can discern*
> *Her scholar is not apt to learn,*
> *Or wants capacity to reach*
> *The science she designs to teach.*

And the conclusion? –

> *But what success Vanessa met*
> *Is to the world a secret yet:*
> *Whether the nymph, to please her swain,*
> *Talks in a high romantic strain,*
> *Or whether he at last descends*
> *To like with less seraphic ends;*
> *Or, to compound the business, whether*
> *They temper love and books together,*
> *Must never to mankind be told,*
> *Nor shall the conscious Muse unfold.*

This was the situation between them, equivocal, undecided, when Swift left for Ireland to take the oaths to the new king. In Dublin he was received in no friendly spirit and was regarded with suspicion; the Whigs had taken over, Archbishop King returned to power as a Lord Justice. In England Bolingbroke was kicked out of office with contumely, and Swift foresaw that worse was to come. He could not resist writing to him, 'it is a point of wisdom too hard for me not to look back with vexation upon past management. Divines tell us often from their pulpits that half the pains which some men take to be damned would have compassed their salvation: this, I am sure, was extremely our case.' To Ford he confided his fears: 'I expect the worst they can compass, and that they will be able to compass it . . . I stay here to forget England and make this place supportable by practice, and because I doubt whether the present government will give me a licence.' He was indeed under observation, his letters being opened – for the new government in England knew that his great friends, Oxford, Bolingbroke and Ormond, had incriminated themselves with the Pretender, though Swift did not know it.

For himself he was dejected and in dismay. To Ford in September, 'I have been hindered by perfect laziness and listlessness and *anéantissement* to write to you. I cannot think nor write in this country . . . Being in England only renders this place more hateful to me, which habitude would make tolerable.' He was not only thrown off his balance, in complete disarray, but was actually ill. In October he was writing strangely 'In Sickness':

> *'Tis true – then why should I repine*
> *To see my life so fast decline?*
> *But why obscurely here alone?*
> *Where I am neither loved nor known.*
> *My life is here no soul's concern.*

How strange! Had he forgotten Stella? Where were the ladies? Were they not near by? His mind was engrossed by English affairs, overset by the disaster to his party, which he had more clearly foreseen than anyone. However, deeply dejected as he was, it is strange to hear him say,

> *Some formal visits, looks and words,*
> *What mere humanity affords,*
> *I meet perhaps from three or four,*
> *From whom I once expected more . . .*

Can these words possibly apply to those whom he had been in the habit of addressing as MD?

On top of all this, while he was ill, depressed and in some apprehension – the English press was full of libels 'In Pursuit of Dr Swift', and so on – Vanessa pursued him to Ireland. She took lodgings in Turnstile

Alley near College Green, and had a country house up the Liffey at Celbridge, where the ale-brown waters flow sounding through the garden. She at once sent a servant to summon him to Celbridge – Kildrought was the Irish name. Swift met the man near Trim, on his way to spend a fortnight with a friend. He replied, 'I would not have gone to Kildrought to see you for all the world. I ever told you you wanted discretion.' He would call on her properly when he returned to town, at her lodgings where there was company, and 'your neighbours can tell me whereabouts'. All the same, he could not help relenting to ask, 'Is Kildrought as beautiful as Windsor, and as agreeable to you as the prebend's lodgings there? Is there any walk about you as pleasant as the Avenue and Marlborough Lodge?'

In reply to further messages, 'I will see you tomorrow if possible. You know it is not above five days since I saw you, and that I would ten times more if it were at all convenient.' After more pressing, 'I will see you in a day or two and, believe me, it goes to my soul not to see you oftener. I will give you the best advice, countenance and assistance I can . . . I did not imagine you had been under difficulties: I am sure my whole fortune should go to remove them. I cannot see you, I fear, today – having affairs of my place to do.' Naturally, the duties of his post came first.

This was not a sufficient excuse for this importunate woman. Her mother had died, leaving the family affairs embroiled; the four children were to share the inheritance, but Vanessa, as the eldest, was having difficulties with the lawyers. There followed reproaches to Swift, who had a good head for business. 'Once I had a friend that would see me sometimes, and either commend what I did or advise me what to do, which banished all my uneasiness. But now, when my misfortunes are increased by being in a disagreeable place, amongst prying, deceitful people, you fly me, and give me no reason but that we are amongst fools and must submit . . . You once had a maxim, which was to act what was right and not mind what the world said. I wish you would keep to it now. Pray what can be wrong in seeing and advising an unhappy young woman? You can't but know that your frowns make my life insupportable. You have taught me to distinguish, and then you leave me miserable.'

And so on and on. Underneath the beseeching one cannot but notice the commanding note, and then the recriminations and reproaches. What a bore such women are! One wonders whether the man so notoriously formidable was not just a little afraid of her; there have been such cases.

The Dean received her letter when he was in company, 'and it put me in such confusion that I could not tell what to do. This morning a woman who does business for me told me she heard I was in love with one —, naming you, and twenty particulars, that little master[1] and I visited you, and that the Archbishop did so . . . I ever feared the tattle of this nasty town, and told you so; and that was the reason why I said to you long ago that I would see you seldom when you were in Ireland.' Then he relents and says that he will see her towards the end of the week if possible, but that he could not visit her 'in so particular a manner', i.e. better in company.

Back came a letter from the boring creature, with the usual incapacity to strike any balance of fairness or justice, completely subjective, no attempt to see the situation from the outside. 'Well, now I plainly see how great a regard you have for me. You bid me be easy, and you'd see me as often as you could. You had better said, as often as you could get the better of your inclinations so much, or as often as you remembered there was such a one in the world.' What justice! And then the usual feminine ploy appealing to pity: 'if you continue to treat me as you do, you will not be made uneasy by me long. 'Tis impossible to describe what I have suffered since I saw you last; I am sure I could have bore the rack much better than those killing, killing words of yours.' She goes on to confess that if anything gives her relief, 'I must give way to it.'

One sees her character well enough in that – utter lack of self-control, and one can guess that, with no father, she had been spoiled by an ambitious and extravagant mother, as well as by Swift. She was a complaining sort of female and that made him angry; then, in a famous phrase of hers, 'there is something in your look so awful that it strikes me dumb.' And more to the same effect. A later missive

---

[1] This refers to Swift's crony, Sheridan the schoolmaster, grandfather of the dramatist.

betrays that there was an element of feminine calculation in her complaining: 'I must chide sometimes, and I wish I could gain by it at this instant, as I have done and hope to do.'

Since all the biographies of Swift have been written by men, it has been usual to treat Vanessa with gallantry, which I find excessive. Most men have been unable to see through her, or think it sufficient justification that she was madly in love. They omit to notice her feminine unreason, her insufferable importunity, a prime case of 'the unspeakable in full pursuit of the uneatable'; my sympathies are with Swift – though he should never have exposed himself to such a type, or been more resolute and pushed her out of his life.

All the more so because he was now under pressure from another quarter – Stella – precisely and naturally on account of Vanessa. Swift was fairly caught between these two women.

Stella was far more deserving of our sympathy, one who, though no grand lady, knew how to conduct herself.

Moreover, the year 1715 – the year of the first Rising on behalf of the Stuart Pretender and of actual invasion – brought grave danger for the leaders of the late ministry and Swift himself was in some apprehension. His friends Ormond and Bolingbroke absconded abroad to the Pretender, Oxford was sent to the Tower. Swift himself had not known of their dangerous dealings, and wrote innocently, 'I am sorry Tories are put out of the King's peace: he may live to want them in it again.' Neither George I nor George II ever did; the party was proscribed from power. Swift could not have guessed how final the disaster was, for the present he abstained from talking politics or looking at a newspaper: 'It is the only receipt I have to possess any degree of quiet.'

Now Swift's letters were opened in earnest; in June he was called in for examination by Archbishop King, whose move it was in the fascinating course their relations took. The Archbishop assured him 'how kind he had been in preventing my being sent to, etc'. Swift said that on his record, he 'expected the protection of the government, and that if I had been called before them, I would not have answered one syllable or named one person.' The Archbishop replied

that that would have reflected upon him. Swift did not care for that –
'I would sooner suffer more than let anybody else suffer by me, as
some people did.' Nor did he fear to write Oxford a grand letter –
'I do not conceive myself obliged to regulate my opinions by the
proceedings of a House of Lords or Commons.' He took the liberty
of assuring him, now in danger, 'of thinking and calling you the
ablest and faithfullest minister, and truest lover of your country
that this age hath produced'. There was some advantage, after all,
in being in the Church.

Nevertheless, he himself was exposed by the letters the Ormonds
wrote him, and 'I have been named in many papers as proclaimed
for £500'.

In these circumstances, an unpopular person – Lord Orrery says
that he was hissed in the streets – he had to exert himself to maintain
his rights as Dean, and subdue Chapter and recalcitrant Vicars-
choral to order. Early in 1716 he was writing to Atterbury – later on
he too had to leave the country – 'I am here at the head of three and
twenty dignitaries and prebendaries, whereof the major part, differing
from me in principles, have taken a fancy to oppose me upon all
occasions in the Chapter-house.' A ringleader contested the Dean's
customary veto and even his right to propose business. Swift had
a further engagement with his Archbishop about this, drawing up a
memorial of 'all his ill-treatment of me, and shown him the injustice
and ingratitude of it . . . if the Queen had lived, he and his favourites
would have used me better.'

Archbishop King was more than equal to this. 'I am heartily sorry
to find that there are some very industrious to sow dissension between
you and me . . . The same was much laboured in your predecessor's
time as he himself can tell you, but he was aware of the snare and
avoided it.' There was one for Jonathan! King followed it with a
very wise response to Swift's acceptance of the rebuke: 'it is not only
an advantage to me and you that there should be a good correspondence between us, but also to the public.' People simply would not
believe that 'we kept any tolerable measures with one another, much
less that there was any good intelligence'. He ended with a generous
sop to Swift's wounded pride, at the same time expressing surprise

that it was precisely Swift's own friends who 'should be so opposite to acknowledge the service you did in procuring the twentieth parts and First Fruits'.

Thus the battle was drawn between the two potentates, each other's nearest neighbour across the wall that divided the Archbishop's palace from the Deanery. This Swift described in a letter to young Pope, with whom he had made friends over his early poem, 'Windsor Forest', with its Tory celebration of the Peace. 'I live in the corner of a vast unfurnished house. My family consists of a steward, a groom, a helper in the stable, a footman, and an old maid, who are all at board wages. And when I do not dine abroad, or make an entertainment, which last is very rare, I eat a mutton-pie and drink half a pint of wine. My amusements are defending my small dominions against the Archbishop, and endeavouring to reduce my rebellious choir.'

It is in this year 1716 that the early biographers place what is a mystery in Swift's life, as to which there is and can be no certainty. Though Orrery, Delany and Deane Swift differ from each other over other aspects of his character, and indeed wrote to correct each other, they are all agreed that Swift went through the empty ceremony of marrying Stella, insisting on absolute secrecy and that they should continue on the same footing as before. These writers agree that the ceremony was performed by Swift's old Trinity tutor, the Bishop of Clogher, in the garden of the Deanery there.

There is now no knowing for certain whether this was true, and no amount of mere discussion will solve the mystery for us. Suffice it to say that Miss Vanhomrigh's coming to live in Dublin – and her feelings for Swift must have been perfectly well known to Miss Johnson, as well as the difficulties they created for him – gave Stella quite enough reason to wish to have her own situation regulated. Though such a ceremony was a pure form, at least it gave her the assurance that he would not marry anyone else. No commentator seems to have noticed that the assurance might have been not unwelcome to him too – provided that everything went on as before.

As it did. His letters this year are fewer than usual, and as usual he was moving about the country. In the rain and slush of February he was at Trim; he read prayers and preached at Laracor, for his curate, 'who could believe it, is laid up with the gout . . . I saw the gardens at Laracor and the grove too – tell Miss Johnson that – and they all look sadly desolate.' In March he was in Dublin, in May back at Trim, when he sends 'service to the ladies' through his Archdeacon, as again in June from Gaulstown, and from Trim in October. That leaves plenty of room for such a brief and formal event that summer.

Some verses attributed to Stella express the emotion of jealousy, which would have been natural enough – she had reason.

> *O shield me from his rage, celestial Powers!*
> *This tyrant that embitters all my hours.*
> *Ah, Love, you've poorly played the monarch's part:*
> *You conquered, but you can't defend, my heart.*

She thought the monster of jealousy banished, but finds that he has usurped the place of love;

> *Or tell me, Tyrants, have you both agreed*
> *That where one reigns the other must succeed?*

The verses seem to fit the situation – or might indeed be applied to both ladies.

It seems also that relations with Vanessa continued as before. She had lodgings in Dublin, as well as her country house at Celbridge. One day Swift was dining with the Provost of Trinity, proposing to call on her in the afternoon. She had, however, told the Provost that she would not be at home. Swift supposed that she had told him that 'so that he might not come tonight. If he comes, you must piece it up as you can – else he will think it was on purpose to meet me, and I hate anything that looks like a secret. I cannot possibly call after prayers, and therefore came here in the afternoon, while people were at church; hoping certainly to find you.' Now Vanessa's sister, Moll, was ill – 'I pray God of Heaven protect you both, and am *entièrement* —'

Swift lapses into a French phrase with Vanessa, and the next letter to survive, from 1719, is entirely in French, with the exaggerated compliments and polite expressions that that language calls forth. What a pity it is that she does not go out into society more! Hidden from the world, her qualities are not known to people; yet no word escapes from her that could be better expressed. '*La coquetterie, l'affectation, la pruderie sont des imperfections que vous n'avez jamais connu.*' It is the style of the old Court days of London and Windsor – those unforgettable memories which they shared.

They continued their former habits of sprightly raillery and teasing, after all a form of affection. Vanessa: 'I should think you knew but little of the world to imagine that a woman would not keep her word whenever she promised anything that was malicious.' She knew it was impossible for him to burn her letters without reading them; and, since she loves frankness, she will try all manner of human arts to reclaim him. 'If all those fail I am resolved to have recourse to the black one, which, it is said, never does . . . When I undertake anything, I don't love to do it by halves . . . Is it not much better to come of yourself than to be brought by force?'

That in itself would have made up my mind to refuse. Swift replied with banter: 'if you write as you do, I shall come the seldomer, on purpose to be pleased with your letters – which I never look into without wondering how a Brat, who cannot read, can possibly write so well.' That kind of thing did not stave off chiding, or 'Governor Huff', as Swift agreeably called her temper. Swift had thought to deflect her, and console her sick sister with a love-letter and verses to cheer her up. Vanessa recognized – this was now in 1720 – that she was not to tease the Dean with too many letters, but 'I cannot defer writing to you any longer . . . I have asked all the questions I used ten thousand times, and don't find them answered at all to my satisfaction.'

His reply to that was, 'prove to me first that it was ever possible to answer anything to your satisfaction, so as that you would not grumble in half an hour.' So far from considering her ill-used, one can only marvel at his patience with such a woman. There follows a change to another mood, which he apparently found difficult to resist. '— — —, Cad, —,[1] you are good beyond expression, and I

[1] These dashes evidently stand for endearments in Vanessa's letters.

will never quarrel again if I can help it.' Of course she did and, with typical female unreason, in the same letter; 'for I must chide sometimes, and I wish I could gain by it . . . I am mightily pleased to hear you talk of being in a huff. I wish I could see you in one.'

Swift responded that August with a fascinating letter, which shows that we might have had a sequel to 'Cadenus and Vanessa', recounting the subsequent story of their relations and all the memories of their experiences together, significantly from their time in England. Here is probably what really bound him to her, the nostalgia for the past of the born writer – which adds a whole dimension for such to the common experience of ordinary folk. 'It ought to be an exact chronicle of twelve years, from the time of spilling the coffee to drinking of coffee, from Dunstable to Dublin. There would be the chapter of the blister; the chapter of Madam going to Kensington [evidently to see the Queen]; the chapter of the Colonel's [her brother] going to France; the chapter of the wedding, with the adventure of the lost key; of the strain; of the joyful return; two hundred chapters of madness; the chapter of long walks; the Berkshire surprise [her visit to Letcombe]; fifty chapters of little times [as in the Sluttery]; the chapter of Chelsea [when he was lodging there]; a hundred whole books of myself and so low [her expression for being depressed]; the chapter of hide and whisper; the chapter of Who made it so.'

What would we not give to possess a poem on these lines, the sequel to the earlier masterpiece? To encourage such a work should have been a proper activity for this woman with time hanging on her hands, who would neither read, nor take exercise, nor go out into society. There were apparently one or two suitable offers of marriage, which would have taken her off Swift's hands; but she remained fixed on him. From Celbridge: '– – – Cad, is it possible you will come and see me? I beg for God sake you will. I would give the world to see you here, and Molkin [her sister] would be extremely happy . . . Do you think the time long since I saw you? . . . Tell me sincerely, did those circumstances crowd on you, or did you recollect them to make me happy?' Again, the reiterated female demand for reassurance, the reference of everything to her own ego, instead of encouraging the writing of a work of art.

All that an intelligent man could do was to recommend her 'to improve your mind and the talents that nature has given you', especially by reading: 'you are not to quarrel and be Governor . . . I have the same respect, esteem and kindness for you I ever professed to have and shall ever preserve, because you will always merit the utmost that can be given you.' This was not enough; letters, sympathy, esteem, consolation were not enough. ' 'Tis now ten long, long weeks since I saw you, and in all that time I have never received but one letter from you, and a little note with an excuse.'

He had other things, immeasurably more important, to think of. In this year 1720, after being stunned by defeat, his mind and spirit were coming alive again; after years in which he could write nothing, his ineradicable political passion was aroused by the appalling distress around, the depression in the woollen manufacture which threw so many weavers out of work and left them to starve. Here was a platform on which public-spirited men like the Dean and the Archbishop could unite. Swift was writing one of his most important and telling pamphlets, proposing that the Irish people should use only their own manufactures in clothes, furniture, etc. and reject English goods. It was a theme that was to reverberate across the centuries, and, before the eighteenth century was out, to be acted upon with the utmost effect by the American colonies. Not only this and other prose pamphlets – with an irresistible outburst of creative energy he was returning to verse. And he was writing *Gulliver's Travels.*

All that Vanessa could think about was herself. 'Oh – – – how have you forgot me! You endeavour by severities to force me from you; nor can I blame you, for with the utmost distress and confusion I behold myself the cause of uneasy reflections to you. Yet I cannot comfort you, but here declare that 'tis not in the power of art, time or accident to lessen the unexpressible passion which I have for – – –. Nor is the love I bear you only seated in my soul, for there is not a single atom of my frame that is not blended with it.'

This was not a happy declaration for an elderly Dean to receive; but it was followed by another. 'How many letters must I send you before I receive an answer? Can you deny me in my misery the only comfort which I can expect at present? Oh! that I could hope to see you here, or that I could go to you. I was born with violent passions, which terminate all in one – that unexpressible passion I have for you.' All this was most unladylike – I know of no other letters from that century in the least like these. Their only value to us is the light, the fierce light, they throw on the man of genius, the rock-ribs and shadows, the inaccessible crevices and unexpected gentlenesses. 'I firmly believe, could I know your thoughts (which no human creature is capable of guessing at, because never anyone living thought like you), I should find that you have often in a rage wished me religious, hoping then I should have paid my devotions to Heaven.' This would have been a consummation devoutly to be wished. Swift's rational Protestantism had nothing to offer here. Only the Catholic Church and strict conventual life might possibly have answered – something like the devotion, the discipline and the ecstasy of Port Royal.

As it was, 'still you'd be the deity I should worship. You are present everywhere; your dear image is always before my eyes; sometimes you strike me with that prodigious awe, I tremble with fear. At other times a charming compassion shines through your countenance, which revives my soul.'

This must have been extremely unwelcome to the Dean, though it is very welcome to us for its revealing picture of him.

At last she elicits some sympathy, for her sister died, leaving her alone in the world. Swift could not give her the consolations of a Catholic priest. All he could say was, 'for God's sake get your friends about you, to advise and to order everything in the forms. It is all you have to do. I want comfort myself in this case, and can give little. Time alone can give it to you.'

Time passed. Nothing changed in her attitude; Swift continued to give her all the rational consolation he could, for what that was worth. And from his last letters of advice, rather than any spiritual direction, we can elicit the principles by which he regulated his own bleak life. 'Cad assures me he continues to esteem and love and value you above all things, and so will do to the end of his life. But at the same time entreats that you would not make yourself or him unhappy by imaginations.' This was in the summer of 1721. 'What is this world, without being as easy in it as prudence and fortune can make it? I find it every day more silly and insignificant.' Here are the mood, and the theme, of *Gulliver*, which he was writing. 'I conform myself to it [the world] for my own ease . . . Shall you, who have so much honour and good sense, act otherwise, to make Cad and yourself miserable? Settle your affairs, and quit this scoundrel island, and things will be as you desire.'

By the death of her two brothers, and now her sister, Vanessa was left in sole possession of the family fortune. It was complicated by legal business and claims upon the government; Swift had again and again helped with business advice and temporary loans. She was now quite well off, but in no mood to change her residence or listen to any proposals from any other quarter. For Swift could not resist assuring her, in French, that *'jamais personne du monde a été aimée, honorée, estimée, adorée par votre ami que vous.'* Evidently she was the one *love* of his life. Then, in lighter vein, 'I drank no coffee since I left you, nor intend till I see you again. There is none worth drinking but yours, if myself be the judge.'

This is the place to say that the suggestive turn that prurient minds like Horace Walpole's have given to the references to coffee-drinking evidently is without justification. The real significance is subtler: it is the symbol of all the good times they had shared, since she had first spilled coffee in the chimney at Dunstable, the succession of happy meetings in the Sluttery: it meant remembered happiness, the pleasure of being together, old associations.

From Clogher next summer, 1722, Swift continued his rational advice as her director. She should see more company and go out into the world more, a lady of parts like hers, not brood alone at home. 'Remember I still enjoin you reading and exercise for the improvement of your mind and health of your body, and grow less romantic, and talk and act like a man of this world.' A revealing phrase – it shows that there was something masculine in her personality, which he approved of. 'God send you through your law and your reference; and remember that riches are nine parts in ten of all that is good in life, and health is the tenth. Drinking coffee comes long after, and yet it is the eleventh' – and he cheers her up by recalling the experiences which would have gone into the poem, if he had written it. The 'sick lady at Kensington' was evidently the Queen; we now learn of an 'indisposition at Windsor', and that the 'strain' (perhaps a hernia) at London came by a box of books – Swift used to box up the books he collected, for transport to Ireland.

Vanessa's next letter begins with the usual reproaches at not hearing from him, then pathetically continues that she had tried to follow his advice and go out into the world; 'and I do here protest that I am more and more sick of it every day.' She was unmanageable, intractable. She goes on to describe the scene of feminine chatter, grimaces and grinning, the gossip about nothing, in terms that show Swift had lent her the manuscript of *Gulliver's Travels*. 'Their forms and gestures were very like those of baboons and monkeys. [The eighteenth century had no idea that they are our cousins.] Just as I was considering their beauty and wishing myself in the country with – – –, one of these animals snatched my fan and was so pleased with me that it seized me with such a panic that I apprehended nothing else than being carried up to the top of the house, and served as a friend of yours was. On this one of their own species came in, upon which they all began to make their grimaces, which opportunity I took, and made my escape.'

Perhaps we may excrete a little more sympathy for the woman, who had been taught to think as Swift did: without inner resources of her own to support it, it incapacitated her from enjoying the boredom of ordinary folks' society. 'For God's sake write to me soon and kindly, for in your absence your letters are all the joy I have on earth. And sure you are too good-natured to grudge one hour in a week to make any human creature happy. – – – – Cad, think of me and pity me.'

Of course, he did. In July 1722 he communicated his own philosophy of how to put up with the company of ordinary humans. 'I see every day as silly things among both sexes, and yet endure them, for the sake of amusements. The worst thing in you and me is that we are too hard to please; and whether we have not made ourselves so is the question.' Here Swift puts his finger on the source of the trouble: as a man of genius he was made like that; but he had made her, a woman of no exceptional talents, like it. One remedy that never failed with him was 'to read I know not how many diverting books of history and travels'. Another was riding: 'I wish you would get yourself a horse, and have always two servants to attend you, and visit your neighbours – the worse the better. There is a pleasure in being reverenced [a very Swift touch], and that is always in your powers, by your superiority of sense, and an easy fortune.' She was a superior woman – very well, behave like one. 'The best maxim I know in this life is to drink your coffee when you can [i.e. enjoy yourself], and when you cannot, to be easy without it.'

The poor lady tried to put this into practice. He had often told her, she said, that 'the best maxim in life, and always held by the wisest in all ages, is to seize the moments as they fly. But those happy moments always fly out of the reach of the unfortunate.' Reading? Since she saw him last she had read more, and 'chose those books that required most attention, on purpose to engage my thoughts. But I find, the more I think the more unhappy I am.' She was a hopeless case; but Swift tried once again: 'at present you want neither power nor skill, but disdain to exercise either. When you are melancholy, read diverting or amusing books: it is my receipt, and seldom fails. Health, good humour and fortune are all that is valuable in this life, and the last contributes to the two former.'

This was masculine common sense; but it did her no good. Nothing could: she was beyond it. Dr Delany, who was in a position to know, said that she took to drink.

Swift was away from Dublin much of the summer of 1722. He wrote these last two letters from Northern Ireland, where he was practising his own precepts. 'Yesterday I rode twenty-nine miles without being weary, and I wish little Heskinage [like Stella, Vanessa seems to have been a little woman] could do as much. Here I leave this letter to travel one way while I go another; but where I do not know, nor what cabins or bogs are in my way.' Travelling rough, he had caught the itch from the ticks that got under his skin. 'I see you this moment as you are visible at ten in the morning; and now you are asking your questions round, and I am answering them with a good deal of affected delays. The same scene has passed forty times as well as the other . . . yet each its *agréments particuliers* . . . I have read more trash since I left you than would fill all your shelves, and am abundantly the better for it.' To amuse her, he went over again the scenes of their English past together: 'Cad thinks often of these, especially on horseback. What a foolish thing is time, and how foolish is man, who would be as angry if time stopped as if it passed.'

This was the last letter to survive in their touching correspondence. Next summer she was dying; she made her will on 1 May 1723, on 2 June she died.

Everything shows that at the end there was an irreparable breach, and of course many stories circulated about it. It is impossible to get back behind to the truth of the matter now. One story was that, hearing a report of Swift's marriage to Stella, she wrote to him to ask if it was true. A more dramatic version was that she wrote to Stella, who sent the letter to Swift; that he rode to Celbridge, flung down the letter, and in fury left without a word. It would be in character.

What looks probable, to account for the drastic step she took at the end, is that she heard of a secret marriage. For she completely cut him out of her will; there is no mention of him, even in the considerable list of friends to whom she left money for mourning-rings in remembrance of her. Most of the people whom she remembered in her will were no friends of his, some of them persons he would disapprove of. The bulk of her fortune she left to a perfect stranger, the philosopher Berkeley, to advance his scheme for a college for the conversion of the Indians in Bermuda, a project Swift thought ridiculous.

It is not true that in her will she gave directions for the publication of 'Cadenus and Vanessa' and Swift's letters to her; but it is perfectly possible, and in keeping with the spirit of the will, that she gave verbal instructions to her executor, who was no friend to Swift.

He and Stella took steps to be away from Dublin at the time – in itself a corroboration of the drama. Stella and Miss Dingley went away to stay for a whole six months with Charles Ford. Swift planned to spend the summer on a long journey through the south of Ireland, where he had never been. On the day Vanessa died he wrote to his friend Chetwode, 'I am forced to leave the town sooner than I expected.'

CHAPTER 6

The Drapier and Ireland

FOR HIS FIRST FEW YEARS after the *débâcle* of 1714 Swift hardly wrote anything – he said that it took him three years to recover his balance. It reminds one of Sir Winston Churchill's vivid description of what it was like to be thrown out of office in 1916, after ten years of ceaseless political activity: he felt like a fish thrown up on the strand, gasping for water, the element in which he lived. Churchill took to painting as an anodyne. Swift sank himself in the duties of his office – he was determined to make a good dean, indeed he needed to; but, in addition, he had a marked aptitude for business: he was very practical, his energetic, activist spirit would have made him a good improving landlord.

He was most attentive to the well-being of his cathedral, and fought for its rights and revenues. We have seen his care to have a good choir; he was no less solicitous about preaching. He favoured a good plain style, exemplified it in his own sermons, and attended those of others to see that they adhered to it. 'For a divine has nothing to say to the wisest congregation of any parish in this kingdom which he may not express in a manner to be understood by the meanest among them.' This gives us a clue to his principle in regard to style in general: 'when a man's thoughts are clear, the properest words will generally offer themselves first, and his own judgement will direct him in what order to place them so as they may be best understood.'

We see this carried out with perfect consistency in the Dean's sermons – a not at all publicized aspect of his life and work. He was not highly regarded as a preacher, for the fashion of his time was for eloquence and rhetoric, which he detested. His sermons are, however, immeasurably better than those that were so popular, and they carry forward into pastoral instruction the principles that governed his life; as such they are most revealing, even when he couldn't live up to them himself.

What these principles were we can see from the 'Thoughts on Religion' he jotted down from time to time. 'I look upon myself, in the capacity of a clergyman, to be one appointed by Providence for defending a post assigned me, and for gaining over as many enemies as I can.' We see that his conception is positive, utterly opposed to the mystical and sacramental, though he submitted himself without question, like a good soldier, to the mysteries of his religion. As to these, the Trinity, for example, he did not pretend to know – neither did anybody else. So he deplored argumentation on such subjects, 'which have multiplied controversies to such a degree as to beget scruples that have perplexed the minds of many sober Christians, who otherwise could never have entertained them.' To what point? 'Men should consider that raising difficulties concerning the mysteries in religion cannot make them more wise, learned or virtuous; better neighbours or friends, or more serviceable to their country.' Swift's was a practical mind, his conception of religion a practical one – and for practice too: we shall see how far he carried out his own precepts in his life.

Even intellectually, he excluded useless doubts and arguings. 'I am not answerable to God for the doubts that arise in my own breast, since they are the consequence of that reason which He hath planted in me; if I take care to conceal those doubts from others [had he done so in *A Tale of a Tub*?], if I use my best endeavours to subdue them, and if they have no influence on the conduct of my life.' It must be allowed that he passes this last test. A High Churchman with regard to the rights and dues of the Church, who always observed the day of the martyrdom of King Charles I – for whom his grandfather had suffered so much – Swift was what we should regard as a Modernist as to doctrine and dogma. 'I have been often offended to find St Paul's allegories and other figures of Grecian eloquence converted by divines into articles of faith.' Sensible man, with a sensible position.

Casually enough, he handed over a bundle of some thirty-five sermons to his crony Sheridan to make use of as he pleased – evidently he did not set a high value on them. Only a dozen have been preserved, but these are excellent of their kind, quite characteristic, some of them with grave ironic jokes. There is one on 'Sleeping in Church', preached with 'the design, if possible, to disturb some part in this audience of half an hour's sleep, for the convenience and exercise whereof this place, at this season of the day, is very much celebrated'. Sermons at St Patrick's were afternoon affairs. His sermon was on the text about the young man in the *Acts*, who, overcome by the length of the Apostle Paul's discourse, fell down from the gallery and was 'taken up dead'; St Paul revived him. 'Preachers now in the world, however they may exceed St Paul in the art of setting men to sleep, fall short of him in the working of miracles.' There follows an admirable discourse on preaching.

The sermon on 'Mutual Subjection' begins with a good joke: 'we may conclude that this subjection from all men to all men is something more than the compliment of course, when our betters are pleased to tell us that they are our humble servants, but understand us to be their slaves.' He goes on to preach, as in several sermons, the duty of good works. 'He who doth not perform that part assigned him toward advancing the benefit of the whole, in proportion to his opportunities and abilities, is not only a useless but a very mischievous member of the public . . . A wise man who doth not assist with his counsels, a great man with his protection, a rich man with his bounty and charity, and a poor man with his labour, are perfect nuisances in a commonwealth.' We see what a moral view of society his was, and we understand the more fully the public spirit that impelled him.

His sermons display, like all the rest of his work, his utter realism without illusions. 'Princes are born with no more advantages of strength or wisdom than other men; and, by an unhappy education, are usually more defective in both than thousands of their subjects.' 'The poor are generally more necessary members of the commonwealth than the rich' – note the scrupulous, and operative, word 'generally'. And there is carefully considered common sense on loving our neighbour. 'We are, indeed, commanded to love our neighbour as ourselves, but not as well as ourselves. The love we have for ourselves is to be the pattern of that love we ought to have towards our neighbour. But, as the copy doth not equal the original, so my neighbour cannot think it hard if I prefer myself, who am the original, before him who is only the copy.' This introduces a very rational disquisition on 'Doing Good', the duty of it, its uses and bounds.

There is constant insistence on duty. 'Even the poor beggar hath a just demand of an alms from the rich man, who is guilty of fraud, injustice, and oppression, if he doth not afford relief according to his abilities.' 'Great abilities of any sort do but make the owners of them greater and more painful [i.e. painstaking] servants to their neighbours and the public.' Swift carried out these precepts himself in the highest degree.

Did he manage to do so well in controlling the impulses of his own temperament? The sermon on 'The Difficulty of Knowing Oneself' enforces that self-knowledge 'teaches a man how to behave himself patiently when he has the ill-fortune to be censured and abused by other people'. I fear Swift was not very patient in this respect. Another advantage is that 'it makes men less severe upon other people's faults, and less busy and industrious in spreading them'. I fear he was very hard upon men's, and women's, faults and was industrious in spreading them in all his writings. Our Saviour commands us 'to forgive our offending brother' – I fear Swift was not very forgiving – and 'to love them that hate us': it does not seem that he tried very hard. But, then, 'Know thyself'? – before the age of Freud not many did.

A sermon like that on 'The Wretched Condition of Ireland' exemplifies Swift's public spirit in action and reads like one of his own pamphlets in the character of 'the Drapier', putting forward the same programme.

Around St Patrick's was an area known as the Liberty, where the Dean was the autocrat and ruler – and a very beneficent autocrat he made. He established a fund of £500 for small loans to deserving tradesmen. By 1715 he was able to say proudly, 'I hear they think me a smart Dean, and that I am for doing good. My notion is that if a man cannot mend the public, he should mend old shoes if he can do no better; and therefore I endeavour in the little sphere I am placed to do all the good it is capable of.' At Laracor similarly, where he had been making improvements from the beginning, he purchased twenty acres for a glebe to help to support the living for his successors. What would not such a man have accomplished for Ireland, if only he had had the power!

Even so, he did his best to encourage others, and, unlike them, was not afraid to admonish the great. The dissolute and nasty Lord-Lieutenant Wharton had a talented son, who was no less dissolute but much nicer. Swift detested the father but liked the son, and one day, when the young Duke was boasting of his mad frolics, took him to task in the most engaging manner, suggesting that he 'take a frolic to be virtuous' – it would do him more honour than all the other frolics of his life. Here speaks the practical moralist. No one has observed what a mass of unrecorded good work this misanthrope did, if only by his exceptional gift for friendship, arising out of his surprising good nature.

In place of the grandees of the Court of Queen Anne – now scattered, but with whom he kept touch by correspondence – he was forming a dependable circle of Irish friends. In Dublin there were two young men who became much attached to him. There was schoolmaster Tommy Sheridan (grandfather of the dramatist), an excellent scholar but very absent-minded and given to gaffes. He committed one such that offended the Dean's dignity. He and Swift were in the habit of exchanging verses, riddles, nonsense rhymes, sometimes in Latin; Sheridan wrote a long set of doggerel verses on the Dean, twenty years his senior, who regarded them as too personal, little less than a lampoon. It was a case of the pot calling the kettle black. The Dean remonstrated with a charming set of verses to Delany, then a Junior Fellow of Trinity, suggesting that he give Sheridan a hint:

> *To you, whose virtues I must own*
> *With shame, I have too lately known;*
> *To you, by art and nature taught*
> *To be the man I long have sought,*
> *Had not ill fate, perverse and blind,*

Placed you in life too far behind –
Or, what I should repine at more,
Placed me in life too far before . . .

What turn of phrase could be more dexterous, or polite? There follows an excellent poem: Swift takes the opportunity, in reproof of Sheridan, of defining the difference between wit and humour, raillery and rudeness. From it we learn, too, how much indebted he was to French writers, in whom he was well read, especially in La Rochefoucauld, where he recognized his own character. He also read Rabelais and Molière; while for raillery – the art he practised, with such dire results, with Vanessa –

Wherein French writers most excel,
Voiture in various lights displays
That irony which turns to praise.

For both these young clerics Swift was able to get useful preferment, when it had been so sourly long in coming for himself.

Out in the country there were a number of close friends, of similar education and interests, in whose country houses he and 'the ladies' could stay for weeks on end. Perhaps, above all, with Charles Ford at Wood Park on the road to Laracor, whose recently discovered correspondence with Swift has thrown much light on the circumstances of the publication of *Gulliver's Travels*, where he went in for more than his usual mystification and employed Ford as a go-between. Ford followed Bolingbroke to France, and on his return was detained for a while. At Loughgall in Northern Ireland was Robert Cope, with whom the Dean maintained a scholarly correspondence and stayed as a guest. At Gaulstown were the Rochforts, and at Woodbrooke the Chetwodes. Like Ford, Knightley Chetwode was a rightwing Tory, and like him got into trouble. Swift intervened, and did his best for him, successfully, with Archbishop King, then a Lord Justice.

When staying with the Rochforts at Gaulstown in September 1721, Swift wrote to console Chetwode: 'for my own part, I have learned to bear everything, and not to sail with the wind in my teeth. I think the folk in power, if they had any justice, might at least give you some honorary satisfaction; but I am a stranger to their justice and all their good qualities, having only received marks of their ill ones.' These men were all Tories, like Swift, in opposition to the Government. But King had a sense of justice – more so than Swift; and Chetwode was able to report to him, 'the Archbishop, in my opinion, has been kind; but it is through you: I had no interest in him.' Swift: 'I am sure I saw my best friends very calm and easy, when I was under worse difficulties than you. A few good offices is all we can expect from others.' When the trouble blew over, we find the austere Dean rallying Chetwode: 'I could find fault with nothing but your paper, which was so perfumed that the company with me could not bear it.' And again, 'your perfumed paper hath been ready to give me an apoplexy; either leave off these refinements, or we will send you to live on a midden in Connaught.'

At this moment Swift was confined to the Deanery with his old ear trouble: 'I have the noise of seven watermills in my ears and expect to continue so above a month. I mope at home, and can bear no company but trebles and counter-tenors.' We must always bear in mind the physical disabilities that offer a counterpoint to his incessant mental activity. He did his best for himself by a temperate diet and regular exercise. He describes himself, in a compliment to the Archbishop, who was suffering from gout: 'I own my head and your Grace's feet would be ill joined, but give me your head and take my feet, and match us in the kingdom if you can. My Lord, I row after health like a waterman, and ride after it like a post-boy.' We have seen that, in the summer of Vanessa's death, he went on a journey to explore the south and far south west. He got as far as the parish of Skull, which was almost the death of him; for, investigating the beauty of the wild cliff scenery, he had to be rescued by his two men-servants. He celebrated these cliffs in a Latin poem, 'Carberiae Rupes', of which, in keeping with the time, he was prouder than of his natural English verse.

Stopping with the ladies out at Quilca – the country living he had obtained for Sheridan – we find him pushing forward improvements. 'Your mason is come, but cannot yet work upon your garden, neither can I agree with him about the great wall.' He was having

Sheridan's lands surveyed for him, and enclosing – the indispensable step towards proper cultivation of the soil. The Dean was engaged in 'stopping gaps and driving cattle from the corn . . . The ladies' room smokes; the rain drops from the skies into the kitchen; our servants eat and drink like the devil, and pray for rain, which entertains them at cards and sleep, which are much lighter than spades, sledges and crows. Their maxim is:

> Eat like a Turk,
>   Sleep like a dormouse;
> Be last at work,
>   At victuals foremost.

Such were Irish entertainments.

That this Anglo-Irishman was not out of touch with the folk-life of the native Irish, or even their balladry, may be seen from his translation of 'O'Rourke's Feast', which someone, perhaps Sheridan, must have translated for him to put into verse:

> O'Rourke's noble fare
>   Will ne'er be forgot,
> By those who were there,
>   Or those who were not.
> His revels to keep,
>   We sup and we dine,
> On seven score sheep,
>   Fat bullocks and swine.
> Usquebaugh to our feast
>   In pails was brought up,
> And an hundred at least,
>   And a madder[1] our cup.

The *Journal* describes a house-party in the summer of 1721 at Gaulstown, of the Rochforts:

> At seven, the Dean, in nightgown dressed,
> Goes round the house to wake the rest;
> At nine, grave Nim and George facetious
> Go to the Dean to read Lucretius.

---

[1] Madder means a wooden cup.

There was a lake in the grounds, for a line comes in several times as chorus:

And then all hands, boys, to the oar!

Once the boat capsized and the Dean fell in; he tells

How Dan caught nothing in his net,
And how his boat was overset,
For brevity I have retrenched,
How in the lake the Dean was drenched.

No one could be more charming than the formidable Dean in unbuttoned mood, writing to Tommy Sheridan: 'You will find Quilca not the thing it was last August; nobody to relish the lake; nobody to ride over the downs; no trout to be caught; no dining over a well; no night heroics; no morning epics; no stolen hour when the wife is gone; no creature to call you names. Poor miserable Master Sheridan! No blind harpers! No journeys to Rantaran!' They clearly enjoyed each other's company, and more – Swift had a fondness for absent-minded Sheridan, indifferent to his own interests. In recommending him for preferment, he said, 'he is a man of good sense, modesty, and virtue. His greatest fault is a wife and four children; for which there is no excuse, but that a wife is thought necessary to a schoolmaster.'

At the Deanery he was also engaged in improving. Encouraging Chetwode to make plantations on his estate and study the right kind of trees and where to place them, he wrote, 'for want of better I have been planting elms in the Deanery garden, and – what is worse – in the Cathedral churchyard where I disturbed the dead, and angered the living by removing tombstones, that people will be at a loss how to rest with the bones of their ancestors.' Some way south of the Deanery there was an empty field, which he called his Naboth's Vineyard. He proceeded to enclose it with a wall, against which he grew fruit-trees. 'I am over head and ears in mortar [this was the summer of 1724], and with a number of the greatest rogues in Ireland, which is a proud word.' They thought to cheat him and scamp the work by putting in bad stone here and there. He let them, as if he hadn't noticed, then made them pick out the bad stone and replace it. The moralist taught them that 'it was in their interest to be honest' – and a good way to deal with lazy, dishonest work-people!

The Dean was at home at the Deanery on Sundays, and not infrequently had people to dinner. Here is a characteristic invitation to his predecessor, whom he had made a bishop, Stearne: 'My Lord, if you do not appoint tomorrow [Saturday], Monday, Tuesday, Wednesday or Thursday to dine at the Deanery with the old club of the Walls and lodges [the Archdeacon and wife, with the two ladies], I believe there may be a mutiny. Therefore pray fix the matter for your own sake.' Like a born writer, Swift expressed himself differently from anyone else, with the stamp of his own personality on everything he wrote.

What was individual to him was that there was nothing he would not say. His spirit was reviving, his genius waking up again, as he recovered from the shock of the catastrophe of 1714 and acclimatized himself to living in Ireland. There is a very naughty poem he wrote in 1722, 'The Progress of Marriage', on an elderly dean, one Pratt, a contemporary of his at Trinity, marrying a haughty young lady not half his age. It might have been Swift's own case with Vanessa.

> Aetatis suae *fifty-two,*
> *A rich divine began to woo*
> *A handsome young imperious girl,*
> *Nearly related to an earl.*

The wedding is ludicrously described:

> *The wedding day, you take me right,*
> *I promise nothing for the night:*
> *The bridegroom, dressed to make a figure,*
> *Assumes an artificial vigour.*

But can he perform his duty by the young creature, as empty-headed as she is lascivious?

> *He wonders what employs her brain,*
> *But never asks, or asks in vain.*

She spends her nights in balls and masquerades; he comes home from church,

> *And meets her hasting to the ball,*
> *Her chairmen push him from the wall:*
> *He enters in and walks upstairs*
> *And calls the family[1] to prayers,*
> *Then goes alone to take his rest*
> *In bed, where he can spare her best.*

The elderly dean is, of course, cuckolded:

> *The Dean with all his best endeavour*
> *Gets not an heir, but gets a fever:*
> *A victim to the last essays*
> *Of vigour in declining days*
> *He dies, and leaves his mourning mate*
> *(What could he less) his whole estate.*

The daughter of an earl, now a wealthy widow, consoles herself with young lovers:

> *Oh, may I see her soon dispensing*
> *Her favours to some broken ensign –*
> *Him let her marry for his face*
> *And only coat of tarnished lace:*
> *To turn her naked out of doors*
> *And spend her jointure on his whores –*
> *But for a parting present leave her*
> *A rooted pox to last for ever.*

There was, indeed, *nothing* that Jonathan Swift would not say – this is what makes him such a wonderful, so universal, a writer. Though this made him uncongenial to the Victorians, and their comfortable society, it makes him very much a writer for our time of break-up and decay, the end of our civilization.

Politics were the breath of life to Swift – he was really made for a politician – and, with the revival of his spirit coinciding with a period of distress around him in Dublin, he could not but take notice of it. A severe depression hit the textile weavers in 1721, with consequent

[1] Family here means household.

unemployment and distress, starvation. Archbishop King describes it for us.

'The poverty of the kingdom is not to be imagined. The cry of the weavers of all sorts, linen, woollen and silk, was intolerable. They sold and pawned all they had for bread – household stuff, clothes, looms and tools, and there remained nothing behind but to starve. They prepared a petition to the Government and Council, who ordered them £100 and a collection in the Church. The numbers of the weaving trade are near 1,700, and the persons near 6,000. What will come of them God only knows. It is true everybody bestirred themselves to get them a supply, the Dissenters, the Roman Catholics, the Deans and Chapters, the College, nay, the Playhouse gave a play which raised £73. So that we have got a fund which, I hope, will amount to near £1,500. But what will this be among so many?'

The good Archbishop, a patriot, took the lead, but his Dean sounded the trumpet-call. He now wrote the first of his historic tracts, which formed ultimately the blueprint for Irish nationalism. He put forward *A Proposal for the Universal Use of Irish Manufacture in Clothes, Furniture of Houses, etc, utterly Rejecting and Renouncing Everything Wearable that comes from England*. Several words in the last line were printed small, so that it looked like *Utterly Rejecting and Renouncing ... England*. Delany tells us that Swift was so moved to indignation by the misery and distress in Dublin that he preached about it, and his talk was full of it. With his temper he one day came out with a dangerous sally, though he said it was somebody else's, that 'Ireland would never be happy till a law were made for burning everything that came from England, except their people and their coals', and then added, 'nor am I yet for lessening the number of those exceptions.'

Swift's proposal was the sensible one of excluding English woollens and silks in order to encourage the Irish manufacture. He urged it with all the passion raised in him by the way the English Government sacrificed the chances of their own Protestant Anglo-Irish, at every point, to selfish English interests. And he broadened the basis of the attack to include absentee landlords, who were given a free hand to depopulate the countryside by converting tillage into pasture. This affected the Church adversely, by diminishing tithes – most of which were already appropriated to the landlords, the rest quite insufficient to support a Protestant clergy – though the accumulation of pluralities enabled English-appointed bishops to live in affluence, their money achieving a high rate of interest where money was so scarce. 'When a divine is sent over to a bishopric here, with the hopes of £2,500 a year, upon his arrival he finds, alas, a discount of 10% or 12%.'

Swift, being Swift, he went further to indict the whole English interest in Ireland, English appointees, English bishops, English landlords, absentees, all who had not at heart the interests of Ireland from which they drew their sustenance: all those 'who by unmeasurable screwing and racking their tenants all over the kingdom, have already reduced the miserable people to a worse condition than the peasants in France, or the vassals in Germany and Poland. So that the whole species of what we call substantial farmers will in a very few years be utterly at an end . . . Whoever travels this country and observes the face of nature, or the faces and habits and dwellings of the natives, will hardly think himself in a land where either law, religion or common humanity is professed.' He concluded with a prophecy: 'nothing is so likely to call down an universal judgement upon a nation as universal oppression.'

What an indictment! And from such a source – from an Anglo-Irishman who regarded himself as English and would much have preferred to live his life in England. Everybody knew who had written it, anonymous as it was; for the first time, in appealing to the latent resources of Irish patriotism, he began to appear as an Irish patriot himself. It was the beginning of a new – and in its ultimate consequences, his most important – career. Actually most of the weavers in Dublin were Protestants; but Swift's defence of their interest could not but extend itself to Catholic weavers too. Where the interests of the *country* were at stake, it was impossible to distinguish between them. The short-sighted selfishness of the English Parliament, dominated by the Whigs for the next half century, was in the end to ruin the Protestant interest in Ireland, destroy all its possibilities of growth and strengthening itself, leaving Ireland, except for the Ulster Scots, a 95 per cent Catholic country.

What a prophet Swift proved to be! No wonder he was lacerated by anger – *saeva indignatio* – when he saw the way things were going and that it was impossible to resist it. All that one could do was to negate, oppose, protest; but in the long run it built up a campaign, a tradition, a literature which destroyed the English in Ireland. This very tract first advocated what came to be known by the Irish term of *boycott*, and was to have an almighty extension all over Ireland in the next century, until the landlords were driven out.

Truly, the English governing class paid a terrible price for their characteristic superciliousness in disconsidering this dangerous man of genius: better to have made him an Archbishop in England than to have relegated him to Ireland, with the Deanery of St Patrick's as base!

The English Government could not but take note of such flagrant defiance. The printer of the pamphlet – the author being 'unknown' – was prosecuted for publishing 'a scandalous, seditious and factious libel'. The Grand Jury, however, brought in a verdict of not guilty; Chief Justice Whitshed, a Whig appointment, sent them back eight times, and only then achieved a postponement of sentence. When the new Lord-Lieutenant arrived, the prosecution was dropped. In those days the circulation of broadsheets was a very effective means of influencing or inciting public opinion. Swift, who appreciated their political use, circulated 'An Excellent New Song', a ballad sung to the tune of 'Packington's Pound', with the refrain:

> *Though a Printer and Dean*
> *Seditiously mean*
> *Our true Irish hearts from old England to wean;*
> *We'll buy English silks for our wives and our daughters,*
> *In spite of his Deanship and Journeyman Waters.*

Thus Ireland received lessons in ungovernability from the greatest of Anglo-Irishmen. It was now to continue for the rest of his life.

While this first campaign was being waged various acts and indications showed the determination of Whig England upon the subordination of Ireland to English interests. Every bishop appointed since George I's accession was an Englishman, except one Welshman, Bishop Evans, Swift's diocesan at Laracor, and his *bête noire*. The Parliament at Westminster quashed the appellate jurisdiction of the Irish House of Lords – Archbishop King described it as 'the enslavement of Ireland'. In the Irish Parliament, the English interest – landlords, bishops, officials – rejected a measure for the encouragement of tillage. In this very year 1720 the Whig Duke of Wharton paid a visit, in which, in two days, he sold his Irish estate for £130,000, which, at forty years' purchase, showed the increasing value of land with a subjugated tenantry.

The next issue to arouse Swift's ire was that for a National Bank of Ireland, with a capital of £500,000, a parallel to that great Whig achievement, the Bank of England. There was a good deal to be said for it on economic grounds; money *was* scarce in Ireland, credit restricted and fetching far too high a rate of interest. But one can see how Anglo-Irish patriotism would oppose it, and Swift in particular: he had always detested the moneyed interest, and thought that its increase upset the balance of society, where his ideal was a broad base of 'substantial farmers' and the rest in proportion: a simply articulated agrarian society.

Archbishop King informs us as to what was coming before the Irish Parliament. 'The Bank, the pernicious Bank, is tumbling upon us. We need no South Sea to drown us, for a little water will do it.' In England the South Sea Bubble had burst, with dire consequences – fortunes for some (including the Marlboroughs and George I's German mistresses), ruin for most.

'France had its Mississippi, and Britain its South Sea, but it is thought this Bubble will be sufficient to do our business. All the speaking men in the House are for it, being concerned as subscribers. Many are against it, but cannot speak their minds. Dean Swift offered to lay me 5 guineas this morning the Bill would pass – for a good natural reason: that it was for private advantage and public mischief.'

Swift wrote to the Archbishop: 'I hear you are to be the sole opposer of the Bank. Bankrupts are always for setting up banks; how then can you think a bank will fail of a majority in both Houses?'

In the event, he was wrong. The Bank was rejected by both Houses of the Irish Parliament. It would probably have been to Ireland's advantage.

Archbishop and Dean, those two great neighbours, were now pulling together and henceforth would continue to do so, in what they considered to be the country's interest, as patriots. A new note of friendship and mutual confidence enters into their correspondence, and there are several tributes to King in verse. The first dates from their co-operation over the Weavers and the Bank:

> *Virtue concealed within our breast*
> *Is inactivity at best;*
> *But never shall the Muse endure*
> *To let your virtues lie obscure,*
> *Or suffer envy to conceal*
> *Your labours for the public weal.*
> *Within your breast all wisdom lies,*
> *Either to govern or advise;*
> *Your steady soul preserves her frame*
> *In good and evil times the same.*

This was no more than the truth.

The next conflict that arose, over Wood's Ha'pence, was intrinsically less important but led to a much fiercer agitation, a more resounding defeat for the British Government, and ended up with the Dean of St Patrick's the most popular figure in Dublin: a folk hero, a strange fate for one who was now a confirmed misanthrope.

Again, there was something to be said for Wood's proposed coinage – but Swift was not the one to say it. It was true that Ireland was short of small change and needed a supply of copper coins, halfpence and farthings. But the circumstances surrounding the purchase of the patent by Wood, as well as the exorbitant profit he would make out of it, made the transaction intolerable, and indeed insulting. In the first place, the Irish Parliament had not been consulted. In the second, Wood's coins would have a smaller proportion of copper than English coins, more brass, and thus, it was calculated, he would make a profit of £40,000 out of it.

He had paid £10,000 for it to the Duchess of Kendal, one of George I's two mistresses. This was the dreadful German, Ehrengard Melusina von der Schulenburg, whom the English called 'the Maypole', she was so tall and lean and cadaverous; the other was the fat Kielmansegge. What they had in common was their rapacity. The Schulenburg was later to receive the enormous bribe of £11,000 from Bolingbroke's French wife, to allow him to return from exile. In the struggle for power between Sir Robert Walpole and the gifted, cultivated Carteret, Kielmansegge supported the latter; but the Schulenburg won with Walpole. So Carteret was pushed out to become Lord-Lieutenant of Ireland, where, it was said, he was not displeased by the agitation against Wood (with his backers!). This was a safeguard to Swift in entering the fray, who was anyway already known to, and respected by, the literate Lord-Lieutenant: they exchanged polite letters in the midst of the rude agitation against the Government.

The manufacture of textiles was immeasurably more important, and here Swift had not succeeded. He despised the passiveness of the Irish, who would not help themselves, either by boycotting English goods or improving their own. Swift did what he could to patronize good workmanship, sending lengths of Irish plaid to the Opposition Court of the Prince and Princess of Wales – the clever Caroline responded by accepting the gift. But the utmost the Irish of themselves would do was negative – obstruct, refuse, oppose. From the first they opposed Wood's patent; both Houses voted against it. But would it be imposed on the country against their wishes?

This is where Swift weighed in with the first of the four famous Drapier Letters: *A Letter to the Shopkeepers, Tradesmen, Farmers and Common People of Ireland*, by M. B. Drapier, assuming the character of a clothier, with its reference back to his previous *Proposal* for boycotting English manufactures. The *Letter* was pure propaganda, full of wild exaggerations. No matter – as the late Fuehrer of the German people, who had a genius for propaganda, said in *Mein Kampf*: when one is offering soap for sale, one doesn't say that someone else's soap is very good too.

The second *Letter* went further, in Swift's manner, and raised the threat of boycott again.

'When the evil day is come (if it must come) let us mark and observe those who presume to offer these halfpence in payment. Let their names, and trades, and places of abode be made public, that everyone may be aware of them as betrayers of their country.'

This suggestion of delation, the sinister character of the informer, was to have a lurid future in Irish politics. What a dangerous man he was, at once charming and utterly ruthless, both compassionate and implacable – all according to whether he had been unforgivably wounded, and where. He was a member of the Church Militant, but hardly a Christian.

Walpole's government in England, nonplussed by the growing agitation and fearful that the new coins would be refused, offered to compromise on a coinage limited to £40,000. This would have been better tactics in the first place. A committee investigated the terms of the patent, and, not unexpectedly, could not 'discover the least pretence to say this patent was passed or obtained in a clandestine or unprecedented manner'. Swift's third *Letter* claimed that the report of the government committee was a fabrication of Wood's; and what wise minister would ignore the universal clamour of a people, 'if that clamour can be quieted by disappointing the fraudulent practice of a single person?' In other words, make poor Wood surrender his patent.

Once more Swift broadened the issue to that of parity of Ireland with England. 'Were not the people of Ireland born as free as those of England? How have they forfeited their freedom? . . . Are they not subjects of the same King? Am I a freeman in England, and do I become a slave in six hours in crossing the Channel?' Pure rhetoric; he knew that the answer was that England had the power to enforce Ireland's subjection.

Meanwhile he was exchanging politenesses with the new Lord-Lieutenant, not yet come over. 'I hope your Excellency will forgive an old humble servant, and one who always loved and esteemed you, for interfering in matters out of his province; which he would never have done if many of the greatest persons here had not, by their importunity, drawn him out of his retirement [!] to venture giving you a little trouble, in hopes to save their country from utter destruction. For which the memory of your government will be blessed by posterity.' And so on, as if he were not the Drapier himself, as everybody knew. Yet when the Lord-Lieutenant delayed a little in replying, he received a rather peremptory reproof, for which Swift subsequently apologized. 'I have discovered in myself somewhat of the bully . . . I am ten years older than I was when I had the honour to see you last, and consequently ten times more testy.' Before setting out for Dublin, Carteret wrote handsomely: 'I shall not be testy but endeavour to show that I am not altogether insensible of the force of that genius which has outshone most of this age.'

When he arrived to take up his government, he was met by news-vendors in the streets hawking the Drapier's fourth *Letter*, which went beyond all bounds. Is it true that the Lord-Lieutenant is coming over to impose Wood's ha'pence on the people of Ireland, and 'put £100,000 into the pocket of a sharper'? But can it be done? He would have to convert the Irish Houses of Parliament, and he has not the means to effect that – except by bribing them all. For there is nothing left to bribe them with – and he gives a list of the great Irish offices in the hands of Englishmen.

In the midst of all this hullabaloo one of the greatest had fallen vacant: the Tory Primate (Swift's appointment) died. Archbishop King was the real leader of the Irish Church, and now – too late – Swift would have liked him to succeed. But Walpole lost no time in appointing a youngish *protégé*, Hugh Boulter, an Englishman, to the highest position in the Irish Church; for the next two decades he remained there, the faithful watchdog of English (and Whig) interests.

The fourth *Letter* went further than before to preach the doctrine of passive resistance. The King no doubt has the prerogative of issuing coins; but 'nobody alive is obliged to take them'. Again, 'I have looked over all the English and Irish statutes without finding any law that makes Ireland depend on England, any more than England does upon Ireland.' He proposed a declaration as 'I, M. B. Drapier, *depend* only on the King my sovereign, and on the laws of my own country'. It was a declaration with revolutionary implications, and was realized for a brief period from 1782 to 1801: the winning of their independence by the American colonies won the recognition of parity for Ireland with England, under a common sovereign. In other words, the equal status of Canada, Australia, New Zealand, within the Commonwealth. If this had been sustained and fulfilled, a century of murder and bloodshed might have been avoided. But it was brought to an end by the suicidal Rebellion of 1798, which instigated the fatal Act of Union of 1801. Swift might well repine at what idiots men are in the mass, and write a work of genius to show it.

Carteret's first measure on arrival was to issue a proclamation offering a reward of £300 for the discovery of the author of the fourth *Letter*, addressed as it was to 'the Whole People of Ireland', challenging English government. Carteret's heart was not in it, but needs must – the administration could not but take action. No one dared attack the unknown author, though his praises were sung in the streets: 'And the people said unto Saul, Shall Jonathan die, who hath wrought this great salvation in Israel? God forbid; as the Lord liveth, there shall not one hair of his head fall to the ground; for he hath wrought with God this day. So the people rescued Jonathan that he died not.' The printer was prosecuted instead. Upon which Swift wrote his *Seasonable Advice* to the grand jury; he was able to assure them that 'his Grace, the Lord Archbishop of Dublin, so renowned for his piety and wisdom and love of his country, absolutely refused to condemn the book or the author'.

This was true and official: the Archbishop had declined to sign the Council's proclamation. In these circumstances it was in vain for Chief Justice Whitshed to discharge the jury which would not find the printer guilty, and recruit another: this only went further and made a presentment, instead, against 'all persons who had attempted to impose Wood's halfpence upon them'. Swift reported gleefully to Ford, 'the government and judges are at their wit's end' – nothing to be done. Still unappeased – he was unappeasable – he wrote a final 'Address to Both Houses of Parliament', grandly setting out 'the universal desires of the nation'. It was a presumptuous claim on his part, but in fact he had become the mouthpiece of the nation and, in the course of the agitation, become the national hero – of a people he despised. For, though the patent was withdrawn, and a minor victory scored, he knew that the Irish Parliament would not follow it up with the constructive measures he desired – the encouragement of Irish manufactures, of tillage, plantation, improvements all over the land, the end of absentee landlordism, at least its limitation, the appointment of born Irishmen to Irish offices in Church and state.

It was a radical programme, revolutionary in its implications. It could only have been carried through by a dictator: had Jonathan Swift been dictator he would have carried it through, or perished in the attempt. As it was, he knew nothing would be done. With Boulter as Primate for the next twenty years the Irish Church was shackled to Whig rule in England; as for the Irish Parliament, Swift expressed his opinion of its increasing subjection to the English interest, roped and tied by bribery and corruption systematized, in the last and most searing of his political poems, 'The Legion Club'.

Meanwhile, in manic mood, he enjoyed the fray; spoiling for a fight, he was reinvigorated. Verses flew to and fro, an immense amount of print and paper was consumed, broadsides, ballads, epigrams – there is a considerable literature on the subject. Swift himself put forth several squibs. There is an amusing one, 'A Serious Poem upon William Wood, Brasier, Tinker, Hardwareman, Coiner, Counter-feiter, Founder and Esquire':

> *When foes are o'ercome, we preserve them from slaughter,*
> *To be hewers of wood and drawers of water;*
> *Now, although to draw water is not very good,*
> *Yet we all should rejoice to be hewers of* Wood.

And so on, all very enjoyable – except for poor Mr Wood.

Chief Justice Whitshed received a lampoon for his pains. Swift was hugely pleased when he observed one day that the motto upon the Chief Justice's coach happened to be *Libertas et natale solum* (Liberty and my native country), for Whitshed was an Irishman born: 'I shall never forget upon what occasion ... at the very point of time when he was sitting in his court and perjuring himself to betray both.' The poor fellow was but doing his duty as Chief Justice – one sees the amenities of Irish politics looming ahead.

138

Archbishop King received another graceful bow, in the meticulous *pas de deux* danced by these two eminent ecclesiastics:

'Great, Good and Just' was once applied
To one who for his country died –

Whether the Whig Archbishop appreciated the comparison with Charles I is not recorded –

To one who lives in its defence
We speak it in a happier sense.
O may the fates thy life prolong!
Our country then can dread no wrong:
In thy great care we place our trust,
Because thou'rt Great, and Good, and Just.

This fracas did not disturb friendly relations between the Lord-Lieutenant and the most formidable figure under his government: Swift attended the levees at the Castle when he felt inclined, and exchanged Latin quips with clever Carteret. The latter made himself very agreeable, listened to the Dean's suggestions for preferments for Irishmen, and interceded with success for some in trouble, including one young officer inclined to Popery. Once, when Swift found himself defeated in argument by Carteret, he is said to have exclaimed, in character: 'What the vengeance brought you amongst us! Get you gone, get you gone! Pray God Almighty send us our boobies back again.' It was an example of

That irony which turns to praise,

which he had defined in the 'Verses to Delany'.

On these amiable terms Carteret's government of Ireland was counted rather a success. From England he continued to correspond with the Dean; he said handsomely that, when folks asked him how he managed to govern Ireland, he answered: 'I pleased Dr Swift.'

The most brilliant person to be recommended to Carteret's attention was the philosopher Berkeley, who already enjoyed the richest deanery in the country, that of Derry. Swift had no sympathy with his philosophy, or with metaphysics at all, but he recognized the younger man's quality and had the justice of mind to speak up for him.

'He was a Fellow in the University here and, going to England very young, he became the founder of a sect there called the Immaterialists, by the force of a very curious book upon that subject. He is an absolute philosopher with regard to money, titles, and power, and for three years past has been struck with a notion of founding a university at Bermuda. His heart will break if his deanery be not taken from him.'

There followed the warmest recommendation of Berkeley's character and attainments – though to Swift he was a Projector, like the philosophers he was writing about in the island of Laputa. He thought his project of a university to convert the West Indians ridiculous – as it was. This did not prevent him from recommending him generously to the Earl of Oxford's scholarly son: 'Dr Berkeley is a true philosopher and an excellent scholar, but of a very visionary virtue, and is endeavouring to quit £1,000 a year for £100 at Bermudas.'

To Swift he provided an example of a type he was writing about in the third Book of *Gulliver's Travels*. For during this period of tumultuous activity he was at the same time finishing and polishing his masterpiece.

CHAPTER 7

The Major Prophet. Gulliver

WHERE *A Tale of a Tub* is an English classic, *Gulliver's Travels* is a world classic. It has been read all over the world for its story and its fantasy, particularly the first two books, dealing with Lilliput, where everything is on a minute scale so that Gulliver appears as a giant, and Brobdingnag, where the inhabitants are on the scale of giants and he is a mere manikin. The extraordinary controlled imagination that could carry through two such projects – one seeing everything through a microscopic lens, the other through an enormous magnifying glass – has never ceased to appeal. People think of them as children's stories, and they have been reproduced scores of times as such. Even Part IV, the kingdom where horses rule, has not been without its popular appeal, suitably edited and censored, for the horse is a noble animal and everybody likes horses. Part III, the voyage to Laputa with the flying island attached, has always been the least popular and is of a more specialized interest; for myself, I find it the funniest, it makes me laugh more than the other books.

The fate and fortune of this masterpiece is not the least of the ironies in the life of this strange man. For what is read as a children's story is the most savage satire written upon human society and upon man himself; and Swift wrote it less to give pleasure than, as he said, to vex mankind. And we can be quite sure that the political reflections, incidents, allusions and morals – which literary critics, even a good one like Middleton Murry, think irrelevant today – are what mattered most to Swift. We shall see, too, how far from irrelevant they are.

The idea of the book went back to the Scriblerus Club, of which Swift was the leading spirit, which was formed in that last winter in London, 1713–14. Arbuthnot, Pope, Gay and Parnell were the other members. They were to write the memoirs of their joint creation, Martin Scriblerus. The project did not get very far. Arbuthnot reported to Swift, in his withdrawal to Letcombe, 'to talk of Martin in any hands but yours is a folly. You every day give better hints than all of us together could do in a twelvemonth. Pope, who first thought of the hint, has no genius at all to it in my mind. Gay is too young; Parnell has some ideas of it, but is idle.' Arbuthnot was to write up the medicine, Swift a voyage and 'the projects of Laputa' – 'all that relates to the sciences must be from you.'

The idea germinated in Swift's mind. Voyages made popular reading throughout the reign of Queen Anne, the most remarkable being those of William Dampier, a West Countryman who had an astonishing career in all the oceans as seaman, buccaneer, pirate and excellent hydrographer. Anyone who has read his *Voyages* – two of them dedicated to members of the Whig Junto, one of them Swift's disappointing patron, Halifax, the other, Orford – will recognize the use Swift made of them. The style Swift adhered to was Dampier's plain, factual, nautical reporting; at one point there is a full-page parody of his hydrographical detail. The maps that accompanied *Gulliver's Travels* are designed to give verisimilitude.

Dampier's voyage to the East Indies and the north coast of Australia took place in 1699; Lilliput and Blefuscu are charted way off in the Indian Ocean from Sumatra and Van Diemen's Land (Tasmania), as discovered in 1699. Dampier was in the Pacific in 1703; Brobdingnag is described as 'discovered A.D. 1703', it is attached to North America, where Alaska is, beyond the fabled Straits of Anian, north of California, which is given Sir Francis Drake's name, New Albion. Laputa, Balnibarbi and Lugnagg, lie in the Pacific off Japan, 'discovered 1701'. 'Houyhnhnm Land' was 'discovered A.D. 1711'– this was the year in which Dampier returned from his voyage round the world, having rescued Selkirk from his solitary confinement on Juan Fernandez. This was the inspiration of Defoe's *Robinson Crusoe*, published in 1719, which had such success that further instalments were demanded.

Swift was not long in following suit. During the years 1722–4 he was comparatively free of his old complaint in his head, giddiness and deafness. Ford was his confidant in regard to writing and publishing *Gulliver*; Swift's first reference to it is in April 1721, 'I am now writing a history of my Travels, which will be a large volume, and gives account of countries hitherto unknown; but they go on slowly for want of health and humour.' With the recovery of his health the pace picked up; the first two books were written in 1721-2; then the fourth book in 1723. Ford must have told Bolingbroke, 'else how should he know anything of Stella or of Horses. I would have him and you know that I hate Yahoos of both sexes, and that Stella and Madame de Villette [Bolingbroke's mistress and subsequent wife] are only tolerable at best for want of Houhyhnhnms.' This was in January 1724: 'I have left the Country of Horses and am in the Flying Island, where I shall not stay long, and my two last journeys will be soon over.'

In August 1725 he writes from Quilca, 'I have finished my Travels and I am now transcribing them. They are admirable things, and will wonderfully mend the world.' He was staying there in Sheridan's parsonage with the ladies, 'reading books twice over for want of fresh ones, and fairly correcting and transcribing my Travels for the public.' It would seem that he was reading *Don Quixote*; while next month he is advising the too confiding Sheridan, 'expect no more from man than such an animal is capable of, and you will every day find my description of Yahoos more resembling.'

To Pope he imparted the principles of his misanthropy, the foundation upon which 'the whole building is erected . . . I have ever hated all nations, professions, and communities, and all my love is towards individuals. For instance, I hate the tribe of lawyers, but I love Councillor Such-a-one, and Judge Such-a-one. So with physicians – I will not speak of my own trade – soldiers, English, Scotch, French, and the rest. But principally I hate and detest that animal called man, although I heartily love John, Peter, Thomas and so forth.'

In short, the Dean was not a Christian but – like that other Anglo-Irishman of genius, Lawrence of Arabia – a Manichee.

In other words, what he detested was Mass-Man – and he had this on his side, that human beings are always to be seen at their most idiotic in their mass-behaviour, as members of the herd, whether nations or churches, political parties, trade unions or, for that matter, universities, even when the individual in himself may be reasonable enough, at times. What Swift detested was the nonsensical belief that men as a whole were rational – their behaviour showed that this was not true. At the utmost, they were capable of reason; then why don't they act on it more? That is the question.

It is really a very complex question, more complex than Swift, who had settled for a rather simple rationalism, perhaps realized – it was another Anglo-Irishman, Edmund Burke, who realized more fully the subtlety of it. Anyhow, the evidences of men's refusal to use what reason they have got were all round him, especially in Ireland, and Swift was right to highlight the evidences of their idiocy. He was a moralist and preacher: he was right to bring home to them again and again the consequences of their folly – how otherwise can, or will, the fools learn? Some of them can learn something some of the time; very well, they should be made to, and if they refuse, they should be lashed for it – it is probable that they understand that better. 'When you think of the world give it one lash the more at my request. The chief end I propose in all my labours is to vex the world rather than divert it.'

Here he may be said to have failed again – the world has never ceased to be diverted by his efforts, when it would have done better to lay them to heart.

Swift may be said to have loved virtue, and recognized it in a man when he saw it. 'Oh! if the world had but a dozen Arbuthnots in it, I would burn my Travels.' As it was, by September 1725 they were ready for the press, 'when the world shall deserve them, or rather when a printer shall be found brave enough to venture his ears.' That in itself should show that the political and social implications of the book were what Swift thought most important about it. 'Drown the world! I am not content with despising it, but I would anger it, if I could with safety. I wish there were an hospital built for its despisers, where one might act with safety, and it need not be a large building, only I would have it well endowed.' He was in time to endow such a building with his life's savings – it would be a lunatic asylum.

1   *Swift as a student at* Trinity College, Dublin, *which he entered in his fifteenth year (1682).*

2   *William III. Swift's patron, Sir William Temple, played an important part in negotiating the marriage which ultimately brought William to the throne.*

3 For ten years Swift's employer and benefactor, Temple was a successful diplomat before his retirement in 1688.

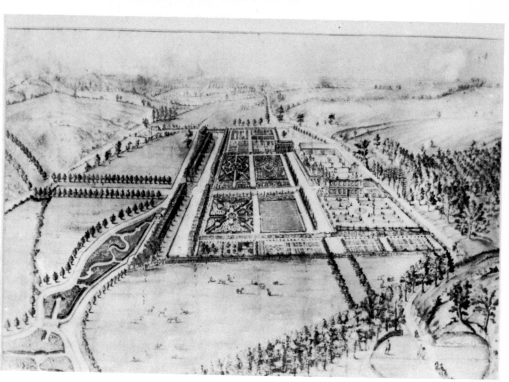

4 The grounds of Moor Park, near Farnham, were landscaped by Temple – a famous gardener – with a canal, walks and avenues in the Dutch style.

· 5   *Esther Johnson (1681–1728), the daughter of Temple's steward, was brought up at Moor Park and, as Stella, was Swift's lifelong friend and protégée.*

6   *St Patrick's Cathedral, Dublin, where Swift got a prebend while vicar of Laracor, and soon became the most active member of the Chapter.*

7   *Archbishop King of Dublin, a formidable personality with whom Swift was to have a long and somewhat ambivalent relationship.*

8 *Swift in early middle age. He was rather short of stature, with piercing, protuberant blue eyes.*

9 *The coffee-house was a regular meeting-place for Swift and his friends in London.*

The Dutchess of Summerset.

10 *An inveterate enemy of Swift, the Duchess of Somerset used her influence with the Queen to block his career.*

11 *Robert Harley, Earl of Oxford, Lord Treasurer during the last years of Queen Anne, and a close friend of Swift.*

12   Queen Anne, despite the efforts of his friends, obstinately refused
preferment for Swift.

13 Henry St John, Viscount Bolingbroke, Secretary of State in Harley's administration. He worked closely with Swift on political pamphlets and articles.

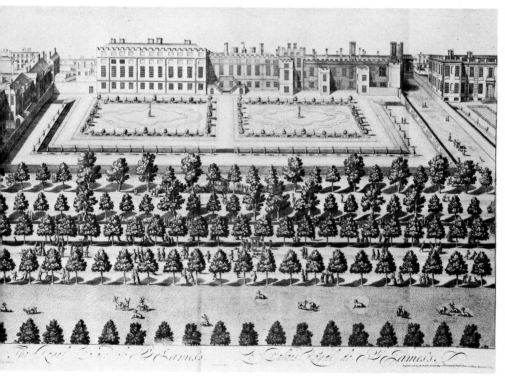

14 For convenient attendance at Court, and daily exercise in the Park, Swift preferred to live close to St James's when in London.

15   *The arrival of George I at St James's.*

Windsor Le Chasteau   *Castle* de WINDSOR

16   *Windsor Castle. Swift spent many summer weeks and weekends at Windsor, engaged in writing on behalf of the ministry.*

*17   Hester Vanhomrigh (1690–1723), called Vanessa by Swift, fell
hopelessly in love with him in London, and followed him to Dublin.*

18 Roubiliac's bust of Dean Swift at Trinity College, Dublin.

19 Swift ultimately became a popular hero famous for his defence of Irish interest.

20 A government-sponsored attempt to foist a new coinage on Ireland (Wood's Ha'pence) was triumphantly resisted by Swift.

21   *Alexander Pope (1688–1744) was for a time Swift's closest friend among writers.*

22   Charles Jervas' portrait of Swift, painted in 1710. Jervas was
an Irish portrait painter fashionable in the London of Queen Anne.

23   *Stella in Dublin. After her death in 1728 Swift wrote: 'her hair was blacker than a raven, and every feature of her face in perfection.'*

24 *A lunatic asylum, to be called St Patrick's Hospital, was Swift's bequest to Ireland. The bulk of his fortune went to its building and endowment.*

25 *With St Patrick's in the background, the immensely famous Dean holds in his hand the patent for Queen Anne's Bounty which he had won for the clergy of Ireland.*

Lord Bolingbroke, whose character had been somewhat reformed by exile, made rather a good point against Swift. 'Pope and you are very great wits, and I think very indifferent philosophers. If you despised the world as much as you pretend, and perhaps believe, you would not be so angry with it.' He went on to say that their mentor, La Rochefoucauld, was a slave to the Court, and his language that of a slighted lover, a disillusioned courtier. There was, in fact, a world of difference between Pope's superficial optimism, and Swift's far more profound view of human nature. But it is true that, an activist spirit, he wished to reform men – and perhaps that was not very rational of him.

'The people of Ireland have just found out that their fathers, sons and brothers are not made bishops, judges, or officers civil or military, and begin to think it should be otherwise. But the government go on as if there were not a human creature in the kingdom fit for anything but giving money.' Was this really necessary? Why this base passivity? No wonder he described the Dean of St Patrick's as 'sitting like a toad in a corner of his great house, with a perfect hatred of all public actions and persons'.

Swift's English friends had remained warmly loyal to him – a tribute to his own warmth of nature – and were desirous to see him in England again. Before he went there was another encounter with Moor Park. He had never forgiven Lady Giffard, who surprisingly had wished to make it up with him: she had been in the wrong over the affair of Temple's *Memoirs* and had not apologized. Swift's old complex about the family now put him in the wrong. Temple's heir was his nephew, now Lord Palmerston, who had, at Swift's request, given a chamber in Trinity College, which was in his patronage, to someone whom Swift recommended: 'for I then had some credit with your lordship, which I am told I have now lost, although I am ignorant of the reason.' This person, now a Senior Fellow, had made over his room to a junior; without sufficiently inquiring into the matter, Swift charged Palmerston with turning the young man out. He was wrong, and opened himself to a dressing down which Temple's nephew evidently relished delivering.

'Your interest with me, if ever lost, such letters will not regain . . . if you had any regard to a family you owe so much to. But I fear you hugged the false report to cancel all feelings of gratitude that must ever glow in a generous breast. No regard to the family was any restraint to you. These refinements are past my low understanding, and can only be comprehended by you great wits.'

There was the source of the trouble; he was in the wrong and, in seeking to justify himself, Swift lays bare the old wound.

'I own myself indebted to Sir William Temple for recommending me to the late King, although without success, and for his choice of me to take care of his posthumous writings. But I hope you will not charge my living in his family as an obligation; for I was educated to little purpose, if I retired to his house on any other motives than the benefit of his conversation and advice, and the opportunity of pursuing my studies.[!] I have found out one secret, that – although you call me a great wit – you do not think me so; otherwise you would have been too cautious to have writ me such a letter.'

One cannot but think that the family scored in this exchange; but how sad that the dear delicious days at Moor Park – to which, in effect, he owed everything – were thus scarred in his mind.

He crossed over to England, taking the manuscript of *Gulliver's Travels* with him, early in March 1726. Pope joined him for a couple of days, and found him in health and spirits, 'the joy of all here who know him as he was eleven years ago'. The misanthrope had the singular faculty of making others happy. Arbuthnot took him on a course of visits through the town, to the leaders of the opposition to Walpole, Lord Chesterfield and Pulteney, thence to Bolingbroke at Dawley and to stay with Pope at Twickenham. At this juncture the Prince and Princess of Wales held their opposition Court at Leicester House; they were on unfriendly terms with George I, and the opposition expected them to overturn the ascendancy of Walpole on the King's demise. Naturally Swift looked to the Princess for the future; this was the highly intelligent Caroline, the brains behind the Hanover family, well instructed, well read, a politician of such competence that old Sarah Marlborough was jealous of her. Swift was successfully presented to the future Queen, though, he said later, not until he had been sent for nine or ten times. Exaggeration or no – what mad pride!

Swift had made it a rule in the days of his power that great ladies were first to seek his acquaintance. No doubt a joke or a pose at first, it became a fixture with him – and, naturally, to others a sign of eccentricity.

Far more important was his meeting at the end of April with Walpole, who now enjoyed complete ascendancy. Swift treated himself as a spokesman for Ireland; 'my principal design was to set him right not only for the service of Ireland but likewise of England, and of his own administration.' The self-appointed ambassador found himself up against an all-powerful minister with decided views of his own, completely at variance with Swift's, 'so alien from what I conceived to be rights and privileges of a subject of England'. Swift put forward his views in the name of liberty, 'a possession always understood by the British nation to be the inheritance of a human creature'. We know what Swift's programme was – the liberties and rights he had demanded for the Anglo-Irish. We are not told what Walpole replied, except that he enlarged very much on the subject. He might well have enlarged it to include the native Irish, whose idea of liberty was complete rejection of English rule. Here was the insoluble dilemma.

Swift had two interviews, the first at Walpole's invitation, 'the second at my desire for an hour, wherein we differed in every point.' Nothing to be done – Swift remained aligned with the opposition. In July he went off on a pleasurable jaunt into the country, seeing old haunts in Windsor Forest, with Pope and Gay, visiting the scholarly Lord Bathurst at Cirencester, a new recruit to the wide circle of Swift's admirers. A reminder of other associations with Windsor came from Ireland with the news that 'Cadenus and Vanessa' was being bandied about in Dublin. Swift tried to de-fuse this explosive item.

'It was a task performed on a frolic among some ladies, and she it was addressed to died some time ago in Dublin, and on her death the copy shown by her executor. I am very indifferent what is done with it, for printing cannot make it more common than it is. For my own part, I forget what is in it. Printing it myself is impossible, for I never saw it since I writ it.' Then – what he really thought: he did not wish to be reminded of it, 'when there is no remedy, and only gives me the ungrateful task of reflecting on the baseness of mankind – which I knew sufficiently before.'

At the same time came news that Stella was desperately ill in Dublin; his letters home are full of grief, alarm and apprehension. He could not bear to be there at the end; one sees that he was no iron stoic, but a passionate man, a prey to fear of every kind. Yet he could not remain away with any peace of mind. He had meant to embark on research into Harley's papers, with a view to writing his life – time was now too short. Always anxious to be an historian, he had nursed the idea of writing a history of Queen Anne's entire reign – that was the project he had put forward in proposing himself for Historiographer Royal. Whatever its merits would have been as history, we have lost a fascinating book, for he knew a great deal of the secret springs of affairs from William III's last years onwards. It reminds one of a greater loss: when Sir Walter Ralegh – with whom Swift had more in common than most – was prevented by Sir Robert Cecil from writing the secret history of Queen Elizabeth's reign.

Nothing remained now but the publication of *Gulliver's Travels*, upon which Swift embarked with more than the usual amount of mystification. He was genuinely apprehensive that ministers would take offence at the political satire and personal references – what he later described as 'the sting' of the book. And indeed the printer took the liberty, in these circumstances, of toning it down, and even inserting mollifying passages – about which Swift complained bitterly later. Though his habit was not to receive money for his writings, he stipulated for the considerable sum of £200 for this, his masterpiece.

Having set the printing of the book in motion, through intermediaries and via the pseudonym of 'Richard Sympson', he departed for Ireland in August, in great anxiety of mind for Stella, and to await the results of publication. We see what a gift for friendship he had in the passionate regrets of his friends, what a vacuum such an outsize personality left. Pope, not over-endowed with emotions, missed him dreadfully: 'it is a sensation like a limb lopped off.' Swift's image was present with him everywhere: 'I shall never more think of Lord Cobham's [Stowe], the woods of Cirencester, or the pleasing prospect of Bibury [in the Cotswolds], but your idea must be joined with them; nor see one seat in my own garden, or one room in my own house, without a phantom of you, sitting or walking before me.'

We have all known such feelings of desolation at the absence of our dearest friends. On arriving in Ireland, Swift was in no better case: he dreamed of England, 'now I can every night distinctly see Twickenham, and the Grotto, and Dawley, and Mrs Blount, and many other *et ceteras*, and it is but three nights since I beat Mrs Pope', Pope's ancient mother whom the Dean amused at cards or backgammon.

Soon the news came over the water of the tremendous hit the book made – as Dr Johnson said, 'a production so new and so strange filled the reader with a mingled emotion of merriment and amazement. Criticism was, for a while, lost in wonder.' For a time the mystification as to its authorship added to the *réclame*; Swift himself kept up the farce of not recognizing it, and only a few people at first were in the know. His friends reported how people were taking it. When Arbuthnot went to see the Princess, 'she was reading *Gulliver* and was just come to the passage of the hobbling Prince, which she laughed at.' There was no difficulty in recognizing the bearing of that passage. The acrimonious party dispute in Lilliput was between High-Heels and Low-Heels, i.e. High Church v. Low Church.

'It is alleged indeed that the High-Heels are most agreeable to our ancient constitution; but, however this may be, his Majesty hath determined to make use of only Low-Heels in the administration of the government, and all offices in the gift of the Crown, as you cannot but observe.' Nobody's heels were lower than his Majesty's (it is doubtful if George I had any religious belief at all, any more than Caroline had – what a contrast with the silly Stuarts!) 'The animosities between these parties run so high that they will neither eat, nor drink, nor talk, with each other. We compute the High-Heels to exceed us in number, but the power is wholly on our side. We apprehend his Imperial Highness, the Heir to the Crown, to have some tendency towards the High-Heels; at least we can plainly discover one of his heels higher than the other, which gives him a hobble in his gait.'

Everybody in politics or society would appreciate the point of that. The Prince of Wales, the future George II, in opposition to his father was holding out hopes to the Tories – at least, some hopes, no one knew precisely how much or of what value: hence one heel high, the other low. This was now the year 1726; next year his father died. What would happen on his accession to the throne? Would the expectations held out to the opposition, which Swift shared – hope springing ever eternal in the breast of this despairer – be fulfilled, Walpole and the Whig monopoly of power at length ended? We shall see.

The joke about heels was carried on in the Princess's circle, as we observe from Swift's correspondence.

Arbuthnot goes on, '*Gulliver* is in everybody's hands. Lord Scarborough fell in company with a master of a ship, who told him that he was very well acquainted with Gulliver, but that he lived in Wapping and not in Rotherhithe. I lent the book to an old gentleman, who went immediately to his map to search for Lilliput.' An Irish bishop was much wiser: he said that the book was full of improbable lies, and 'for his part, he hardly believed a word of it'.

The reaction of the old Duchess of Marlborough was much to her credit, after all that Swift had written against the Duke. 'She says she can dream of nothing else since she read it. She declares that she has now found out that her whole life has been lost in caressing the worst part of mankind, and treating the best as her foes. If she knew Gulliver, though he had been the worst enemy she ever had, she would give up her present acquaintance for his friendship.' It must not be supposed that the old Duchess had any more justice of mind than Swift had, even less; her enthusiasm was partly due to the fact that she too had moved over to the opposition against her former *protégé*, Walpole. We see how personal spite enters into people's judgments, even remarkable people, who should know better.

Some of the party politicians felt themselves touched, even among Swift's friends. Lord Harcourt thought 'in some places the matter too far carried' – but he was a stuffed shirt. Lord Bolingbroke 'is the person who least approves it, blaming it as a design of evil consequence to depreciate human nature; at which it cannot be wondered that he takes most offence, being himself the most accomplished of his species.' This was good-humoured irony; but, in fact, the political gambler, who had gambled away the whole future of his party at the end of Queen Anne's reign, was now engaged in making for himself a second career as a benevolent philosopher, and could not accept Swift's view of human nature.

'The politicians to a man . . . agree that the satire on general societies of men is too severe' – they would, since their profession was to represent what societies are, and their practice of it necessarily depended on political cant and humbug. 'Those of them who frequent the Church say his design is impious, and that it is an insult on Providence by depreciating the works of the Creator.' Lady Mary Wortley Montagu, egregious woman, had to be different: 'Here is a book come out that all our people of taste run mad about: 'tis no less than the united work of a dignified clergyman, an eminent physician, and the first poet of the age.' We see that this eminent lady was taken in, and could not quite make it all out, but, 'I cannot help suspecting some very powerful motive at the bottom of it'. As to that she was right – there was indeed!

The generality of people were delighted, since they had not the sense to know what the motive was. Pope and Gay reported that the book 'has been the conversation of the whole town' ever since its publication. 'The whole impression sold in a week, and nothing is more diverting than to hear the different opinions people give of it, though all agree in liking it extremely. It is generally said that you are the author; but I am told the bookseller declares he knows not from what hand it came. From the highest to the lowest it is universally read, from the cabinet-council to the nursery.'

Like all universal books, it has always retained that width of appeal. Arbuthnot, judicious as ever, summed it up: '*Gulliver's Travels*, I believe, will have as great a run as John Bunyan.'

It certainly has had, and more, in the recession of religious belief; while it is, of course, far more relevant in the breakdown of standards in a mass-civilization, when we are face to face with what men in the mass really are.

For, to Swift, the moral content of the book was immeasurably more important than the story in which it was framed, entertaining as that was.

In Lilliput, which occupies the first book – always the most popular, it has added a word to the language, lilliputian, for what is diminutive – human society and its affairs are reduced to scale and made to look ridiculous by being shown up as so small. Anyone who knows the history of the time can detect the references to real events and persons. In the preparatory letter by Captain Gulliver, Dampier is referred to by name as his cousin and his book cited by its title. The Emperor of Lilliput had reigned seven years; so had George I when this book was written. The inventory of the contents of Gulliver's pockets, when the Man-Mountain is examined, is a parody of the findings of the secret committee to examine into the Jacobite dealings of Oxford, Bolingbroke and Ormond. The qualification for high office is rope-dancing, at which the most skilful performer is Flimnap, i.e. Walpole.

The prizes awarded, so many coloured ribbons, were the ribbons of the Orders of the Garter, the Thistle, and the Bath. What nonsense they were! But since donkeys need carrots to entice them along, Walpole had recreated, or invented, the Order of the Bath. There were not enough Garters to go round for the asses who wanted them; anyone who knows the history of the eighteenth century will know the heart-burnings it gave rise to, not to be awarded a Garter. So Walpole created what his clever son Horace called 'a bank' of honours – a red ribbon instead of a blue – as a *pis aller* for unsuccessful aspirants, and condescended to accept a red ribbon himself, instead of a blue, to set the example and *pour encourager les autres*.

Civil War was waged between the Big-endians and Little-endians, on the vital issue whether to break one's egg at the big end or the small. In these disputes one Emperor lost his life, another his crown, i.e. Charles I and James II.

'It is computed that eleven thousand persons have, at several times, suffered death rather than submit to break their eggs at the smaller end. Many hundred large volumes have been published upon this controversy; but the books of the Big-Endians have been long forbidden, and the whole party rendered incapable by law of holding employments.'

This refers to the proscription of Catholics by Protestants after the Reformation, and the hundreds of volumes of senseless religious controversy. Of course, Catholics had burned thousands for denying the 'truth' of Transubstantiation, as Protestants had hanged hundreds of Catholics for upholding Papal Supremacy. Eleven thousand in Lilliput was a diminutive number compared with those who killed, or were killed, for these nonsense issues. Here they were reduced to their proper perspective.

At the Court of Lilliput Gulliver extinguished a fire in the Empress's apartment by voiding a stream of water from an improper engine. He was not forgiven for this: 'the Empress, conceiving the greatest abhorrence of what I had done, removed to the most distant side of the Court, firmly resolved that those buildings should never be repaired for her use and, in the presence of her chief confidants, could not forbear vowing revenge.' Queen Anne's confidant in religious matters was Archbishop Sharp: in *A Tale of a Tub* Swift had pissed on their religious beliefs.

The beliefs of the people of Lilliput were absurd; but, 'if they were not so directly contrary, I should be tempted to say a little in their justification. They bury their dead with their heads directly downwards; because they hold an opinion that, in eleven thousand moons, they are all to rise again. In which period the earth – which they conceive to be flat – will turn upside down; and by this means they shall, at their resurrection, be found ready standing on their feet. The learned among them confess the absurdity of this doctrine, but the practice still continues, in compliance to the vulgar.' We are not told, in so many words, what this implies as to the Christian doctrine of the resurrection of the dead, but Swift makes very clear the obvious distinction between what is thought by the intelligent among us, and what is believed by the idiot people. Their beliefs are nonsense.

As to children, the people of Lilliput did not recognize that a child had any obligation to his parents for bringing him into the world – 'which, considering the miseries of human life, was neither a benefit in itself, nor intended so by his parents, whose thoughts in their love-encounters were otherwise employed.' The second proposition is true enough. Hence the conclusion, they think 'nothing can be more unjust than for people, in subservience to their own appetites, to bring children into the world and leave the burden of supporting them on the public'. In Lilliput, poor people contributed a small portion of their monthly earnings, by way of insurance, to maintain their own children. What would Swift have thought of a society like today's, where people are swaddled in social insurance from the cradle to the grave? The question is rhetorical: we know well enough what he would have thought.

Gulliver set sail on his second voyage in a ship commanded by a Cornishman, Captain John Nicholas, in 1702. East of the Moluccas they were driven off course in a great storm, which gave Swift the opportunity to incorporate a page of technical sea terms straight out of Sturmy's *Compleat Mariner* – and very laughable it is. They were driven 'five hundred leagues to the east, so that the oldest sailor on board could not tell in what part of the world we were.' They held on course till they discovered the land of Brobdingnag. Here, in a land of giants, Gulliver was a Lilliputian; the scale was reversed in the other direction, so that size magnified human horrors. A child picked up the tiny manikin to play with, who was afraid the horrid boy 'might do me a spite, well remembering how mischievous all children among us naturally are to sparrows, rabbits, young kittens' – we who live in the country might add, to birds, hedgehogs, moles, anything innocent and small that they can kill.

The large scale showed up human imperfections under the magnifying glass. A woman giving suck to a child disgusted Gulliver by her breast exposed: 'it stood prominent six foot, and could not be less than sixteen in circumference. The nipple was about half the bigness of my head, and the hue both of that and the dug so varified with spots, pimples and freckles that nothing could appear more nauseous.' This enabled Swift to reflect on 'the fair skins of our English ladies, who appear so beautiful to us only because they are of our own size, and their defects not to be seen but through a magnifying glass'. Swift applied the magnifying glass – as in such realist poems as 'The Progress of Beauty', or 'A Beautiful Young Nymph Going to Bed', in which he undresses her completely, false hair, false eyebrows, false teeth, false complexion:

> *Up goes her hand, and off she slips*
> *The bolsters that supply her hips.*
> *With gentlest touch she next explores*
> *Her shankers, issues, running sores,*
> *Effects of many a sad disaster;*
> *And then to each applies a plaster.*

For the nymph is revealed as a poxed prostitute:

> *Corinna in the morning dizened,*
> *Who sees, will spew; who smells, be poisoned.*

That Anglo-Irish writer of today, Samuel Beckett, in his portraits of human deliquescence and decay, is not so effective.

Size showed up every horror. 'There was a woman with a cancer in her breast, swelled to a monstrous size, full of holes, in two or three of which I could have easily crept. There was a fellow with a wen in his neck, larger than five wool-packs. But the most hateful sight of all was the lice crawling on their clothes. I could see distinctly the limbs of these vermin with my naked eye, much better than those of an European louse through a microscope, and their snouts with which they rooted like swine.'

Smells were similarly heightened. The Maids of Honour at Court 'would often strip me naked from top to toe, and lay me at full length in their bosoms. Wherewith I was much disgusted; because, to say the truth, a very offensive smell came from their skins.' He supposed that 'those illustrious persons were no more disagreeable to their lovers, or to each other, than people of the same quality are to us in England'. One of these large creatures took liberties with the manikin: 'a pleasant frolicsome girl of sixteen would sometimes set me astride upon one of her nipples – with many other tricks, wherein the reader will excuse me for not being over-particular.' What with one thing and another – evidently, not for Swift the joys of the marriage-bed!

The King of Brobdingnag inquired into the institutions of Gulliver's native country, particularly into Parliament. Gulliver described the House of Lords, with lords temporal and lords spiritual – the eighteenth-century House of Lords was much smaller, immensely more powerful, and the bishops formed a more important part of it. 'These were searched and sought out through the whole nation among such of the priesthood as were most deservedly distinguished by the sanctity of their lives, and the depth of their erudition: who were indeed the spiritual fathers of the clergy and the people.'

And the House of Commons? The members were all 'principal gentlemen, freely picked and culled out by the people for their great abilities and love of their country, to represent the wisdom of the whole nation.' What would Swift say of the spectacle presented to us in our time – when, before the war, this assembly, under Tory rule, sacrificed the interest of their country for their own class interest, appeasing Hitler because they thought he was anti-Red, and so enabled him to make his war in the most favourable circumstances?

The King of Brobdingnag was not impressed. He wanted to know why people were so anxious to get into Parliament. Whether an outsider with a longer purse might not prevail on the vulgar voters against the better man? Whether the claim to greater public spirit was always sincere – or whether humbug was not more successful? (English politics never produced a greater artist in this element than Stanley Baldwin, the most powerful figure in Britain in the decades that led to the war.) The King could not understand how a country could become bankrupt and 'run out of its estate like a private person. He asked me, who were our creditors; and where should we find money to pay them.' (Swift would be incredulous at the answer – the Arab nations.)

And one day, 'when I happened to say there were several thousand books among us written upon the art of government, it gave him a very mean opinion of our understandings.' He did not think that government needed endless discussion and dispute – palaver and argy-bargy, cant and humbug; but, above all, common sense and reason, a sense of fairness and speedy decision. In any case, he gave it as his opinion that 'whoever could make two ears of corn, or two blades of grass, to grow upon a spot of ground, where only one grew before, would deserve better of mankind, and do more essential service to his country, than the whole race of politicians put together.'

How whole-heartedly we must agree to this! The man who deserved best of his country in the miserable decades that led to the war was not one of the whole race of politicians but the great agricultural expert, Sir George Stapledon, who did precisely what Swift desiderated, and made two blades of grass grow where only one grew before.

The voyage to Laputa also took place in a ship commanded by a Cornishman, this time Captain William Robinson. This third book of *Gulliver's Travels* is the part that goes back to the original memoirs of the Scriblerus Club, from which Swift put the materials together. Hence it has more diversity, a less unified impact than the other three parts, and has from the first been less appreciated. Its targets are more diversified, one might say more specialized; I find it the most diverting of the books, and even more apposite to targets of today.

The inhabitants of Laputa were philosophers; 'their heads were all reclined either to the right or the left; one of their eyes turned inward, and the other directly up to the zenith . . . The minds of these people are so taken up with intense speculations that they neither can speak, nor attend to the discourses of others,' unless their attention is attracted by a flapper hitting them with a blown-up bladder. They were so wrapped in cogitation, so absent-minded, that they needed a flapper to prevent them from falling off the pavement, or in a ditch.

In a lifetime amongst academics I have known many such: a professor who would travel up to London absent-mindedly in his carpet-slippers; or a Fellow of All Souls who ran into the college in the black-out, not knowing it was there, skinning his nose half off; or another, having learned (improbably) to drive a car, on his first drive out, ran straight into a telegraph-pole. But there are too many tales of such people: they all needed Swift's flappers with bladders to attract their attention.

The Court here was devoted to mathematics. The King paid no

attention to the intruder from another sphere, for 'he was then deep in a problem, and we attended at least an hour before he could solve it'. When dinner appeared, 'there was a shoulder of mutton, cut into an equilateral triangle, a piece of beef into a rhomboid, and a pudding into a cycloid'. Clothes were scientifically calculated. When a suit was made for Gulliver, the tailor 'first took my altitude by a quadrant, and then with a rule and compasses described the dimensions and outlines of my whole body, all which he entered upon paper; and in six days brought my clothes very ill made, and quite out of shape, by happening to mistake a figure in the calculation. But my comfort was that I observed such accidents very frequent, and little regarded.' We in our time of adding-machines and computers, a mechanized and standardized society, observe such accidents more frequently still: few can add up any more or keep their own accounts, individual quality has gone from clothing, furnishings etc., and the community is at the mercy of those who control its technical equipment, frequently enough held to ransom at every stage.

In Laputa people no longer made their own music, they listened only to the music of the spheres – as it might be radio, or drug-addicted to television. The houses of these intellectuals were very ill-constructed, 'the walls bevil [sloping], without one right angle in any apartment, and this defect ariseth from the contempt they bear to practical geometry, which they despise as vulgar and mechanic.' We remember the contempt expressed by a devotee of pure mathematics, G. H. Hardy, in *A Mathematician's Apology*, for applied mathematics: he called it Hogben-mathematics, after the author of *Mathematics for the Million*. These people were 'dexterous enough upon a piece of paper in the management of the rule, the pencil and the divider', yet 'I have not seen a more clumsy, awkward and unhandy people, nor so slow and perplexed upon all other subjects'. We have noticed that, too, among such persons.

These intellectuals, so useless in the practical concerns of life, are yet insufferably conceited and arrogant about public affairs – as it might be, a Bertrand Russell, almost always wrong. They are for ever arguing and discussing, 'giving their judgments in matters of state, and passionately disputing every inch of a party opinion'. Swift here makes an acute observation: the disciplines of mathematics and politics, the abilities required for either, are utterly different; those qualified for one are practically disqualified *ipso facto* for the other. The itch for people like Bertrand Russell, with a specialist gift for mathematics, to lay down the law about politics in general – where, as the historian Trevelyan used to say, Russell was a perfect 'goose' – springs from 'a very common infirmity of human nature, inclining us to be more curious and conceited in matters where we have least concern, and for which we are least adapted either by study or nature'.

Whether from abstraction or no, or just not noticing, these people are constantly in bed with each other's wives, such philosophers notoriously in the public prints over their divorces, pupils and tutors exchanging or seducing their respective spouses. Sometimes the husband is so 'rapt in speculation that the mistress and lover may proceed to the greatest familiarities before his face'. It is not an unfamiliar picture at the universities today.

Naturally, in a society run by such intellectuals, the country was neglected, in a squalid run-down condition, while they were given up to their projects. In Laputa some of their resources went into extracting sun out of cucumbers – but nothing like so much as the Ground-nut Scheme, on which the 1945–51 Labour government wasted hundreds of millions; or *Concorde*, on which governments of both parties have spent a thousand million. Oh, for a Swift to describe what is happening today! (However, George Orwell did very well to point out the end of the road in his *1984*.)

It is astonishing how unerringly Swift pointed to the consequences of such fatuity, in 1726. There were the jerry-builders, 'who had contrived a new method for building houses, by beginning at the roof, and working downwards to the foundation'. How many jerry-built apartment buildings have we seen in our time collapsing, with considerable loss of life? Then there was the agricultural projector, 'who had found a device of ploughing the ground with hogs, to save the charges of ploughs, cattle and labour.' Swift describes the technique with gravity, and then: 'it is true, upon experiment they found the charge and trouble very great, and they had little or no crop.' At a university which shall be nameless there was a Professor of

Political Science who experimented just this way with pigs and potatoes on ground outside the city: he was known to the locals as 'Starve-Hog—' for the pigs did not prosper, neither did the potatoes or the ground itself.

Laputa had a school of political projectors, one of whom proposed that members of Parliament should deliver their speeches and then vote directly contrary. This might have been a good idea in the 1930s: the large Tory majority in favour of appeasing Hitler would have done well to vote against, whatever they *said* – what they said makes sickening reading in Hansard today. On the other side, the lunatic fringe of the Labour left who were fixed on disarmament, when Hitler's Germany was working all hours to re-arm, would have been far more sensible to vote clean contrary to their irrelevant convictions.

Nor is Swift any less apposite in the absurdity to which he reduces projects for taxation – taxing people on their follies and vices, taxing highest those who have most success with women, etc. The projects which have come from the Cambridge economists – the Selective Employment Tax (which had to be dropped, it was so inoperable) – and others, like VAT or the projected Wealth Tax – have all had a creeping effect in undermining incentive, ruining efficiency, crippling the economy.

Not that Swift had any illusions about democracy – he had much too clear a view of average human nature. I merely make the point how relevant his views are today, precisely because they were based on a view of human nature without illusions. He would have seen, as Dostoievsky did – and exposed the whole process in *The Possessed* – that liberal illusions are the parents of anarchy, violence and social catastrophe. Swift knew that societies cannot exist without discipline. Later on, there were student disturbances at Trinity in the course of which one Fellow was shot dead; Swift put his finger on the cause – the poor discipline under a feeble Provost.

In his account of the Academy in Laputa he exposes the perfectibility nonsense of the progressives. Relevant as ever, chemists attend 'to administer to each of them lenitives, aperitives, abstersives, corrosives, restringents, palliatives, laxatives, cephalalgics, icterics, apophlegmatics, acoustics, as their several cases required'. It reminds one of the accounts given of the drug addiction of students at the modern universities, or indeed the vast extension of drug-taking in contemporary mass-civilization. Naturally ordinary people do not know what is good for them and are incapable of operating without direction. Without direction, society falls apart – as Communist Russia or China knows, since Communists do not suffer from liberal illusions about human nature.

What could be more apposite than Swift's account of the computer? 'Everyone knew how laborious the usual method is of attaining to arts and sciences.' Here was a short cut, very useful for those incapable of attaining to them and a perfect expression of a mechanized age. By this contrivance, 'the most ignorant person at a reasonable charge, and with a little bodily labour, may write books in philosophy, poetry, politics, law, mathematics, and theology, without the least assistance from genius or study.' Some of this has already come to pass. In America I have seen specimens of computer poetry. An example of computer history, from Harvard, I have myself reviewed in *The English Historical Review*.[1] The Americans tried to run their war in Viet Nam on computer lines. It was not very successful.

The projectors were bent on a 'universal language to be understood in all civilised nations'. But we do not now need this boon – the world enjoys it in the form of a vulgarized English or, rather, American. Swift has told us elsewhere what he thought of critics and in how little estimation he held them. Here he speaks only of ancient critics, who had 'horribly misrepresented' the meaning of the classics: Homer found simply that 'they wanted a genius to enter into the spirit of a poet'. And Aristotle was 'out of all patience' with the Schoolmen and commentators who misunderstood him. In these matters Swift was a conservative, and a stickler for strict grammatical usage. He could not bear the use of 'don't, won't, can't etc' coming increasingly into practice; and he always corrected people who said 'he behaved' for 'he behaved himself' – 'behaved – what?', he would say sharply.

[1] cf. my *Discoveries and Reviews*, pp 181–3.

Nor did he subscribe to the worship of science, the veneration accorded in his time to Newton. Gassendi's Epicurianism and Descartes' vortices were equally exploded, and he predicted the same fate for Newton. 'New systems of nature were but new fashions, which would vary in every age; even those who pretend to demonstrate them from mathematical principles would flourish but a short period of time, and be out of vogue when that was determined.' The vogue of Newton would be determined, or ended, by the vogue of Einstein.

However, Swift's deepest concerns were political and social; he ends with a scathing account of nobility and family pride. 'I confess it was not without some pleasure that I found myself able to trace the particular features by which certain families are distinguished, up to their originals. I could plainly discover from whence one family derives a long chin, why a second hath abounded with knaves for two generations, and fools for two more; why a third happened to be crackbrained, and a fourth to be sharpers.' Anyone who knows the inner history of certain peerages, and not peerages only – knowing here the incursion of a groom, there a touch of the tar-brush, here again a political colleague, or the husband's own brother – will savour Swift's reference: 'neither could I wonder at all this, when I saw such an interruption of lineages by pages, lackeys, valets, coachmen, gamesters, fiddlers, players, captains and pickpockets.' To what point their fatuous family pride, to this outsider of genius – of no family himself – but who knew their humbug through and through? What a radical this Tory was!

He knew too well 'the true causes of many great events that have surprised the world, how a whore can govern the backstairs, the backstairs a council, and the council a senate'. The whole background of Charles II's reign – virtuous Queen Anne's uncle – was a background of whores: Lucy Walters, from whom the Monmouths and Buccleuchs were descended; Barbara Villiers, with her numerous bastards, among them the Graftons and all the Fitzroys; Nell Gwynn, with the St Albans dukedom; Louise de Kéroualle, made Duchess of Portsmouth for her services. With James II there was a similar tale and a whole progeny of Berwicks, Waldegraves, Falmouths. Nor did Swift omit the physical effects of pox on the generations – with which both Charles II and James II were touched.

James I not, for obvious reasons; he was not interested in women, but had had a whole succession of boy-friends, Esmé Stuart, James Hay, Robert Carr, George Villiers. They had all made their fortune; indeed the infatuation of three generations of Stuarts for three generations of Villiers, in both sexes, has proliferated the strain in a large section of the English peerage. And we learn, from a later reference in Swift's correspondence, that he knew what the tastes of the Whig hero, William III, really were – about which he was so secret that historians have never been sure. No one was in a better position than Swift to know. And he ends up, with poker face, 'I hope I may be pardoned if these discoveries inclined me a little to abate of that profound veneration which I am naturally apt to pay to persons of high rank, who ought to be treated with the utmost respect due to their sublime dignity, by us their inferiors.'

More important than this, however, was the keeping out of men of the greatest ability from power for the benefit of the second-rate. Here Queen Anne's reign furnished no such disastrous object-lesson as did England between the wars, when the two men of genius who were available – Lloyd George, who was right on domestic and economic issues, as was Winston Churchill in regard to Germany and the urgent necessity for a Grand Alliance, not Appeasement – were kept out of power for the benefit of an inferior run of average politicians. Such options are dangerous and, in the event, proved disastrous.

Since men are like that, Swift went on to describe them as such in Part IV, the country where horses ruled over men, the scandal of which has gone on reverberating ever since. People object to the view of human beings put forward. It is true that they do not *have* to be like that – even Swift did not think so: they *could* be more sensible, they *could* be more reasonable; they do not have to be such idiots and make themselves and others miserable, if only they took a little more thought. Every one of us could do better if he tried. In this sense Swift was not a complete despairer; nor am I. But we are not subject to illusions.

In the last voyage the Houyhnhnms are the horses, the Yahoos the men subject to them – *they* are the beasts of burden; another word, Yahoo, has been contributed to the language. We should take note that Swift's disgust is directed towards Mass-Man, for the Yahoos are hardly individualized – in itself a sufficient reflection on the mass of men. The first distinction made is that the horses have no word for lying – they can only call it 'the thing that is not'. Lying is a human propensity – Swift was disgusted by it, as all elect persons are. Not only will ordinary people lie, but they can hardly ever recount an event correctly. In statement, they do not care whether what they say is true or no; and as for thinking, in the exact sense of the word, they are mostly incapable of it. The joke is of course that they do not know it.

Gulliver's equine master has to have the fact of human war, the causes for the killings, also explained – it is not understood in the world of horses (though how many of these poor creatures have suffered from men's insanity, in war, one's heart bleeds to think). Gulliver-Swift explains that in the long European war that had gone on through William III's and Queen Anne's time, almost without break from 1689 to 1713, 'about a million of Yahoos might have been killed in the whole progress of it, and perhaps a hundred or more cities taken, and thrice as many ships burnt or sunk'. In the two world wars inflicted by Germany in our time, in the insane attempt to achieve world power – the chief factor in the recession of civilization, the relapse to barbarism and the spread of violence, the ruin of the twentieth century – we should have to multiply these figures of destruction by fifty or a hundred. So much for progress.

And what are the causes? 'Sometimes the ambition of princes, who never think they have land or people enough to govern.' This accounts for such aggressors as Philip II or Louis XIV or Napoleon, or the Germany of Bismarck, the Kaiser or the Fuehrer – for the objectives were continuous, European ascendancy, to which twentieth-century Germany added the aim of *Lebensraum*, the depopulation of Eastern Europe by Slavs for Germans to take their place. There are, too, religious or ideological wars: 'difference of opinions hath cost many millions of lives: for instance, whether flesh be bread, or bread be flesh; whether the juice of a certain berry be blood or wine.' We see what nonsense he thought the issue of transubstantiation to be, over which so many lives had been sacrificed in the religious wars of the sixteenth and seventeenth centuries.

Swift's analysis of the causes of war goes further. 'Sometimes the quarrel between two princes [or powers] is to decide which of them shall dispossess a third of his dominions.' This was a prime factor in the Thirty Years War, and was to be exemplified again, in the later eighteenth century, in the wars set going by Prussia's seizure of Silesia, and over the Partition of Poland. Sometimes a war is set off out of fear that the other will get in his blow first – the threat that grows ever more dangerous with the possession of nuclear weapons. 'Sometimes a war is entered upon because the enemy is too strong, and sometimes because he is too weak.' An historian can think of such cases. 'Sometimes our neighbours want the things which we have, or have the things which we want.' We think of the war the Americans forced on Mexico in 1846, in order to get hold of Texas, New Mexico, Arizona and Southern California – covering up the naked aggression with the humbug of 'Manifest Destiny'. Or, again, their aggression against Spain in 1898, which landed them with Cuba and the Philippines.

To the instances which Swift gives we may add the further refinement in our time of the campaign for the extermination of the Jews in Europe led by the most powerful nation of the Continent, in the central strategic situation, which should have been the keystone in the arch of European civilization. Instead of which . . . Germany ruined Europe.

Gulliver's equine master observed that 'the Yahoos were known to hate one another more than they did any different species of animals.' But, though they could wound each other with tooth and nail, they did not have the advantages of civilized men; 'they seldom were able to kill one another, for want of such convenient instruments of death as we had invented.' There is an amusing passage on this agreeable theme at the beginning of Sir Winston Churchill's *History of the English-Speaking Peoples*, on the replacement of Stone Age man by those who had bronze implements, and Bronze Age men by the

Iron Age, to which happy phase we still, for a time, belong. 'Men armed with iron entered Britain from the Continent and killed the men of bronze. At this point we can plainly recognise across the vanished millenniums a fellow-being. A biped capable of slaying another with iron is evidently to modern eyes a man and a brother. It cannot be doubted that for smashing skulls, whether long-headed or round, iron is best.'

Jonathan Swift was not amused; and he would have regarded his worst apprehensions of the future of humanity as fulfilled if he could have known of the discovery of nuclear fission – by the scientists he despised – which, for the first time in history, has put it within the power of man to end the human race and destroy the planet. It is now not beyond the bounds of possibility.

Swift contented himself with observing that, for want of foreign war to engage their attention, or absorb their aggressions – as in the halcyon days of James I and Charles I – 'for want of enemies' the Yahoos 'engage in what I call a civil war among themselves'. The Yahoos are recognizably men all right, and men are Yahoos.

And in other respects too. Swift disliked extravagance, all forms of waste, and vulgar ostentation. The Tory Churchman has radical observations to make on the subject. 'The rich man enjoyed the fruit of the poor man's labour, and the latter were a thousand to one in proportion to the former. The bulk of our people were forced to live miserably, by labouring every day for small wages to make a few live plentifully.'

Anyone who knows the vulgar opulence of the Edwardian upper classes in England – the over-feeding of aristocracy, upper middle-class, country gentry, while working people were in actual want (in the village of my youth some folk simply had not enough to eat) will have witnessed an almighty revenge in the society of today. Still more vulgar and extravagant was the Gilded Age in America, the world of Astors, Vanderbilts, Belmonts, Goulds, Fricks, Huntingtons, Morgans, Mellons – they, too, have seen the writing on the wall.

The boot is now on the other foot. Swift would no more have approved of senseless waste on the part of the people. He disliked intemperance and drink; he has a very pertinent passage on the wasteful extravagance of burdening the economy with luxury imports. There is a further stricture of deeper import on the absurdity of magnifying our wants. But the Yahoos were as idle and lazy, as they were mischievous and vicious. Work is good for Yahoos – so they do their best to avoid it.

Their sexual appetites are similarly inordinate and uncontrolled. This is the part of the book that has given most offence, for everyone feels touched by it. And also Swift has given expression to his disgust for female sexuality. One day, when he stripped stark naked for a bathe, a female Yahoo, inflamed with desire, pursued him into the water (once again, the woman is the pursuer). He had already noticed that, at such a juncture, a female Yahoo had 'a most offensive smell; and when any of the males advanced, would slowly retire, looking often back, and, with a counterfeit show of fear, run off into some convenient place where she knew the male would follow her.' Now Gulliver found himself embraced 'after a most fulsome manner', and had to be rescued from his humiliating plight. The hair of this creature was 'black as a sloe', like Stella's; Middleton Murry considered that, consciously or no, Swift was cauterizing her from his mind. I can only say that Vanessa should have been alive to read this passage, after all he had had to put up with at her hands. That Swift was capable of such meanings we may be sure, from what he says about red-heads, 'more libidinous and mischievous than the rest' – a final kick at 'Carrots'.

People have been shocked, too, by Swift's disgust for normal copulation. The point of this encounter was its final proof for Gulliver that he was of the same species as the Yahoos. Hence his horror at the 'facts of life' on his return home, 'when I began to consider that by copulating with one of the Yahoo species, I had become a parent of more, it struck me with the utmost shame, confusion, and horror.'

Reproduction was a matter for the exercise of rational control, or there would soon be overpopulation. 'Caution is necessary to prevent the country from being overburdened with numbers.' In the country of the horses these matters were regulated, whereas 'one half of our natives were good for nothing but bringing children into the world'. Gulliver cited 'the custom we had of castrating horses when they were young, in order to render them tame . . . the operation was easy and safe.' Why not use the invention for the benefit of the Yahoos? Why not indeed? – when the population explosion has become almost as much of a threat to the future of the human race as nuclear fission itself and, short of rational measures of control, idiot humans will out-eat their means of subsistence upon the planet.

This is the subject of an alarming look into the future by a distinguished scientist, Darwin's grandson, Sir Charles, in *The Next Ten Million Years*. It is obvious that food resources will not provide for an indefinite expansion of the species – quite apart from the exhaustion of other resources, such as oil and minerals. Darwin's argument assumes that man is essentially a wild animal, and will not control his appetites, that the population explosion will carry on to planetary disaster. But men *could* control their proliferation if they *would* – without resorting to Swift's rather old-fashioned device. The question then is, will they do so in time?

We are back at the fundamental issue behind *Gulliver's Travels*, that runs through all Swift's work, and was the prime concern of his life, the raw nerve of his mind – the place, the character, and the use of reason in man. He had no use for men's opinions – quite rightly, for what they suppose themselves to think is usually nonsense. 'Controversies, wranglings, disputes, and positiveness in false or dubious propositions' were unknown in the country where Gulliver found himself. Similarly, systems of philosophy, all differing among themselves, were of no account – fancy valuing oneself upon 'the knowledge of other people's conjectures, and in things wherein that knowledge, if it were certain, could be of no use . . . I have often since reflected what destruction such a doctrine would make in the libraries of Europe, and how many paths to fame would be then shut up in the learned world.'

And a very good thing, too, is the implication, for many of these pursuits are purposeless, and the reputations made in pursuing them bogus. A useful clearance is made of what merely encumbers the mind, and clutters up its more pointful functioning. In a sentence which gives the whole *clou* to Swift we read: 'Neither is reason a point problematical as with us, where men can agree with plausibility on both sides of the question, but strikes you with immediate conviction, as it must needs do where it is not mingled, obscured, or discoloured by passion and interest.' In other words, it is total judgment, into which intuition, discrimination, memory enter along with reason – somewhat analogous to Newman's illative sense.

What a tremendous work! No wonder the world has gone on discussing it ever since – and much of it highly entertaining and amusing.

With this book Swift became a figure in European literature. The Continent was as yet not much in the habit of reading English writers; but *Gulliver's Travels* was at once translated into French – by the Abbé Des Fontaines, a Jesuit – and thence flew over Europe. Bolingbroke's French wife sent to Swift 'some fans just arrived from Lilliput, which you will dispose of to the present Stella, whoever she be', so Bolingbroke wrote with some lack of tact. Swift thought of paying a visit to France, where he had never been; Voltaire, who was a great admirer and thought that Swift possessed the *ridiculum acre* in the highest perfection, commended him to the Secretary of State at Versailles, as '*un des hommes les plus extraordinaires que l'Angleterre a produit*'.

This was no polite exaggeration.

CHAPTER 8

Stella

ALL THIS WHILE Stella continued to be – what Swift had educated and trained her for – the dependable companion providing the framework of his life, filling not the background but the foreground, providing the sense of security this insecure man so sorely needed. His intellect was incessantly occupied by his work, but his daily thoughts were with 'the ladies', by whom he meant essentially Stella – though the letters were addressed to the senior of the two, Dingley, whom he called 'Bec'. The two together were addressed jointly as MD in the *Journal*, which provides the fullest evidence we have – for he destroyed all Stella's letters to him – of his constant care for them.

Amid the pressures of the glorious years in London he frequently dreamed of them, and hoped they dreamed of their Presto. Now he is buying an apron for Stella or a pound of chocolate without sugar; he has been given a fine ivory snuff-rasp for Miss Dingley, and sends her 'a large roll of tobacco, which she must hide or cut shorter out of modesty', with 'four pair of spectacles for the Lord knows who' – Stella again. He executed commissions with her mother down at Farnham – Stella wants her writings and a picture from thence sent over by Swift. The 'little language', with which he concluded his letters is not only pet-language, but a form of petting himself and reposing upon the security of their devotion to him. 'Do you ever read? Why don't you say so? I mean does Dd [Dingley] read to ppt? [poppet, i.e. Stella] Do you walk? I think ppt should walk for Dd, as Dd reads to ppt. For ppt oo must know is a good walker, but no so good as pdfr [podifer, i.e. Swift] . . . Farewell deelest lole deelest MD MD MD MD MD FW FW FW Me Me Lele Me lele Me lele lele lele Me.' [i.e. love me.]

Though Swift was determined to keep Stella fixed in his mind as his little ungrown-up girl – without further complications, as with the passionate Vanessa – Stella was a woman of character, much respected and admired. Though small of stature, she was spirited and brave; she adored riding, and was not afraid to tackle burglars. While the ladies were lodging in William Street on the outskirts of Dublin, 'in a new house which stood solitary, a parcel of rogues, armed, attempted the house, where there was only one boy. Having been warned to apprehend some such attempt, she learned the management of a pistol; the other women and servants being half dead with fear, she stole softly to her dining-room window, put on a black hood to prevent being seen, primed the pistol fresh, gently lifted up the sash, and taking her aim with the utmost presence of mind, discharged the pistol, loaden with the bullets, into the body of one villain, who stood the fairest mark. The fellow, mortally wounded, was carried off by the rest, and died the next morning.' Thus Swift, in pride at her more than feminine courage. However, after this the ladies moved into the centre of the town, by St Mary's church: hence the 'St Mary's ladies' as they are frequently referred to in the letters he wrote to his friends to look after them whenever he was absent.

His own care characteristically extended to the minutest concerns, particularly financial. He was convinced that, without his supervision, the ladies would overspend themselves: it was to avoid that, and consequent poverty, that he had brought them to Ireland. Certainly, without him, they could never have lived like ladies. His own accounts are filled with expenditure on their behalf – by far the most frequent items. There was not only the allowance of £50 a year he paid them quarterly, but there are frequent payments for 'treats', occasionally 'coaches' and regular dinners, sometimes once a week. The only letter of his to Stella to have survived by chance – apart from the *Journal* – admits us into their domestic interior. On an April day in 1721 Stella suddenly announced that they were descending on him for dinner.

'You should have sent your messenger sooner; yes, I think the dinner you provided for yourselves may do well enough here, but pray send it soon. I wish you would give a body more early warning, but you must blame yourselves. Delany says he will come in the evening, and – for aught I know – Sheridan may be here at dinner. Which of you was it that undertook this frolic? Pray do not serve me these tricks often. You may be sure if there be a good bottle you shall have it.' There follows a postscript with a reference to a French writer they had been reading together, Margaux: 'Margoose, and not Mergoose: it is spelt with an *a*, simpleton.'

What a contrast to the letters being wrung out of him by Vanessa, contemporaneously! This letter is one of easy, relaxed domesticity. And such is the tone of the frequent references to the ladies in Swift's letters to their common acquaintance. Occasionally one pricks up one's ears at a hint, but no more. On settling into the Deanery on his final return in 1714, the Dean was having servant trouble; he had managed to get an ugly old woman, 'since the ladies of my acquaintance would not allow me one with a tolerable face though I most earnestly interceded for it.' Chetwode thought that they were a little hard 'to tie you down to ugliness and age. But you know best if not just.' There followed a tell-tale sentence struck out: 'Since the world says you may command a very agreeable one and yet defer it.'

This was a normal man's point of view; but Swift was not a normal man.

Stella was very dark; we find Swift referring to her at this time, 'if the black lady does not find amendment in her health they had better come where company is stirring, and so I told them in a letter I writ to them three days ago.' And again to his Archdeacon, 'I leave the rest to your black Privy Councillor – be not frightened, I mean only Miss Johnson. My humble service to Gossip Doll [the Archdeacon's wife] and the ladies.' He was anxious that they should have a widening circle of acquaintance, and they did indeed have many friends, Archdeacon Walls and his wife, Bishop Stearne and his, the Stoytes, Raymonds, Jacksons, Worralls, Stopfords, Sheridans. Most of these were clerical, and of them the closest and dearest were the Sheridans, with whom the ladies and Swift stopped now and again in the country at Quilca.

Country life was apt to be rough out there, though Swift made the most of it in verse, 'The Blunders, Deficiencies, Distresses and Mis-fortunes of Quilca'. No fire in Stella's bedroom for the grate was broken; no milk for her breakfast for the men would not milk the cows before 11 a.m. – the Dean had to engage battle – *bellum lacteum*. He also had to use his greatcoat to stop the wind coming down the chimney; no lock to the door, a hole in the floor, and a draught to blow out a candle on the calmest day. 'Miss Dingley full of cares for herself, and blunders and negligence for her friends.' No doubt Swift was exaggerating as usual, but she declared she would rather have a cellar in Dublin than a palace in the country. We see the kind of person she was, with her snuff-taking habits and her addiction to the card-table – we hear of her japan-board.

Swift was convinced that exercise was the panacea for good health, and Stella stayed around in the country every summer: with the St George Ashes at Finglas, at Templeogue and Donnybrook, with Swift's cousin at Swanton, at Wexford, then a spa, for the waters – when he was anxious that she should go to Bath or Tunbridge, or even try Montpellier.

Little as we are allowed to know about her life directly, we catch a glimpse of her gestures. 'I am sorry the Bishop [Stearne] went out of town before I came. Read that last sentence to Miss Johnson and observe whether she turns up her forehead and dabs her hand on the table or on her knee' – evidently a way she had at the card-table. She never received visits in the morning, and did not drink wine. We know that she had a mind of her own, though under the surveillance of her mentor, and a sharp turn of phrase. When 'Cadenus and Vanessa' became public property in Dublin, someone had the misfortune to say to her that the woman who inspired such a poem must have been very remarkable: Stella turned this corner swiftly with, 'It is well known that the Dean could write well upon a broomstick.' When people involved themselves in noisy argument, she dealt with them as they deserved; she made a habit of agreeing with them: it saved noise and time, she said. Even in her last illness, when her doctor assured her his medicine would get her to the top of the hill, she said – but she would be out of breath before she got there.

In Dublin – unlike Vanessa who lived much to herself – Stella was never in want of company. Swift says, 'her own lodgings from before twenty years old were frequented by many persons of the graver sort who all respected her highly, upon her good sense, good manners, and conversation.' And until she was forty she enjoyed fairly good health. When young she had been beautiful, though inclined to be plump. Now Swift urged, 'use exercise and walk; spare pattens and spare potions; wear out clogs and waste claret.' Like most people of the time, she was too much given to potions. From 1723, when she was forty-two, she lost appetite and grew thin; Swift began to be alarmed: 'the ladies are as usually; Miss Johnson eats an ounce a week, which frights me from dining with her.' This was in February 1723.

In 1719 Swift began the charming practice of celebrating her birthday in verse – though, never reliable about dates, he reduced her age out of gallantry or for the exigencies of rhyme:

> Stella this day is thirty-four [actually thirty-eight]
> (We won't dispute a year or more)
> However, Stella, be not troubled,
> Although thy size and years are doubled,
> Since first I saw thee at sixteen
> The brightest virgin of the green:
> So little is thy form declined
> Made up so largely in thy mind . . .

Next year Swift himself was ill, and Stella nursed him tenderly, with the brave spirit characteristic of her:

> What Stella by her friendship warmed
> With vigour and delight performed:
> My sinking spirits now supplies
> With cordials in her hands and eyes,
> Now, with a soft and silent tread,
> Unheard she moves about my bed.

Swift himself had less courage:

> When on my sickly couch I lay,
> Impatient both of night and day,
> Lamenting in unmanly strains,
> Called every power to ease my pains,

> *Then Stella ran to my relief*
> *With cheerful face and inward grief;*
> *And, though by Heaven's severe decree,*
> *She suffers hourly more than me . . .*

We see well here the situation between them – the woman more courageous and stoical, and far less self-pitying, than the man.

This same year, in a poem to celebrate her collecting and transcribing his verses, this strange man chides her for what he chooses to regard as her only fault, her spirited objection to reproof. How much of that she had had to put up with from him! – it is good to think that she was not at all afraid to answer him back:

> *Your spirits kindle to a flame,*
> *Moved with the lightest touch of blame,*
> *And when a friend in kindness tries*
> *To show you where your error lies*
> *Conviction does but more incense:*
> *Perverseness is your whole defence –*

Very feminine of her. But he must have been intolerable at times, as he was certainly intolerant. He goes on,

> *Truth, judgement, wit give place to spite*
> *Regardless both of wrong and right.*
> *Your virtues all suspended wait*
> *Till time hath opened Reason's gate.*

There was his god – Reason. What we learn from this is that they had their quarrels, their temporary breaches.

> *And what is worse, your passion bends*
> *Its force against your nearest friends,*
> *Which manners, decency, and pride*
> *Have taught you from the world to hide.*

We are glad to know that she was no door-mat for him, that she could hold her own against this formidable man – and even that a shade of resentment entered into it. The poem itself gave reason enough for that:

> *Thou, Stella, wert no longer young*
> *When first for thee my harp I strung –*
> *Without one word of Cupid's darts,*
> *Of killing eyes, or bleeding hearts.*

We remember that Cupid's darts had been for Vanessa, still at this time living not far away, and still in hot pursuit of the evasive Dean. *His* principle with regard to both women – in spite of a world of difference between them in character, and even a shade of difference in his feelings for each – remained as he said candidly:

> *With friendship and esteem possessed,*
> *I ne'er admitted love a guest.*

Swift prided himself, as we saw in his verses to Delany, in being able to pay a compliment in the form of a detraction, to praise someone ironically by mentioning a defect – a risky art, akin to the raillery which was the fashion of the time and with which he infected his Irish friends, especially those closest to him, like the Sheridans. But it meant something more to Swift: it chimed with the remorseless realism of his outlook and the bent of his mind to reduce everything to what was displeasing or disgusting in *la condition humaine*. Voltaire called him the master of the *ridiculum acre*, and so we must take his mingling of beauties and blemishes.

For Stella's next birthday, her fortieth, he wrote:

> *Now this is Stella's case in fact:*
> *An angel's face, a little cracked –*
> *Could poets or could painters fix*
> *How angels look at thirty-six.*

It is possible that, apart from the needs of rhyme, he did not know how old she really was. Still –

> *every virtue now supplies*
> *The fainting rays of Stella's eyes:*
> *See at her levee crowding swains*
> *Whom Stella freely entertains*

With breeding, humour, wit and sense,
And puts them to so small expence,
Their minds so plentifully fills,
And makes such reasonable bills,
So little gets for what she gives
We really wonder how she lives.

Remember, she would never have had such an agreeable social life if it had not been for Swift – he carried her up a certain way with him, if not to the heights of his grand acquaintance. As for marriage, his biographers, who have been all men, have gallantly assumed that he was treating her badly by not marrying her. But not every woman is mad to be married, nor every man either. Virginia Woolf saw, from a woman's point of view, that there were compensations in not being married – or, alternatively, if there had been a formal marriage (as to which no one can tell), in not cohabiting with such an impossible man.

Meanwhile, he did his best to help in every way, but one. The ladies were not very good managers to begin with, and Swift regarded their St Mary's establishment as more than they could afford: 'you'll be as poor as rats: that place will drain you with a vengeance.' So he was anxious to save them expense by occupying his lodgings, and then the Deanery, when he was absent. These changes must have added further interest to their way of life; they were rarely tied to one place for long. By the time Swift was settled into the Deanery he had incited Stella to keep meticulous accounts like himself; so that, with his regular help and his looking after her own small finances, the fear jested at in the poem never came about:

And, had her stock been less, no doubt
She must have long ago run out.

Then come the compliments, ambivalently phrased in terms of her being no chicken:

should you live to see the day
When Stella's locks must all be grey,
When age must print a furrowed trace
On every feature of her face –

yet, however young another may look,

> All men of sense will pass your door
> And crowd to Stella's at fourscore.

It seems that this year, 1721, Stella herself celebrated Swift's birthday in verse:

> St Patrick's Dean, your country's pride,
> My early and my only guide . . .
> When men began to call me fair
> You interposed your kindly care;
> You early taught me to despise
> The ogling of a coxcomb's eyes,
> Showed where my judgement was misplaced,
> Refined my fancy and my taste.

On each of her birthdays Swift turned out verses for the occasion. Then in October 1723, on the ladies' return from their six months' stay with Charles Ford at his country house, they were greeted by cheerful verses which give one a pretty picture of their way of life:

> Don Carlos in a merry spite
> Did Stella to his house invite:
> He entertained her half a year
> With generous wines and costly cheer.

There follows an inventory of all the good things they had to eat and how nice they grew in their taste – turned up their noses at partridges unless they tasted of the corn, or venison unless it had the right *fumette*. Don Carlos had much ado to make her try this pigeon's leg, or prevail on her to touch a quail. After all the luxuries of Wood Park,

> But now arrives the dismal day,
> She must return to Ormond Quay:
> The coachman stopped, she looked and swore
> The rascal had mistook the door.
> At coming in you saw her stoop,
> The entry brushed against her hoop;
> Each moment rising in her airs
> She cursed the narrow winding stairs.

Settled in once more, she summoned company to supper to keep her spirits up, striving in vain to ape Wood Park:

> Two bottles called for (half her store:
> The cupboard could contain but four);
> A supper worthy of herself,
> Five nothings in five plates of Delft . . .
> Thus for a week the farce went on –
> When all her country-savings gone,
> She fell into her former scene:
> Small beer, a herring, and the Dean.

The poem ends with a fine compliment: apologizing for depreciating her fare – poets 'regard not whether false or true' if it gives them a subject:

> For though my raillery were true,
> A cottage is Wood-Park with you.

New Year 1724 brought verses for Dingley – 'Bec' – evidently a humble soul, absent-minded, easily distracted, unable to concentrate for long, devoted to her lap-dog Tiger; we learn that Stella too had a dog, Pug, and there is a sufficiently revealing reference, even in jest, to 'Stella's magisterial pride' – clearly a superior spirit. On her birthday Swift was ill in bed again:

> She tends me like an humble slave;
> And, when indecently I rave,
> When out my brutish passions break,
> With gall in every word I speak,
> She with soft speech my anguish cheers,
> Or melts my passions down with tears.

Then Swift states the conclusion we have already arrived at:

> Although 'tis easy to descry
> She wants assistance more than I,
> Yet seems to feel my pains alone,
> And is a stoic in her own.

For, by 1725, Stella's illness, whatever it was, had gained upon her and was entering its final phase, though Swift did not recognize it.

In 'A Receipt to Restore Stella's Youth' he recommended country air and exercise as usual:

> *Why, Stella, should you knit your brow,*
> *If I compare you to the cow?*
> *'Tis just the case, for you have fasted*
> *So long till all your flesh is wasted,*
> *And must against the warmer days*
> *Be sent to Quilca down to graze,*
> *Where mirth and exercise and air*
> *Will soon your appetite repair.*

She did pick up there, though it was a bad summer and rained incessantly. She swore it would rain till Michaelmas, but is 'generally much better . . . and in spite of the weather, which is worse than ever was heard of, we make a shift to walk and use exercise.' We have a glimpse of her there, wearing a small pick-axe – she and Swift were seeing to improvements there in Sheridan's absence: 'she is so pleased with her pick-axe that she wears it fastened to her girdle on her left side, in balance with her watch.' What is so interesting, a matter of some subtlety, is to notice the authority she exerts – just as if she were Mrs Dean Swift. She admonishes Sheridan, of whom she is fond; but he was feather-headed and an ill manager. He really must retrench his expenses: 'this is Stella's advice, as well as mine. She says now you need not be ashamed to be thought poor.' They both pressed him 'to make a great appearance of temperance', while away from home. Apparently he was going to the Bishop of Cork. 'Miss Johnson and I say, you must needs observe all grave forms, for the want of which both you and I have suffered . . . Miss Johnson put me in mind to caution you not to drink or pledge any health in his company, for you know his weak side in that matter.'

Later, 'Miss Johnson does not understand what you mean by her stamped linen, and remembers nothing of it; but supposes it is some jest. The ladies are well.' Then Miss Dingley, bless her, discovered what this housekeeping matter referred to.

From London Swift heard from his grand friend, Lord Bolingbroke, that Charles Ford was coming over. 'Your Star will probably hinder you from taking the same journey.'

It did not next spring, when Stella was somewhat better and Swift was able to cross over in March 1726, as we have seen, bringing *Gulliver* with him. He kept in constant touch with the ladies, as in the years of the *Journal* – but, alas, all the later letters were destroyed. He evidently reported to them all his doings in London, renewing acquaintance and paying his addresses to the Princess and leaders of the opposition; for he writes to Worrall, his factotum: 'the ladies have told you all my adventures, and I hear you are ruining me with dung' – this was for Naboth's Vineyard, the field some way south of the Deanery, which he was turning into a pleasaunce. 'I have writ several times to the ladies, and shall soon do so again.' Worrall was a Vicar-choral at St Patrick's; Swift reported that he had failed to get a choirman at Oxford, but was trying to get one in London.

Early in July, 'I find the ladies make the Deanery their villa. I have been told that Miss Johnson's health has given her friends bad apprehensions . . . but their secretary, Dr Sheridan, just tells me she is much better, to my great satisfaction. I wonder how you could expect to see her in a morning, which I, her oldest acquaintance, have not done these dozen years, except once or twice in a journey.' Swift kept in touch with news of her health through Sheridan and Archdeacon Walls too. To Sheridan he confessed his uneasiness, but the Archdeacon assured him she was better. He therefore imparted the news, 'because I know Miss Johnson would be pleased with it', that he had mentioned to the Princess the £1,000 debt he considered owing to him, on the promise of Queen Anne's last ministry, for the expenses of his installation at St Patrick's, the sum by which he was out of pocket. He had bidden the Princess to tell Walpole, but 'I scorned to ask him for it'. Of course he never got it – others, for far less services, carried off thousands from the state.

He had been offered a good piece of private preferment, 'which, if I were ten years younger, I would gladly accept, within twelve miles of London and in the midst of my friends. But I am too old for new schemes, and especially such as would bridle me in my freedoms and liberalities.' I think this shows his acceptance, at last, that his fate was irrevocably committed to Ireland. As Dean of St Patrick's he was freer to speak his mind than he would be anywhere else, and his liberalities would mean his present charities and those he intended for the future. He had, too, an offer of 'a fine house and garden, and park, and wine-cellar in France' – i.e. at Lady Bolingbroke's seat – for the winter. 'If Miss Johnson were not so out of order I would certainly accept of it; and I wish she could go to Montpellier at the same time.'

The next news that came was alarming – evidently Stella was despaired of; Swift was unnerved, as we see from the overwrought letters he sent, among the most revealing he ever wrote.

'What you tell me of Miss Johnson I have long expected, with great oppression and heaviness of heart. We have been perfect friends these thirty-five years. Upon my advice they both came to Ireland, and have been ever since my constant companions. And the remainder of my life will be a very melancholy scene, when one of them is gone whom I most esteemed, upon the score of every good quality that can possibly recommend a human creature. I have these two months seen through Miss Dingley's disguises. And indeed, ever since I left you, my heart is so sunk that I have not been the same man, nor ever shall be again, but drag on a wretched life till it shall please God to call me away.'

We see that the two women had done their best to keep the truth from him; this shows that they knew how passionate a man he really was, nothing like so strong as he fancied, his nerves exposed to every ill gust, slight or injury, sickness or grief. He paid a terrible price in nervous strain for the iron control he sought to impose on his nature – and was never successful in wholly imposing. The result was the self-pity that reeks in him, as it did in that comparable exemplar of self-repression in our time, Lawrence of Arabia. To anyone inured to normal human responses to suffering, it must make an unpleasant impression when Swift says that, if Stella is going to die, he cannot bear to be in Ireland at the time. 'I would not for the universe be present at such a trial as seeing her depart. She will be among friends that, upon her own account and great worth, will tend her with all possible care, where I should be a trouble to her, and the greatest torment to myself.'

He is thinking of himself – that is what makes the most unfavourable impression; he is not thinking, as a priest should do, of the departing soul and the consolation he should bring. But, then, he never speaks of himself as a priest, and he was very little of a Christian. His best excuse was, indeed, what he said himself – that he would only be a trouble to her. And, even at such a moment, he thought in terms of discretion. 'In case the matter should be desperate, I would have you advise that they should be lodged in some airy healthy part, and not in the Deanery – which besides, you know, cannot but be a very improper thing for that house to breathe her last in.'

There is something pathetically inadequate in what follows: 'let her know I have bought her a repeating gold watch, for her ease in winter nights. I designed to have surprised her with it; but now I would have her know it, that she may see how my thoughts were always to make her easy.' It needs no psychological sophistication to detect the element of propitiation in that, or the self-protection uppermost in the conclusion: 'I am of opinion that there is not a greater folly than to contract too great and intimate a friendship, which must always leave the survivor miserable.'

Shakespeare exposed himself to everything in life; Swift took the opposite course, hoping to shield himself from the blows life gives one: he did not avoid suffering, he suffered all the more.

The one thing he gained – if it is a gain – was perfect clarity about himself and the trap in which he was caught. He could not bear to witness her death; yet he could not bear to be away if she were dying. 'If I were now near her, I would not see her; I could not behave myself tolerably, and should redouble her sorrow.' We must respect that as the truth, and the clear-mindedness with which he confessed, 'all my preparations will not suffice to make me bear it like a philosopher, nor altogether like a Christian.' It is something that he knew his own inadequacy; and very touching when he breaks down and the man comes through, in quite unaccustomed language to a friend, 'dear Jim, pardon me, I know not what I am saying; but believe me that violent friendship is much more lasting, and as much engaging, as violent love.'

Unexpectedly, on his return, Stella rallied, and they were able, for

one last year, to resume their old accustomed ritual. In March 1727
Swift presented the last and much the most tender of his birthday
poems to her:

> *This day, whate'er the fates decree,*
> *Shall still be kept with joy by me:*
> *This day then, let us not be told,*
> *That you are sick, and I grown old.*

He must have recognized that her loss was inevitable now:

> *Although we now can form no more*
> *Long schemes of life, as heretofore,*
> *Yet you, while time is running fast,*
> *Can look with joy on what is past.*

Here is the form his consolation takes, the remembrance of her good
deeds, her numerous charitable acts:

> *Say, Stella, feel you no content*
> *Reflecting on a life well spent?*
> *Your skilful hand employed to save*
> *Despairing wretches from the grave;*
> *And then supporting from your store*
> *Those whom you dragged from death before . . .*
> *Your generous boldness to defend*
> *An innocent and absent friend;*
> *That courage which can make you just*
> *To merit humbled in the dust . . .*
> *That patience under torturing pain,*
> *Where stubborn stoics would complain.*

There were her qualities, tersely summed up by this truth-telling
pen; all recognized in her a remarkable woman, well worthy the
devotion of a man of genius, so strange a story. With the usual egoism
of the male he ends:

> *Me, surely me, you ought to spare,*
> *Who gladly would your suffering share,*
> *Or give my scrap of life to you*
> *And think it far beneath your due –*
> *You to whose care so oft I owe*
> *That I'm alive to tell you so.*

In April, in preparation for Swift's return to England, 'the ladies are with me, being now come to live at the Deanery for this summer'. Next month, from London: 'I hardly thought our friend would be in danger by a cold. I am of opinion she should be generally in the country, and only now and then visit the town.' In London the Dean was received well by the Princess, and reported it all as usual to Stella, though we have not the letters he wrote to her. We learn from those to other friends of the bantering relations he was on with this clever woman, who understood her man. She taxed him with being the author of a bad book, evidently the *Drapier Letters* just collected and issued together. 'But she assures me that both she and the Prince were very well pleased with every particular. But I disown the whole affair . . . only gave her leave, since she liked the book, to suppose what author she pleased.' What the Princess really thought of him she told charming Mrs Howard, her lady-in-waiting and her husband's official mistress – a very good friend of Swift's: Caroline thought him 'an odd sort of a man' . . . 'But I forgive her, for it is an odd thing to speak freely to princes.'

He was on the eve of going at last to France, when George I died and they were all in the midst of a political crisis, with all the hopes and long-deferred expectations of the opposition in a fine frenzy. 'I writ to Stella the day we heard the King was dead, and the circumstances of it.' Swift was again setting out for France when he was 'with great vehemence dissuaded from it by certain persons whom I could not disobey'. He was suffering from his old enemy – 'I believe this giddiness is the disorder that will at last get the better of me; but I would rather it should not be now.' For his old political enemy was at last threatening to fall; the new King and Queen conferred power upon the opposition hope, Spencer Compton. At this juncture Swift reported, 'I am like a great Minister, in a tottering condition.' But it was Spencer Compton who tottered: George II had called in a ninny, who could not even present the business to be undertaken. Sir Robert Walpole genially did it for him, and was rewarded with the confidence of both George and Caroline, which was not withdrawn as long as they lived. There was no future for the opposition.

At the end of August Sheridan wrote that Stella's illness had entered its final phase: no recovery was possible. Swift's reaction was one of fatalist resignation.

'I shall be perfectly content if God shall please to call me away at this time. Here is a triple cord of friendship broke, which hath lasted thirty years, twenty-four of which in Ireland . . . These are the perquisites of living long: the last act of life is always a tragedy at best, but it is a bitter aggravation to have one's best friend go before one. I long knew that our dear friend had not the *stamina vitae* . . . I brought both those friends over that we might be happy together as long as God should please; the knot is now broken, and the remaining person has ill answered the end [so much for Rebecca Dingley] . . . The other, who is now to be lost, is all that was valuable.' In September he was every day expecting news of her death, and again wrote to Worrall, this time in Latin, that it might not take place in the Deanery, for he had enemies who would place a sinister interpretation upon it.

On his way back to Ireland that month he was held up at Holyhead by bad weather for a week, in which he scribbled verses in a pocket-book still preserved.

> *I never was in haste before*
> *To reach that slaveish, hateful shore:*
> *Before, I always found the wind*
> *To me was most malicious kind.*
> *But now, the danger of a friend*
> *On whom my fears and hopes depend –*
> *Absent from whom all climes are cursed,*
> *With whom I'm happy in the worst –*
> *With rage impatient makes me wait*
> *A passage to the land I hate.*

Stella lingered on into the new year. We have some of the prayers Swift composed for his own use at her bedside – he could not evade his duty, it waylaid him, caught by the inevitable demands of life in the end.

In these prayers we look into his very soul, and we see what it was that he most valued in Stella in commending her to God. 'We beseech Thee also, O Lord, of Thy infinite goodness to remember of this Thy servant; that the naked she hath clothed, the hungry she hath fed, the sick and fatherless whom she hath relieved, may be reckoned according to Thy gracious promise as if they had been done unto Thee.' Stella's had been a very different life from Vanessa's, with her selfish concern only with and for herself. 'And now, O Lord, we implore Thy gracious favour towards us here met together: grant that the sense of this Thy servant's weakness may add strength to our faith that we, considering the infirmities of our nature and the uncertainty of life, may by this example be drawn to repentance before it shall please Thee to visit us in the like manner.'

In October, when it was evident that there was to be no reprieve or mercy for her: 'give her grace to continue sincerely thankful to Thee for the many favours Thou hast bestowed upon her: the ability and inclination and practice to do good, and those virtues which have procured the esteem and love of her friends, and a most unspotted name in the world . . . Continue to her, O Lord, that firmness and constancy of mind wherewith Thou hast most graciously endowed her, together with that contempt of worldly things and vanities that she hath shown in the whole conduct of her life . . . Pity us, the mournful friends of Thy distressed servant, who sink under the weight of her present condition, and the fear of losing the most valuable of our friends.' Fifteen years older than Stella, the useless Dingley would continue for years, supported by Swift.

And then, last, in November: 'give her strength, O Lord, to support her weakness, and patience to endure her pains, without repining at Thy correction . . . Forgive the sorrow and weakness of those among us who sink under the grief and terror of losing so dear and useful a friend.' What strange words to use at such a moment – the rational control of the word 'useful', the 'terror' of life without her! In those two contrasting words we have the whole paradox, the tension within Swift's nature.

Many are the stories told of Stella's last days, entangled as her life was with so memorable a man. We cannot give credence to them, for they lack firm evidence, and we shall never know. The least improbable is that Swift offered to make public the marriage; in another version that she asked it – in either case, the knell of the words 'too late' sounded. But this, brief as it is, depends on the assumption of a ceremony – all agree that, if it did take place, it was a mere formality.

In December she made her will, and here we are on firm ground. She abided by Swift's wishes: she did not go against them, as Vanessa had done. We learn from it that she had been maintaining a charity-child, 'who now lives with me'; she provided for his apprenticeship to a trade. She left to Dingley her little watch and chain, and twenty guineas; to Swift all her papers and her strong-box, with her savings, £150 in gold. The bulk of her fortune, after a life-interest to her mother, she left to Dr Steevens' Hospital, in accordance with the Dean's wishes, to support an unmarried chaplain. She was only forty-six when she died, on 28 January 1728.

Swift's only consolation, as always, was in writing: that night he sat down to write his character of her.

'This day, being Sunday, about eight o'clock at night, a servant brought me a note, with an account of the death of the truest, most virtuous, and valuable friend that I, or perhaps any other person, ever was blessed with. She expired about six of the evening of this day; and as soon as I am left alone, which is about eleven at night, I resolve, for my own satisfaction, to say something of her life and character.'

Sunday evening, we know, was the Dean's time for receiving company; when they had all gone, he sat down to write till midnight – it was his way of keeping control of himself. 'Her hair was blacker than a raven, and every feature of her face in perfection.' There follows an account of her early days – neither Moor Park nor Sir William Temple is mentioned – and her withdrawing into Ireland, 'with her dear friend and companion, the other lady'. 'I cannot call to mind that I ever once heard her make a wrong judgement of persons, books, or affairs. Her advice was always the best, and with the greatest freedom, mixed with the greatest decency . . . There seemed to be a combination among all that knew her to treat her with a dignity much beyond her rank.'

After paying tribute to her courage and staunchness, the devotion she elicited from her servants, 'she spoke in a most agreeable voice, in the plainest words, never hesitating, except out of modesty before new faces, where she was somewhat reserved; nor, among her nearest friends, ever spoke much at a time.' However, 'in an afternoon or evening's conversation, she never failed, before we parted, of delivering the best thing that was said in the company.'

In spite of the smallness of her fortune, 'her charity to the poor was a duty not to be diminished . . . She bought clothes as seldom as possible, and those as plain and cheap as consisted with the situation she was in; and wore no lace for many years . . . I have heard her say, she always met with gratitude from the poor: which must be owing to her skill in distinguishing proper objects, as well as her gracious manner in relieving them. . . .

'By returning very few visits she had not much company of her own sex, except those whom she most loved for their easiness or esteemed for their good sense. But she rather chose men for her companions, the usual topics of ladies' discourse being such as she had little knowledge of, and less relish . . . Wise men, through all her modesty, whatever they discoursed on, could easily observe that she understood them very well, by the judgement shown in her observations as well as in her questions . . . She loved Ireland better than the generality of those who owe both their birth and riches to it. She had indeed reason to love a country where she had the esteem and friendship of all who knew her, and the universal good report of all who ever heard of her . . . She detested the tyranny and injustice of England, in their treatment of this kingdom.'

Here we come back to Swift – is this not rather Swift than Stella? He wrote in little bits and pieces in the days after her death, 'as I found time'.

> January 29. My head aches, and I can write no more.
> January 30. Tuesday. This is the night of the funeral, which my sickness will not suffer me to attend. It is now nine at night, and I am removed into another apartment that I may not see the light in the church, which is just over against the window of my bed-chamber.

It is the language of desolation and despair.

CHAPTER 9

Literature and Life

THE 'SCRAP OF LIFE' that remained to Swift extended to another eighteen years, of which the last three, 1742–5, were sunk in mental debility. There was indeed a certain tragic propriety in his end – as he had foretold one day to the poet Young, pointing to a tree that had been struck, he would go like that, dying from the top. He must have had extraordinary vital energy to have lasted as he did, to his seventy-fifth year, before he was felled, after the life-long illness he suffered from, all the strains and stresses he endured and put upon himself. All the same, these last long years are something in the nature of an epilogue. The main themes of his life had long taken shape, his greatest works been written; his interests continued the same – politics both English and Irish, defeat registered with regard to the first, with regard to the latter more vehement and enraged than ever; writing, both prose and verse; scribbling incessantly, rhymes, riddles, doggerel; conducting a large correspondence with friends; performing his duties at St Patrick's; and more active than ever in good works, but in and for Ireland.

There is no deterioration in mental faculties or style until his breakdown, and it would be a mistake to underestimate the quality of his literary production, though on a smaller scale and more scrappy. His 'Verses on the Death of Dr Swift' were as good as anything he ever wrote, and were more widely acclaimed on publication; his last poem, 'The Legion Club', more savage and biting. In prose, the *Modest Proposal* of 1729 was as masterly a piece of irony, as absolute and terrifying; two years later he was putting together and polishing two characteristic works in a totally different vein, the *Polite Conversation* and *Directions to Servants*, the latter left unfinished.

His letters remained as good as ever, always something interesting in every one.

For the rest, one notices some change. After Stella's death, he becomes more misogynistic, more anti-women in theory – though he continued to have women friends, both great and small. His disgust for *la condition humaine* did not prevent him from doing many kindnesses in many directions. But his work became more scatological and nasty: he tortured himself with disgust at necessary human functions – even when he had a point, for example, observing the contrast between the droppings of horses, shapely and inoffensive, and human excrement, the filth of the Yahoos. One simply does not know how to account for his obsession – apart from the consequences of an inhuman repression; even there, the repression stoked up his energies, as well as fuelled the tensions. He would have made a wonderful subject for a Freud.

The extraordinary thing is that – even after the English equivalent of Richelieu's Day of Dupes, and the relegation of Spencer Compton to the Speakership while Walpole engrossed all power – Swift did not for some years give up all hope. In 1730 he was writing, 'I see nails, that I thought might be pulled out, now more strongly riveted than ever.' To Gay, 'does Walpole think you intended an affront to him in your opera [*The Beggar's Opera*]? Pray God he may, for he has held the longest hand at hazard that ever fell to any sharper's share, and keeps his run when the dice are changed.'

It was to continue for a good many more years yet. Swift described him as monopolizing 'the regal power' – true in its way, and he operated by a most effective system of corruption, which infuriated the virtuous, like Bolingbroke, and the wits, intellectuals who, because they could write better, thought they could govern better. Swift called Walpole's Excise Bill of 1733 'execrable'; in fact, it was one of the best measures to be proposed in that century – and was defeated by the appeal to popular prejudice. Walpole did not try again; he held on to power instead.

Swift repined at his fate: to Bolingbroke, 'you think, as I ought to think, that it is time for me to have done with the world; and so I would, if I could get into a better before I was called into the best,

ot die here in a rage, like a poisoned rat in a hole. I wonder
ʌre not ashamed to let me pine away in this kingdom, while
ʌre out of power.' And there was some reason in his complaint
ʌrs Howard, for it was she who positively directed him to remain
in London at George II's accession in 1727, hinting that 'I might
reasonably hope for a settlement in England. Which, God knows,
was no very great ambition, considering the station I should leave
here of greater dignity, and which might easily have been managed
to be disposed of as the Crown pleased.' He thought of his English
friends as his real ones – his Irish friends were a poor substitute for
Pope and Gay, Bolingbroke, Bathurst and Oxford. Only Orrery and
Delany came anywhere near them. Moreover, now that Stella was
gone, there was no strong tie to hold him.

He confessed to Bolingbroke that nothing could cure his itch for
meddling with public affairs, except his frequent returns of deafness.
He regarded the people around Queen Caroline as 'the most impudent
in forgetting their professions that I have ever known'. He hardly
dared to charge her as yet – in itself an indication that he had not
given up all hope; but Walpole was her man. 'I remember, when I
was a little boy, I felt a great fish at the end of my line which I drew
up almost on the ground. But it dropped in; the disappointment vexes
me to this very day, and I believe it was the type of all my future
disappointments.' His later letters occasionally yield significant
biographical details like this; it is only now that he tells us that he
was never so possessed by the passion for fame as when he was young.
That throws a retrospective light on his years at Moor Park and his
resentments there. Nothing consoled him – not even the magnificent
tribute of Carteret in 1735, when he was very famous, the most
famous man in one kingdom and hardly any other to compete in
the other. 'As for futurity, I know your name will be remembered
when the names of Kings, Lords Lieutenants, Archbishops and Parliament politicians, will be forgotten.'

So he was thrown back on Ireland, with his insatiable desire to be
up and doing. Here, what enraged him was the passivity of the people:
he could not get them to be up and doing for themselves. We shall
see that he was far from being merely denunciatory and destructive;

he was essentially constructive, and in his own sphere, where he could see to things himself, he accomplished many practical jobs for Ireland. But he had a bigger programme of action: tax absentee landlords at 5s in the pound on what they took out of the country; encourage Irish manufactures, make Irish people use their own manufactures, instead of paying for English; control luxury imports to keep a satisfactory balance of trade and stop the drainage of currency from the country; improve the quality of Irish goods; improve the land and agriculture. He could get none of this taken up by the Irish legislature, bought and sold in the English interest. And frustration maddened him.

Like Froude later, he challenged the Irish to act for themselves; he would not respect them until they did. In one or two letters one sees the Anglican Dean encouraging law-breaking: this would have a very effective future in Ireland, and when one thinks of the way in which independence was eventually achieved . . . the way of assassination, a murder campaign, as a Chief Justice of the Irish state subsequently admitted! Gay had been in Scotland with the Queensberrys. 'Who could write to you in Scotland? Yet I am glad you were in a country nine times worse than this, wherein I speak very favourably of the soil, the climate, and the language. But you were among a brave people and defenders of their liberty, which outbalances all our advantages of nature.'

And the condition of Ireland? 'A bare face of nature, without houses or plantations; filthy cabins, miserable, tattered, half-starved creatures, scarce in human shape; one insolent, ignorant, oppressive squire to be found in twenty miles riding; a parish church to be found only in a summer day's journey; a bog of fifteen miles round; every meadow a slough, and every hill a mixture of rock, heath and marsh . . . There is not an acre of land in Ireland turned to half its advantage, yet it is better improved than the people; and all these evils are effects of English tyranny.' Swift exaggerated, in both terms – but one sees what a place this Anglo-Irishman has in the tradition of Irish nationalism.

As the eighteenth century progressed there was considerable improvement, but at the time he was writing, earlier, there was a vicious circle. The poverty of the country encouraged moral degeneration, which again encouraged poverty and squalor. How to break it? The English were not alone responsible. In so far as they were Swift went for them tooth and nail; he never ceased to inveigh against the utter lack of public spirit among the Irish themselves. Even in his sermons he preached against bad workmanship. In pamphlets he confessed, 'it hath never been once my good fortune to employ one single workman who did not cheat me to the utmost of his power in the materials, the work and the price. . . . This, I must own, is the natural consequence of poverty and oppression. These wretched people catch at anything to save them a minute longer from drowning.'

And there were too many of them – another consequence of squalor and lack of self-control. Out of his fury at frustration came the most savage of his essays in irony: *A Modest Proposal for Preventing the Children of Poor People from being a Burden to their Parents and for Making them Beneficial to the Public*. Since there are too many of them, and people are starving, why not eat them? Regarded by everyone as an ironic masterpiece it makes sickening reading – particularly in a world overrun by the population explosion: when science has produced effective devices for controlling it and idiot humans will not use them – or more wicked idiots, on ideological persuasions, refuse to make use of them.

We need go no further in exploring what has been called 'the appalling impact of this masterpiece' – its relevance today, especially to uncontrolled and uncontrollable societies like India, is all too obvious. Even Swift's side-swipes at humans make one shudder, there is such a deadly truth in the cool recitation pointing out men's pretty little ways: 'men would become as fond of their wives during the time of their pregnancy, as they are now of their mares in foal, their cows in calf, or sows when they are ready to farrow, nor offer to beat or kick them – as it is too frequent a practice – for fear of a miscarriage.' One does not need to resort to the newspapers to learn of the beating of women by their husbands, or the cruel maltreatment of children – I knew of the fact from my youth in village life. Swift was merciless in his exposure of humans; but what he said of them was justified. It was true. This famous tract has been described as 'a lucid nightmare'; but the nightmare is all round us – if we look, and do not close our eyes to the facts.

The refusal of the Irish Parliament to do anything about it brought down upon its head the last and most furious of Swift's poems. The Parliament was an assembly of landlords, many of them partly absentee and, not content with having taken most of the tithes from the Church, were bent on further depredation. This brought Swift's feeling to boiling point in 'A Character, Panegyric and Description of the Legion Club'.

> As I stroll the city, oft I
> Spy a building large and lofty,
> Not a bowshot from the College,
> Half the globe from sense and knowledge.
> Tell us what this pile contains?
> Many a head that holds no brains –

as it might be the unspeakable assembly at Westminster in the 1930s, that went on with Appeasement until the year was 1939, which sounded the knell for Britain.

> Let them, when they once get in
> Sell the nation for a pin . . .

(they got in all right, with overwhelming majorities in the 1930s, and they sold the nation for less than a pin.)

> See, the Muse unbars the gate;
> Hark, the monkeys, how they prate!

Clio is the Muse of history, and she keeps the record. One should read now the record of the 1930s, as recorded in Hansard.

> What, said I, is this the mad-house?
> These, she answered, are but shadows,
> Phantoms, bodiless and vain,
> Empty visions of the brain.

True enough, but it is the business of history to record their doings. Swift records their doings, and by name, in the 1730s; it wants, it still needs, a Swift to do justice to those responsible for far greater disaster to this nation in the 1930s.

> *How I want thee, humourous Hogarth!*
> *Thou, I hear, a pleasant rogue art!*
> *Were but you and I acquainted*
> *Every monster should be painted.*
> *You should try your graving tools*
> *On this odious group of fools,*
> *Draw the beasts as I describe 'em,*
> *From their features while I gibe them.*

Now for the constructive side. We have seen the improvements made at Laracor; in addition, he left in his will lands which he had purchased for £260 to improve the living. There were the works he put in hand for Sheridan at Quilca, the encouragement he gave to his friends among country gentlemen, like Chetwode and Ford, in planting and parking and paling. The Archbishop of Cashel was repairing and restoring at that historic spot: he was anxious to get Swift's approval for what he was doing in putting St Cormac's old chapel and buildings in order, spending a good deal of money on the work. He invited the scholarly Dean to come and stay, and approve the plans. Archbishop King had been succeeded in Dublin by Hoadley in 1729, brother of the notorious Whig and very latitudinarian bishop, a favourite with Queen Caroline. Swift cannot have approved of his new neighbour, but he was won round by Hoadley's improving the Archbishop's country estate at Tallaght, building a residence there and setting a good example.

He sought to do so very notably himself. In England in 1727 Queen Caroline had invited him to inform her of matters of concern in Ireland – it meant nothing, of course, just the usual royal humbug. 'The woollen manufacture of this kingdom sat always nearest my heart,' he said. On his return he sent her a valuable present of Irish silks for her and the Princesses. Apparently she used the material for dresses, and promised him a medal for his collection of coins. Nothing came of it. The Hanoverians were notoriously stingy – and the medal became quite an obsession with Swift, as it would.

In Dublin there were his own improvements, making a garden

of Naboth's Vineyard, and planting fruit-trees. We have seen his care for the cathedral, its services, sermons and the choir; every morning, when in residence, he was in his stall at 9 a.m. He now had a regular campaign for the restoration of the monuments. The most grandiose, the one occupying most space, was that of the 'Great Earl of Cork', who had made a vast fortune out of Irish land. This had come down to the Earl of Burlington. Swift wrote and wrote to get a subscription out of him – and got a rather arrogant response. At this the irascible Dean blew up and sent him a tart message: 'pray tell him this in the severest manner, and charge it all upon me, and so let the monument perish.' He got it repaired: there it still is. The ablest of Dutch William's aides was old Marshal Schomberg, killed at the battle of the Boyne. He was buried in St Patrick's, and Swift considered that he ought to have a memorial. He sued again and again to his daughters to put one up – in vain. So he put one up himself, and wrote a Latin inscription arraigning the family for the indignity, 'that thou, O stranger, mightest know in how poor a cell the ashes of so great a general lie neglected, to the reproach of his heirs.'

We know of Swift's fund from which loans were made to deserving tradesmen in the Liberty of St Patrick's; in addition, the charities and gifts of this prudent manager, so careful with his money, were numerous. He had a regular 'seraglio' of poor old women he supported, and whom he adorned with characteristic names, Cancerina, Stumpanympha, Stumpantha, Pullagowna, Friterilla, etc. Their very names bring them before our eyes. His correspondence is full of good deeds, recommendations of deserving clergymen for preferment, of charity boys for a place. Some of this was, in a sense, official and proper to his position – he served for years as a governor of the Blue Coat School, for example. But most of it was personal, and reflected pure kindness of heart – or sense of duty.

In some ways ungenerous, in others he was a generous man – to the deserving, or the genuinely helpless. And his good nature over-rode party prejudice, as with Archbishop Hoadley. When Lady Betty Germain's kinsman, the Duke of Dorset, was Lord-Lieutenant Swift wrote on behalf of a young soldier who was 'as great a Whig as the father . . . You will have several requests for this post . . . but you are to observe only mine, because it will come three minutes before any other. I think this is the third request I have made to your Grace. You have granted the two first and therefore must grant the third. For when I knew Courts, those who had received a dozen favours were utterly disobliged if they were denied the thirteenth. Besides, if this be not granted, the Grattans will rise in rebellion, which I tremble to think of.' So – may 'the young Whig have the barrack of Kinsale, worth £60 or £70 a year?' Let this serve for an example – the style is irresistible.

Then, too, he helped various writers who had not much luck. He was a persistent patron to the Pilkingtons, until their matrimonial infidelities became a public scandal and he had to withdraw his countenance. They were not without talents; Matthew Pilkington was a clergyman, not very well suited to the cloth; Laetitia, Swift rather admired for her talents and the brave face she put on things. Swift recommended them to his grand English friends too. Bolingbroke, who had become respectable with age, warned Swift against being too free with his recommendations. Mrs Barber was a more virtuous character, with a large and sickly family. She had no luck with her poems; so Swift gave her the manuscript of his *Polite Conversation*. Since it was in dialogue form, a play was made of it and acted in Dublin; it produced quite a sum of money for the relief of Mrs Barber.

A Dublin doctor, Michael Clancy, who published a volume of memoirs, had lost his sight. Having written a play, some friends lent it to Swift, who responded charmingly. 'I read it carefully, with much pleasure, on account both of the characters and the moral. I have no interest with the people of the playhouse, else I should gladly recommend it to them. I send you a small present, in such gold as will not give you trouble to change' – a considerate touch; it was £5, all in small pieces – we should multiply by perhaps twenty for current value. Clancy replied, 'when I strive to express the thorough sense I have of your humanity and goodness, my attempt ceases in admiration of them. You have favoured my performance with some degree of approbation, and you have considered my unfortunate condition by a mark of your known benevolence.'

Scores, more probably hundreds, of people had reason to be grateful to the paradoxical public figure for his known benevolence. The misanthrope was a patriot. At seventy he is most anxious to commemorate the public spirit and services of a recent Lord Mayor, Humphrey French: 'I will, although I am oppressed with age and infirmities, stir up all the little spirit I can raise to give the public an account of that great patriot, and propose him as an example to all future magistrates, in order to recommend his virtues to this miserable kingdom.' It was patriotism on Swift's part that made him write several times to the Duke of Chandos to ask him to bestow the Clarendon Papers in his possession – those of the second Earl, who had been Lord-Lieutenant – upon 'the University here, because Irish antiquities are of little value or curiosity to any other nation'. He obtained a copy of Rymer's indispensable *Foedera* for the library. On his persuasion Stella had bequeathed the reversion of her fortune to Steevens' Hospital. We can infer that, if it had not been for the breach at the end, Vanessa's would not have gone to a college in the Bermudas. And now Swift was making the arrangements to leave the bulk of his much larger fortune to found a lunatic asylum for the Irish.

It was much needed.

No wonder – paradoxical as it is – that Swift became a popular hero, a legend in his own lifetime; he certainly achieved all the fame he had so passionately desired when young, and became after his death a figure of folklore. All round the country there were spots associated with him – not only at Laracor or Trim, Wood Park or Howth, but as far afield as Kilroot or Gosford in the north, where there were the Dean's Walk and Dean's Seat. In the Deanery at St Patrick's, in my time, his skull ornamented the sideboard in the dining-room, a secular relic upon which Yeats wrote a play, as he translated the famous Latin epitaph into English verse. Swift's presence looms behind much in modern Irish literature. But I am concerned with his life, not his tradition, living as that is.

As early as 1729, on his return from a long absence with the Achesons in the north, he was 'received with great joy by many of our principal citizens, who also on the same occasion caused the bells to ring in our cathedrals, and had bonfires and other illuminations'. It became the custom to celebrate his birthday regularly in this way – while he as regularly sat at home and read the third chapter of the Book of Job on that day. This year the Dublin corporation presented him with the freedom of the city in a gold box – it did not give unadulterated pleasure to the Government. When, in 1737, the corporation of Cork conferred the freedom of that town upon him, they sent him a silver box without any inscription or parchment specifying what services the freedom was for. A typical Irish oversight – he sent it back again for either an inscription, or for some more worthy person than himself.

In 1734 there was a fracas over yet one more measure in Parliament designed against tithes. The Dean was not personally affected, but had a petition presented against it on behalf of the Church. Serjeant Bettesworth spoke up against the petition, and for his pains was lampooned about the town:

> Thus at the bar the booby Bettesworth,
> Though half a crown o'er pays his sweat's worth,
> Who knows in law nor text nor margent,
> Calls Singleton his brother Serjeant.

We need not pursue the dog in the doggerel, but merely point out that Swift's verses were recognizable from their uncommon, out-of-the-way rhymes, apart from anything else.

The Serjeant-at-law, a rather pompous person, took great offence and pursued the Dean to an evening party at someone's house, where there ensued an altercation, a scene. Swift did not altogether get the best of it; the Serjeant made a point when he compared Swift to his own Yahoo climbing up to a height from which to squirt filth on all mankind. When Bettesworth threatened the Dean, however, twenty or thirty inhabitants of the Liberty banded together to protect him. He could not be touched – as Walpole found later that year, on the publication of some libel in London. He had Pilkington, Mrs Barber and Motte the printer, who were involved, taken into custody. When he was considering sending a messenger to

Dublin to attach the Dean, he was warned that the attachment of the Drapier could not be effected in Ireland with safety by less than ten thousand men.

He had become the country's sacred bull, safe in the Liberty of St Patrick's.

He was hardly less famous in England. His grand acquaintance, social, political and literary, remained loyal – a tribute to what they felt for him; as old friends died new ones recommended themselves. From the haughty Countess Granville he received what we should call fan mail: 'I never wished so much as I do now that I were bright and had a genius which could entertain you, in return for the many excellent things that entertain me daily, which I read over and over with fresh delight.'

She called him 'the charming Dean', a side to him we are apt to overlook. Other unknown admirers wrote too. His oldest grand friend, Lady Betty Germain, whose friendship went back to early days at Dublin Castle, kept in regular, affectionate touch. Among newer acquaintance were Gay's patroness, the Duchess of Queensberry, who also tried to lure Swift over to stay, and delightful Mrs Howard, now to become Countess of Suffolk – deaf like Swift, but more philosophic about it: she did not allow it to spoil her natural good humour.

Among writers Pope had become Swift's closest friend; there is no doubt that Swift was fond of the little monkey, brilliant, *maladif*, forced to live a most careful, abstemious life, with his background of women – his aged mother and the Blount sisters. They were all Catholics; and the friendship had begun in typical Swift fashion by his offering Pope twenty guineas to change his religion. Pope knew how to take this joke. Then, if only he would come over and stay in the Deanery, he could have the Catholic Dean of St Patrick's, who was twice Swift's age, as his confessor. The raillery continued – until, in the end, Pope played Swift a characteristic trick over the publication of his letters, the inwardness of which the candid Dean did not suspect.

Pope persuaded Swift to publish a miscellany of their verse together, most of which was Swift's: 'at all adventures, yours and my name shall stand linked as friends to posterity, both in verse and prose,' wrote Pope. Swift was proud of having suggested the idea of the *Dunciad* to him: 'I am one of everybody who approve every part of it, text and comment.' Both Pope and Swift were constantly attacked in print by inferior writers – they had this in common, along with their politics. Swift once said that if he wrote about a straw, some ass would rise to answer him. Pope's superior talents aroused the jealous envy of those who hadn't many; he positively delighted in provoking them, and then they provided subjects for his *Dunciad*, like flies embalmed. Swift was more philosophic about being attacked, or more inured to it; he simply said once that it was the natural concomitant of distinction: if one stood out, one was a target for fools.

From a literary point of view dealing with Pope was rather tricky. 'If I am your friend', Swift wrote flatteringly, 'it is for my own reputation, and from a principle of self-love.' There then followed a hint: 'I do sometimes reproach you for not honouring me in letting the world know we are friends.' Pope was so ambitious as a writer that he did not want to share his acknowledged pre-eminence as a poet with anyone. (The Hanoverians were such Philistines that they made Stephen Duck their Poet Laureate; the first writers of the age were in opposition.)

Though Pope was the greater poet, with much wider range, nothing of his prose would last. Here, too, he was over-ambitious, engaged in devious schemes to get back his letters, rewrite them and publish them for posterity. Swift did not realize all that he was up to, or capable of, in this way and confided to him innocently his own conviction. 'I find you have been a writer of letters almost from your infancy, and, by your own confession, had schemes of epistolary fame. Montaigne says that if he could have excelled in any kind of writing, it would have been in letters. But I doubt they would not have been natural, for it is plain that all Pliny's Letters were written with a view of publishing. And I accuse Voiture himself of the same crime, although he be an author I am fond of.' There follows a devastating conclusion: 'they cease to be letters when they become a *jeu d'esprit*.' This does for Pope as a letter-writer; he rewrote his letters, until they became self-conscious and artificial, stilted and empty, pompous essays instead of letters. It was a fashionable fault in the eighteenth century – one notices it in the letters of Young (whom Swift did not much like), as well as in Bolingbroke's.

Swift, on the other hand, as a letter-writer is superb – along with Horace Walpole, the best of English letter-writers. This aspect of his genius and writing has hardly been appreciated: precisely because his letters are so natural, they are the most complete expression of the man. Their range is magnificent, from the simple to the most eloquent; there are grand formal letters of consolation like those to Oxford when in the Tower, set-pieces, but at the same time sincere, full of pride and indignation, loyalty and affection. There are touching words of condolence to people in trouble, like those to his cousin, Mrs Whiteway, on the death of a son – Swift's concern for her is real and transparent. So was his concern for Vanessa and Stella – his letters to them express everything: awkwardness, embarrassment, apprehension, emotion in the case of the one; security, affection, relaxation, fun in the case of the other; love, his own kind of love, reasonable and under control, for both. And there are letters of pure linguistic virtuosity to Sheridan: sometimes in Latin, or dog-Latin; sometimes dividing up the syllables differently, so that it looks like Esperanto or, possibly, Yahoo. Once, Sheridan wrote him a letter with thirteen words ending in -ing; Swift responded with a letter where there are one hundred and sixty. What virtuosity! What a natural gift for language – and the influence of it has gone on to this day with Joyce and his perverse monument, *Finnegan's Wake* (along with the coprophily).

In their thirst for fame both Pope and Bolingbroke ceased to be the good companions they had been, when young. 'My Lord Boling-broke and Mr Pope press me with many kind invitations. But the former is too much a philosopher; he dines at six in the evening, after studying all the morning till afternoon and, when he hath dined, to his studies again.' Evidently a very different man from the 'Colonel' of the glorious, anxious last days of Queen Anne! And, 'Mr Pope can neither eat nor drink, loves to be alone, and hath always some poetical scheme in his head. Thus the two best companions have utterly disqualified themselves for my conversation, and my way of living.' Though he longed for England, his own way of life was best for him, he wrote to Gay and his Duchess. 'I must have horses to ride, I must go to bed and rise when I please, and live where all mortals are subservient to me. I must talk nonsense when I please. I must ride thrice a week, and walk three or four miles besides every day.' To Bolingbroke he wrote that he loved *la bagatelle* more than ever and scribbling verses at night, when company had gone. (His Sunday evening receptions cost him six bottles of wine; his cider was good Herefordshire cider he stocked from Goodrich.)

With Gay there were no complications as with Pope, and one sees Swift's literary generosity, where Pope had none. Swift wrote, '*The Beggar's Opera* has knocked down *Gulliver*; I hope to see Pope's *Dulness* [*Dunciad*] knock down *The Beggar's Opera*, but not till it has fully done its job.' They were all anti-Walpole. Swift praised Gay's *Fables* to the skies; no one could compete with him in that *genre* he had made his own. He had himself tried again and again, but was so dissatisfied with his efforts that he had torn them up. But he had overlooked his own 'Baucis and Philemon', one of the best of its kind.

Swift's last decade produced a couple of his most admired productions. Goldsmith regarded 'On Poetry: a Rhapsody' as one of the best versified poems in the language. The title is ironical: so far from being rhapsodic it is regular in measure, and in place of romance is sarcasm. Dr William King of Oxford said that it would have procured him favour at Court, 'if Lord Hervey had not undeceived Queen Caroline and taken some pains to teach her the use and power of irony.' It did not need Lord Hervey to point out the reward she and her spouse received for their meanness:

> *Fair Britain in thy monarch blest,*
> *Whose virtues bear the strictest test,*
> *Whom never faction could bespatter,*
> *Nor minister, nor poet flatter.*
> *What justice in rewarding merit?*
> *What magnanimity of spirit?*

Beside him:

> *The consort of his throne and bed –*

(i.e. when it was not occupied by Mrs Howard) –

> *A perfect goddess born and bred:*
> *Appointed sovereign judge to sit*
> *On learning, eloquence and wit.*

And the minister who ruled George II's kingdom for him –

> *Now sing the minister of state*
> *Who shines alone, without a mate –*

i.e. Walpole lived with an Irish mistress, Maria Skerrett.

We need not go through Swift's survey of contemporary letters – his parallel to Pope's *Dunciad*, but merely note that Dryden is not forgotten, at this late date:

> *Read all the Prefaces of Dryden,*
> *For these our critics much confide in –*
> *Though merely writ at first for filling,*
> *To raise the volume's price a shilling.*

We may couple this with a last informative passage about Dryden, from a letter of 1735, in which Swift discusses points of criticism, revealing in detail his extraordinary meticulousness about the correct use of words. In rhyming Swift called the triplet, 'a vicious way of rhyming, wherewith Dryden abounded and was imitated by all the bad versifiers in Charles II's reign. Dryden, though my near relation, is one I have often blamed as well as pitied. He was poor, and in great haste to finish his plays, because by them he chiefly supported his family. He likewise brought in the Alexandrine verse at the end of the triplets. I was so angry at these corruptions that above twenty-four years ago I banished them all by one triplet, with the Alexandrine, upon a very ridiculous subject.' So – the famous conclusion of the 'Description of a City Morning' had been another jeer at Dryden. 'I absolutely did prevail with Mr Pope, and Gay, and Dr Young, and one or two more, to reject them.'

Dr William King, leader of the Oxford Jacobites – until he met the Old Pretender on a visit *incognito* to London, which disillusioned him – became a new friend of Swift's after meeting him in Dublin. King tells us that no poem of his had such a reception as his auto-biographical poem, 'Verses on the Death of Dr Swift'. It was based on a maxim of La Rochefoucauld, which had had but too much influence on his mind: '*dans l'adversité de nos meilleurs amis nous trouvons quelque chose qui ne nous déplaît pas.*' The poem is a brisk survey of Swift's life and career, which betrays his illusions about himself no less than about others. For example:

> *Had he but spared his tongue and pen*
> *He might have rose like other men:*
> *But power was never in his thought,*
> *And wealth he valued not a groat.*

One can only gasp at the self-deception, if that was what he really thought – I suspect it was, not merely what he would like others to think.

On the other hand, he summed up in one short line what he had achieved as the Drapier:

> *Taught fools their interest how to know.*

Not only that, it may be taken as the prime purpose of political, or at least electoral, activity. (I took it for motto in the whole decade I spent as a political candidate in the 1930s, trying to open the eyes of the electorate to the folly of Appeasement and of the working class, bemused by Baldwin, to their own interest. One sees the relevance of Swift to politics and society at every turn.)

A good deal of the poem is good fun, and has the colloquial tone of Mrs Harris's Petition:

> *My female friends, whose tender hearts*
> *Have better learned to act their parts,*
> *Receive the news in doleful dumps:*
> *'The Dean is dead (and what is trumps?)'*
> *'Then Lord have mercy on his soul.*
> *(Ladies, I'll venture for the vole)' [i.e. all the tricks]*
> *'Six Deans, they say, must bear the pall*
> *(I wish I knew what King to call.)'*

An amusing round is made of how the news was taken by different people; Queen Caroline's promise is not forgotten:

> Kind Lady Suffolk in the spleen
> Runs laughing up to tell the Queen.
> The Queen, so gracious, mild, and good,
> Cries, 'Is he gone? 'Tis time he should.
> He's dead, you say; why, let him not;
> I'm glad the medals were forgot.
> I promised them, I own, but when?
> I only was the Princess then.
> But now as Consort of the King,
> You know 'tis quite a different thing.

So much for the vanity of royal promises. Nor, at the end, did he avoid the subject that had done him harm all through his life. Some would say,

> He doth an honour to his gown
> By bravely running priestcraft down:
> He shows as sure as God's in Gloucester

(a proverb going back to the cult of the Holy Blood at Hailes)

> That Jesus was a grand imposter,
> That all his miracles were cheats,
> Performed as jugglers do their feats.
> The Church had never such a writer –
> A shame he hath not got a mitre!

The conclusion is not without some admixture of delusion:

> Perhaps I may allow, the Dean
> Had too much satire in his vein,
> And seemed determined not to starve it,
> Because no age could more deserve it.
> Yet, malice never was his aim:
> He lashed the vice but spared the name.
> No individual could resent
> Where thousands equally were meant.

Once more we gasp – and once more are forced to agree:

> His satire points at no defect
> But what all mortals may correct.

Swift entrusted the publication to his new friend, Dr William King, who was able to report that 'none of your works have been better received by the public than this poem'. Abroad, in France he was no less admired: Cardinal Polignac summed up pithily, '*il a l'esprit créateur.*'

When the rumour of the existence of the *Polite Conversation* reached London, people were very anxious to see it. The idea went back to the glorious years in London, when so much of his work was adumbrated. There can be no doubt that he kept a notebook in which he entered the inanities which passed with polite people for conversation – there were few to add to his collection on coming back to Ireland. Out at Quilca – alone, without Stella – in the summer of 1731 he passed his time reducing to order the collections he had made. If one watches ordinary people's talk with the lynx eyes and cats' ears of a Swift or an Evelyn Waugh, one notices that they cannot express themselves except in clichés. It is not only the inanity of what they have to say that is funny, but the fact that they cannot say it except in the worn-out coin of phrases that are used by everybody a million times over. In the first lines of the work people cannot meet someone they have just been talking about without saying, 'Talk of the devil –'; while 'a parson would say, "I hope we shall meet in heaven".' And so it goes on, 'it's an ill wind that blows nobody any good', while the next 'can't see the wood for the trees'.

The extraordinary thing is that, with mingled virtuosity and relentlessness, Swift carries it on for pages and pages. It was published in 1738 as *A Complete Collection of Genteel and Ingenious Conversation according to the Most Polite Mode and Method now Used at Court and in the Best Companies of England.* With a reference back to Bickerstaff, the author is given as Simon Wagstaff. The fatiguing thing about this book is that it is so complete, though no doubt Swift could have gone on further. One is simply battered down by it all – one can no more finish it than one can finish *Bouvard et Pécuchet.*

Swift introduces the work, with grave poker-face, as from one having begun to frequent society from 1695, the sixth year of King William III, 'of ever-glorious and immortal memory, who rescued three kingdoms from popery and slavery' – but had not given him a prebend. On leaving company he immediately entered into his table-book, 'the choicest expressions that passed during the visit'. (Evelyn Waugh was often silent in company, making mental note of the nonsense that was uttered.) Polite noises and gestures are also useful to observe, so as to be 'never at a loss upon any emergency, the true management of every feature, and almost of every limb, is equally necessary' – to avoid the awkward postures one notices; some standing on one leg, others not knowing what to do with their hands, stretching back in a chair until the back is broken, and a hundred other little ways humans have of making themselves objectionable in company – coming too close to one, putting their hands familiarly on one's shoulder, breathing on one, pressing one into a corner, practically boarding one, etc.

Proverbs are to be distinguished from those polite speeches which beautify conversation; these last will 'wholly avoid the vexations and impertinence of pedants, who affect to talk in a language not to be understood'. (As it might be the jargon of sociologists or economists.) One must be very sparing of *doubles-entendres*, 'because they often put ladies upon affected constraints, and affected ignorance.' Swift does not miss a point; women understand well enough, but affect not to. He does not go on to the further implication that they think it is their due to pretend to be shocked, when they are not; in fact, men are really more shockable than women.

After a long Introduction there follows the body of the book in three dialogues, after the form of a play.

Swift's last prose work, *Directions to Servants*, was unfinished. He seems to have been working at it in the country in 1731 and perhaps in 1732, but by 1738 he had mislaid the manuscript. It was published, uncompleted, in the year of his death, 1745. I find it much more amusing than the *Polite Conversation*; it is a return to the lower-class, below-stairs humour of which he was such a master. His odd way of life had early equipped him for it. He had always had a habit of putting up in cheap, threepenny inns (though he carried his own clean sheets) and he was often on the roads. So there was nothing he did not know about low life, or 'the facts of life', though he does not seem to have operated on these last. He was non-operative – hence the tensions, never satisfied.

Though there are no servants in our very equal society, the booklet is no less *à propos* than others of his works. And, come to think of it, why no domestic servants? What is wrong with domestic service? It is much more in keeping with the genius of ordinary people than anything else – their conversation, for instance. Who would want their conversation? – compare Swift's *Polite Conversation*. So many of the humorous *Directions* are still so apposite. 'If a corner of the hanging wants a single nail to fasten it, and the footman be directed to tack it up, he may say he doth not understand that sort of work, but his honour may send for the upholsterer.' How very *à propos* in a world run by trade union regulations, when an electrician may not touch the end of a pipe belonging to the plumber's job, or the strict demarcation between welder and fitter, or who not? And 'whoever, out of malice to a fellow-servant, carries a tale to his master, should be ruined by a general confederacy against him.' Very recognizable practice against a non-union man.

It is evident that Swift built up his book from observation and actual incidents. An unworked-up note tells us that Lord Peterborough's steward pulled down his house, sold his materials, and charged My Lord with repairs. We have all known builders who have made similar depredations at the expense of their client. Another note refers to stewards taking their lords' money 'for forbearance from tenants'. The late Duke of Westminster used to be presented with such 'forbearing' leases to sign in a hurry, just as he was about to leave on a journey. Always use the best materials for yourself is a good rule, and leave the inferior for the master – one has observed that often enough practised upon oneself. As if it made any difference! – however well-dressed they may appear, the moment they open their mouths one knows who is who.

'If an humble companion – a chaplain, tutor, or a dependent cousin happened to be at table – whom you find to be little regarded by the master and the company (which nobody is readier to discover than we servants), it must be the business of you and the footman to follow the example of your betters, by treating him many degrees worse than any of the rest. And you cannot please your master better, or at least your lady.' There is a naughty observation which yet has its truth: women *are* more snobbish than men.

'When your master and lady go abroad together, to dinner or on a visit for the evening, you need leave only one servant in the house, unless you have a blackguard boy to answer at the door, and attend the children.' The newspapers today headline the misdoings of baby-sitters, who not infrequently murder or make off with the wretches in their charge; and there is the incomprehensible but popular habit of baby-snatching from perambulators. Swift would find more variations on his themes in a more complex society.

'If you singe the linen with the iron, rub the place with flour, chalk, or white powder; and if nothing will do, wash it so long till it be either not to be seen, or torn to rags.' It reminds one of the attempts to cover the hole burnt by a cigarette in a hostess's counterpane by a sluttish guest, Lucky Jim, in Kingsley Amis's novel of that name – a work symptomatic of the squalor of our time, by a descendant of one side of Swift's genius. People have been amused, or scandalized, by the jokes in this book – about warming the plates under your armpits, or washing the glasses with your own water, to save salt; or wet-nurses contriving to be with child as soon as they can, 'while you are giving suck, that you may be ready for another service when the child you nurse dies, or is weaned.' The real interest of the book again is the observation of human society, and the insight into human motives.

One side to Swift's mind is hardly at all noticed – the scholarly side. He was extraordinarily widely read, and one must place the emphasis on the width of his intellectual interests. We know that at Moor Park he laid in a stock of reading sufficient to last a lifetime, mainly in the classics both Latin and Greek, though he read Greek authors often in Latin translation. He read Lucretius three times in the year 1697–8 – enough to undermine anyone's faith. One can see the direction his mind was taking from the reading it fed on: Hobbes, 'Hudibras' Butler, Rabelais, Lucian. He often made notes on his reading, sometimes scathing, as in his comments on Bishop Burnet's *History*; a marginal note in Latin tells us how much he laughed at the fabulous absurdities and lies of Philostratus; with his quite different taste in style, he corrected Clarendon's magnificent, orotund English. It is a pity that his notes on Hobbes's *Leviathan* are lost: they would have been piquant. In 1711 he bought for Stella a French translation of Lucian in three volumes, but could not bear to part with it. Some of her books, choice reading, came to him after her death.

His constant precepts both to her and Vanessa to occupy their minds with reading he acted on himself: he was always reading (or writing). Once out at Quilca, with nothing more to read, he asked Sheridan to send him a bundle of his scholars' Latin exercises. In 1729 we find him ploughing through Baronius, of whom there were twelve volumes; his lonely domestic state gave him the time. What is remarkable is not the reading in the classics, except for its range, for that was regular with scholarly persons of the time; nor his reading in divinity. He had a fair collection of seventeenth-century divines, and possessed Archbishop Sharp's Sermons, it is amusing to notice. His own sermon style was a world away from theirs, weighed down with innumerable quotations in Latin and Greek, to show off their learning in the Early Fathers and the Schoolmen. Swift, as we have seen, went in for no such absurdity – and was so much better.

A man's books are a good index of his mind, and Swift's whole bias was towards history, politics in the broadest sense, and literature. He read books of travel, as we should expect; he gave away his medical books to his doctor. His library was not that of a scholar, in the specialist sense of the word, but that of a writer; his reading of the Latin poets was not for the sterile purpose of turning out Latin verses, but using them for the creative purpose of writing English verse. Paradoxically he appreciated Plato – more, we may be sure, for his politics than for his metaphysics. Again, he was too big a man himself not to admire the greater genius of Milton, for all his republicanism and acrid Nonconformity.

The most noticeable thing, for a man of the time, was his wide reading in French – a debt to Sir William Temple; both Swift and Stella spoke French, Vanessa read it. We have seen the mark made on his mind by La Rochefoucauld, who appealed so bitterly to his disillusionment with human beings. Swift was hardly less indebted to

Rabelais, Montaigne, St Evremond and the naughty Bussy Rabutin. He admired Voiture and Malherbe, and was also well read in the French dramatists and French memoirs. His writings and references in his letters show how familiar a companion Don Quixote was to his mind.

Swift's work was over.

In May 1740 he made his will; it is long and full of good deeds, like his life. The bulk of his fortune went to building and endowing 'an hospital large enough for the reception of as many idiots and lunatics as the annual income of the said lands [recited] and worldly substance shall be sufficient to maintain; and I desire that the said hospital may be called St Patrick's Hospital.' In fact, it is usually referred to as Swift's. His first provision was an annuity of £20 for Rebecca Dingley. He provided handsomely for his cousin, Mrs Whiteway, the intelligent good woman who looked after him in his last years – there always seems to have been some good woman in the background to look after him. There were bequests of money to Mrs Whiteway's sons, to enable one to become a lawyer, the other a surgeon; the daughter to have his plain gold watch, the Japan writing-desk given him by Lady Carteret's mother, 'my square tortoise-shell snuff-box, richly lined and inlaid with gold, given to me by the right honourable Henrietta, now Countess of Oxford, and the seal with a Pegasus, given to me by the Countess Granville' – a thoughtful, symbolic trinket.

There were many such objects, with interesting associations. He chose to bestow on the then Earl of Oxford two antique gold seals, 'because they belonged to her late most excellent Majesty Queen Anne, of ever glorious, immortal and truly pious memory, the real nursing-mother of all her kingdoms.' What a change the years had brought, from 'the royal prude' of 1714! To his 'dearest friend, Alexander Pope', he left his miniature of their friend, Robert, Earl of Oxford' – but Pope was dead before Swift was. To Orrery he left his enamelled silver plates for various wine-bottles; to Deane Swift his writing materials; to Delany, his silver medal of Queen Anne;

to a lawyer friend, the gold box in which was the freedom of the city of Dublin; prebendary John Grattan, the silver box of the Cork freedom, 'in which I desire the said John to keep the tobacco he usually cheweth [Ugh!] called pigtail.'

There were many bequests to other clerical colleagues in the Chapter: to one, his Van Dyck portrait of Charles I, and a bird picture given to Swift by the Earl of Pembroke; to another his gold bottle-screw and his strong-box; to a third, books, thirteen Persian miniatures and a silver tankard; to a fourth, a large gilt medal of Charles I, with the crown of martyrdom. We see revealed how Swift's Cavalier ancestry prevailed, atavistically, over the Whiggery of his education and upbringing with Temple.

'I bequeath all my horses and mares to the Reverend Mr John Jackson, Vicar of Santry, together with all my horse furniture; lamenting that I had not credit enough with any chief governor (since the change of times) to get some additional church preferment for so virtuous and worthy a gentleman. I also leave him my third best beaver hat.' Other beaver hats to others; a medal of Queen Anne and Prince George went back to Mrs Barber; his housekeeper, Miss Ridgeway, daughter of his former housekeeper, Mrs Brent, was provided for.

All these things, and more, point to the essential loyalty of his own nature, which in return he elicited in those nearest to him.

A few years before, he had burned most of his writings and papers – including, we must suppose, what we most regret, Stella's letters. The publication of the *History of the Four Last Years of the Reign of Queen Anne* was left to the care of Dr King; it led to a good deal of correspondence, for Bolingbroke – for all his humbug of philosophic benevolence – still hated Oxford's memory. After some emendation and omissions the book was published, but not till years after Swift's death. Mrs Whiteway loyally opposed the publication of his letters, for fear of their being tampered with as well as for expediency's sake: 'The Letters to and from Dr Swift had been printed long ago, but for me. I opposed it publicly at the Dean's table, as I did often privately to himself, and with that warmth which nothing could have excused but friendship . . . There is a time in life when people can hear no reason and, with a sigh, I say – this is now the case with our dear friend.'

In October 1742 he had what looks like a stroke, or his old disease struck him a mortal blow. One night his left eye swelled as large as an egg, and large boils appeared on his arms and body. 'The torture he was in, is not to be described. Five persons could scarce hold him for a week.' When the pain subsided, he recognized Mrs Whiteway and took her by the hand; she asked if he would give her a dinner, to which he replied, 'to be sure, my old friend.'

His vitality was such that he survived another three years, walking, for ever walking, ten hours a day up and down the stairs and rooms of the great house, his mind gone. There were some broken gleams of self-recognition, recorded by Deane Swift: rocking himself to and fro in a chair, repeating, 'I am what I am; I am what I am;' one day, unable to bring out a word he wanted, 'I am a fool.' Towards the end, he told Deane Swift, 'Go, go,' pointing to the door, and then, raising his hand to his head, as if in apology, 'My best understanding . . .'

On 19 October 1745, a month from his 78th birthday, he died. He lay in some state in the hall in the Deanery, when crowds came to look upon him, the coffin open; until someone cut a lock of hair from his head for a relic. The Deanery was then closed, and he was buried privately, as he desired, and in the cathedral at night – as Stella had been – on 22 October 1745.

There he lies in the vault, not far away from her.

Further Reading

THE MOST IMPORTANT THING is to read the works of Swift himself. The best and latest edition is that of Herbert Davis in many volumes (published by Basil Blackwell, 1964). An earlier edition by Temple Scott (Bohn's Standard Library, published by Bell, 1908) in several volumes is still quite good, and separate volumes can be picked up second-hand. Only a few of Swift's works can be obtained separately in popular editions – fortunately *Gulliver's Travels* can be; some of his essays appear in miscellaneous collections. *A Tale of a Tub* has a full edition, edited by D. Nichol Smith (Oxford, 1920 and 1958); *Swift's Satires and Personal Writings*, edited by W. A. Eddy (Oxford, 1932) offers a useful selection.

The best edition of Swift's poems is that by Harold Williams in three volumes (Oxford: Clarendon Press, 1937); but the one-volume *Swift's Poetical Works*, edited by Herbert Davis (Oxford Standard Authors, 1967), is more practical and quite sufficient.

The Correspondence of Jonathan Swift, edited by Harold Williams, five volumes (Oxford: Clarendon Press, 1963) is now the standard edition. Elrington Ball's edition in six volumes (published by Bell, 1914) remains excellent, especially for Swift's Irish background and friends; upon these the footnotes are invaluable.

Two biographies may be recommended: Irvin Ehrenpreis, *Swift; the Man, his Works, and the Age* (London, 1962), and J. Middleton Murry, *Jonathan Swift: A Critical Biography* (London, 1954). Good biographies of Swift's friends are Peter Smithers, *The Life of Joseph Addison* (2nd edition, Oxford 1968); Willard Connely, *Sir Richard Steele* (London, 1934); George Sherburn, *The Early Career of Alexander Pope* (Oxford, 1934). See also, *The Correspondence of Richard Steele* (Oxford, 1941), edited by Rae Blanchard, five volumes; and *The*

Correspondence of Alexander Pope (Oxford, 1956), edited by George Sherburn, five volumes.

For the background of Moor Park read Julia G. Longe: *Martha, Lady Giffard, Her Life and Correspondence* (London, 1911). Unfortunately there is no full-length biography of Sir William Temple: a gap to be filled, a good subject for someone competent to do it. For Ireland, read W. E. H. Lecky, *History of Ireland in the Eighteenth Century* (London, 1892); *A Great Archbishop of Dublin, William King* (London, 1906), edited by C. S. King; and Louis Landa, *Swift and the Irish Church* (Oxford, 1954).

For historical and literary background read G. M. Trevelyan, *England under Queen Anne* (London, 1932; new edition 1965); K. G. Feiling, *History of the Tory Party, 1640–1714* (Oxford, 1924), and *The Second Tory Party* (London, 1938); G. N. Clark, *The Later Stuarts* (Oxford, 1934); Leslie Stephen, *English Literature and Society in the Eighteenth Century* (London, 1904; new edition 1963).

For subsidiary figures follow up the biographies in the *Dictionary of National Biography*.

List of Illustrations

19 Allegory on Swift's services to Ireland; contemporary engraving. British Museum.

20 Wood's Ha'pence; cartoon, 1724. British Museum.

21 Alexander Pope with Miss Blount; painting by Charles Jervas. National Portrait Gallery, London.

22 Jonathan Swift; portrait by Charles Jervas, c. 1718. National Portrait Gallery, London.

23 Esther Johnson, contemporary portrait by an unknown Irish painter. National Gallery of Ireland.

24 St Patrick's Hospital; engraving after J. Aheron, c. 1762. National Library of Ireland.

25 Jonathan Swift, Dean of St Patrick's; mezzotint by Andrew Miller after Francis Bindon, 1743. British Museum.

Index